QADDAFI'S WORLD DESIGN
Libyan Foreign Policy,
1969–1987

To My Parents

QADDAFI'S WORLD DESIGN

Libyan Foreign Policy, 1969–1987

Ronald Bruce St John

Saqi Books

Library of Congress Cataloging-in-Publication Data

St. John, Ronald Bruce.
 Qadhdhafi's world design.

 Bibliography: p.
 1. Libya——Foreign relations. 2. Qaddafi, Muammar.
I. Title.
DT236.S8 1987   327.61′2   87-9886

British Library Cataloguing in Publication Data

St. John, Ronald Bruce
 Qaddafi's world design : Libyan foreign
 policy, 1969–1987.
 1. Libya——Foreign relations
 I. Title
 327.61′2   DT236

ISBN 0-86356-161-6

First published 1987 by
Saqi Books, 26 Westbourne Grove, London W2 5RH
and 171 First Avenue, Atlantic Highlands, New Jersey 07716

Printed in Great Britain by
Billing & Sons Ltd
Worcester

Contents

Preface   9

1. Introduction   **11**
  The setting   12
  The foreign policy of the Idris regime   14
  National identity   16
  Early statements of the RCC   17

2. Arab Nationalism and the Third Universal Theory   **21**

  Sources of Arab nationalism   21
  Development of Arab nationalism   23
  Pan-Arabism   24
  Qaddafi's approach   26
  Third Universal Theory   28
  Changing role of Islam   30
  Islam and Arab nationalism   33

3. Qaddafi's Holy War   **35**
  Reorientation   35
  Fatah   37
  Palestine before unity   38
  The unregenerate rejectionist   40
  Beirut, 1982   42
  Qaddafi and terrorism   45
  Policy failure   48

4. Quest for Arab Unity   **49**
  The new pan-Arab leader   49
  The Tripoli Charter   51
  The Benghazi Declaration   54
  Swing to the Maghreb   57
  Arab disunity, 1975–80   58
  Phase two   61
  Return to the Maghreb   63
  The Treaty of Oujda   66
  Assessment   69

5. Positive Neutrality   **71**
  Early expression of positive neutrality   71
  Early Soviet contacts   73
  Arms build-up   74
  Deepening Soviet relationship   75

Strains in the Soviet-Libyan relationship 77
Reluctant allies 78
Early relations with the United States 79
The redirection of US policy 81
Dénouement 84
Qaddafi and Europe 85
Europe's response to Reagan 88

6. The Third Circle **93**
Target Israel 94
The failure to consolidate 98
Setbacks 100
More of the same 102
Observations 105

7. The Primacy of Oil **107**
First moves 107
The September agreements 109
Tehran–Tripoli agreements 111
Increased participation 114
War and embargo 116
Oil revenues and foreign policy 118
Falling oil revenues 120
Oil policy and foreign policy 123

8. The Foreign Policy Process **125**
Libyan policy environment 125
The structure of government 126
Evolution of the political system 128
The Arab Socialist Union 129
Popular revolution 130
General People's Congress 132
Revolutionary Committees 134
Political parties 136
The military 137
Petit bourgeoisie 138
Organized opposition 139
New foreign-policy process 140

9. Conclusions **143**
Early continuity 144
Policy innovation 145
Constant principles 146
Tactical flexibility 147
Political isolation 149

Notes 151

Select Bibliography 173

Index 175

Preface

This book is intended to fill a gap in the literature on Arab foreign policies. Its objective is to underline the basic tenets of the foreign policy of the Socialist People's Libyan Arab Jamahiriya, more commonly known as Libya, and to place them in a regional and extra-regional context. Primarily intended to be a textbook or general introduction to the subject, it is also hoped the analysis will be of interest to specialist students of the foreign policies of Arab or other Third World states.

In place of the more conventional chronological approach, the author has opted for a thematic structure. While the available literature on Libyan foreign policy remains limited, the plethora of information available on the September 1969 Revolution means we can assume a certain familiarity with the chief events and personalities in Libyan and Middle Eastern affairs which is necessary for a thematic approach to succeed. Equally important, a series of analytical chapters on key aspects and themes of contemporary Libyan foreign policy is the best way to demonstrate its underlying consistency while highlighting the subtle changes which have occurred in the last 18 years. Therefore, the advantages of a thematic approach appeared to outweigh its major shortcoming, which is that selected topics, such as United States policy, are relevant to more than one of the themes discussed.

It may be of interest to the reader to know that no similar study of Libyan foreign policy exists in any language. As such, this book is a preliminary statement which it is hoped will encourage additional research on the subject. In the interim, it is hoped this study offers a meaningful contribution to the growing volume of serious study of Arab foreign policies and that it will be a source of encouragement to others to explore this field of study.

The author has used accepted spellings where they exist; and where they do not, he has rendered foreign words and names into English according to accepted scholarly methods. Diacritical marks have been omitted. For the sake of simplicity, regions and countries are generally referred to by their current, popular names as opposed to official designations. In addition to their standard purpose, the references also serve as a bibliography of the available literature relevant to the study of Libyan foreign policy.

This book is the product of some 10 years of observation, investigation and reflection which began in 1977 when the author first visited Libya. Over this time, he has published several articles which have dealt with selected aspects of the present work. Consequently, he would like to thank the editors who have allowed various earlier approximations of parts of the present material to appear under their auspices. He would also like to thank his wife and two sons for the encouragement and support they have given him. A work of this sort requires an enormous amount of time and energy, much of which would otherwise have been theirs.

1
Introduction

What has taken place in Libya is a revolution.
Muammar al-Qaddafi

On 1 September 1969, a small group of Libyan army officers, calling themselves the Free Unionist Officers' Movement, executed a successful coup d'état against an aging monarchy and initiated a radical reorientation of Libyan foreign policy. The movement was led by a 12-man central committee which designated itself the Revolutionary Command Council (RCC). At first, the leadership of the RCC remained anonymous, but Colonel Muammar al-Qaddafi soon emerged as chairman and *de facto* head of state.

The RCC abruptly terminated the loose association the Libyan monarchy had maintained with the Middle Eastern alliance system established by the United States, and initiated an intense, often stormy, association with the rival Arab system. Thereafter, the Libyan government pursued a complex, aggressive and increasingly violent foreign policy, remarkable for the broad scope of its objectives and activities. Seeking a wider audience than its predecessor, the RCC repeatedly found it difficult to establish a meaningful relationship between aspirations and accomplishments. Addressing diplomatic problems of overwhelming complexity with naive, simplistic solutions, it grew increasingly frustrated as its policies were greeted outside Libya with widespread disbelief or lack of interest and largely rejected.

In the meantime, Colonel Qaddafi, the chief ideological innovator and initiator of the RCC, refined his control of the revolutionary government and increasingly personified Libyan foreign policy. A growing fascination with the self-proclaimed Leader of the Revolution — often described as bizarre, irrational or quixotic — distorted the continuity which characterized Libyan foreign policy after 1969. While that policy evidenced a measured tactical flexibility, its architects remained deeply committed to tenets and objectives articulated at the outset of the revolution. It was this rigidity in the face of changing realities in Africa and the Middle East which helped explain the singular lack of success of Libyan foreign policy.

The setting

Libya is located on the north central coast of Africa. It is bordered on the north by the Mediterranean Sea, on the east by Egypt and Sudan, on the west by Tunisia and Algeria, and on the south by Niger, Chad and Sudan. Southern Libya includes a large part of the Sahara desert, which extends across northern Africa from the Atlantic Ocean to the Red Sea. With an area of 680,000 square miles, Libya is both the fourth largest state in Africa and the fourth largest in the Arab world. One-quarter the size of the continental United States, it is larger than the combined areas of France, Spain, Italy and West Germany.

Libya rests on the periphery of three worlds — Arab, African and Mediterranean. Its location has given it some flexibility as to where it will play a regional role, as well as creating considerable uncertainty as to where it belongs. At independence, the Kingdom of Libya comprised three provinces which were not ruled as a single unit until the twentieth century. In the pre-independence era, the largest province, Cyrenaica in the east with 27 per cent of the population, looked towards Egypt and beyond to the Mashrek (Arab east). In the west, the province of Tripolitania, one-third the size of Cyrenaica but containing 68 per cent of the Libyan people, looked westward towards the three Arab states comprising the Maghreb (Arab west). The south-western province of the Fezzan, which was the most sparsely settled, holding only five per cent of the population on one-third of the total area, directed its attention towards little beyond the Sahara desert, of which it was inseparably a part, as well as the African states bordering the Sahara. Geographically, this political division was reinforced by the physical split of the nation's two major provinces by the Gulf of Sirte and the great Sirte desert.[1]

The location of Libya in a strategically important area of the world contributed to its visibility on the world stage and gave its foreign policy an extra-regional importance it would not otherwise have had. Positioned in an area where the interests and ambitions of the superpowers crossed after World War II, it was continuously involved in the interplay of power politics after 1945. Of course, the importance of its geographical position heightened the political foreplay which preceded independence. In the end, it was the inability of the Big Four (the United States, the Soviet Union, Britain and France) to reach an agreement on a trusteeship for the area which was the decisive factor in the decision to grant Libya independence.[2]

Demography has compounded the constraints which geography has imposed on Libya's foreign policy. For a large country with an ambitious leadership, a population of between three and four million citizens concentrated in a few detached urban centres has been debilitating. Because of Libya's small population, Colonel Qaddafi has occasionally referred to himself as a leader without a country.[3] Compared to its neighbour Egypt, for example, Libya has 75 per cent more territory but only five per cent as many people. Consequently, it has proved difficult for the Libyan government both to meet its development targets and to build the military force it feels is necessary to promote the national interest. Libya's limited demographic resources have influenced a number of controversial labour and security policies over the last two decades, including universal conscription, the forced repatriation of migrant workers and the recruitment of mercenaries.

The Islamic religion penetrated North Africa as a result of the Arab conquest around AD 642. In subsequent centuries, the North African shore, especially the area which is now Libya, assumed a deepening Arab-Islamic character. In 1842 Muhammad ibn Ali al-Sanusi founded the Sanusiya order, an Islamic revival movement, in Cyrenaica. Sanusism achieved a widespread following in eastern and southern Libya, as well as spreading into central and western Africa. More a religious than a political movement, it aimed at purifying Islam and educating its adherents in Islamic principles. Devotion to Islam underlay Cyrenaican resistance to Italian colonial rule, added continuity and legitimacy to the monarchy and became the second foundation for Qaddafi's Third Universal Theory as well as a tool of contemporary Libyan foreign policy.

Libya includes three climato-geographic zones. The thin Mediterranean littoral is the most heavily populated and the most suitable for agriculture. But it is also the smallest, containing only three per cent of the country's total area. Around six per cent of Libya is semi-desert chiefly suitable for grazing. The remaining 90 per cent is a desert zone which contains only a few scattered oases. An appreciation of the arid nature of Libya is best conveyed by the fact that no river or stream in the country has a permanent flow. To correct a popular misconception, less than 20 per cent of Libya's deserts are covered by sand dunes. A much greater part is occupied by rocky and gravel plains.[4]

Despite the limitations of terrain and climate, three-quarters of the Libyan population in the early 1950s was forced to support itself by herding or farming. Only 20 per cent lived in urban areas. The largest part of the rural sector was settled in villages, but a substantial number of nomads and semi-nomads existed. Libya's capacity to generate foreign-exchange earnings in this period was so limited that a significant contribution came from the export of esparto grass and the scrap metal collected from disabled World War II armoured vehicles. While the discovery of oil in commercially viable quantities in 1959 later modified the Libyan economy, in the early years of the monarchy Libya was aptly referred to as the desert kingdom.[5]

The foreign policy of the Idris regime

The United Kingdom of Libya, under the rule of Muhammad Idris al-Mahdi al-Sanusi, achieved independence on 24 December 1951. It was the first North African nation to attain statehood and the first state to emerge under the auspices of the United Nations. Regionally and extra-regionally, Libya enjoyed the initial advantage of having no aggravated boundary disputes or other outstanding quarrels.

Unfortunately, tranquillity did not last, and the Libyan government and people became increasingly enmeshed in the growing politicization of the Arab world. Contemporary events — especially the colonial struggles that linked Libya, the Palestine conflict, increased Soviet interest in the Middle East, the growth of Nasserist and Baathist pan-Arabism, and anti-royalist movements throughout the Arab world — were simply not propitious for the orderly political development of a conservative, traditionalist monarchy. The extremely limited anti-colonialist credits of the monarchy were soon used up as its dependence on income from British and American air bases fostered a policy of co-operation with and support for the West. At the same time, the legitimizing force of nationalism which stemmed from the achievement of independence was increasingly challenged both internally by opposition groups and externally by pan-Arab movements.[6]

The Libyan monarchy emphasized Libyan-Arab brotherhood and solidarity, but this seldom exceeded lip service unless under extreme pressure. For example, the king blocked Libyan membership of the Arab League until 1953, and his administration always fell short of offering tangible support for the Arab cause in the Middle East. Threatened by growing Egyptian influence, the monarchy took steps to reduce Egyptian propaganda in 1956, temporarily closing Egyptian government information centres.

In 1957 Libya and Tunisia signed a bilateral treaty which the two states hailed as a model of bilateral collaboration, as well as the framework for a broader scheme of multilateral co-operation with other North African countries. Critics of the treaty, especially the Arab nationalist supporters of President Nasser of Egypt, denounced the treaty as little more than an instrument for harmonizing the policies of the signatories with the West.

The appearance and reality of the monarchy's dependence on the West rested heavily on the income and financial assistance generated by British and American air bases in Libya. In 1953 Libya agreed to a 20-year treaty of friendship and alliance with Britain in which Libya ceded extensive jurisdictional and extraterritorial rights in return for long-term financial assistance. A year later, the governments of Libya and the United States signed an agreement which granted the latter the use of Wheelus base outside Tripoli until 1970, in exchange for a programme of economic, technical and military assistance. Thereafter, the governments of Britain and the United

States occupied paradoxical positions in Libya for the remainder of the decade. Although the Libyan government embraced the Eisenhower doctrine, whereby the United States sought to build anti-communist alliances, official opinion towards the United States was not as warm as it was towards Britain, while popular opinion in Libya and elsewhere in the Arab world was not as hostile to the United States as it was towards Britain.[7]

The existence of large Western bases in Libya and the dependence of the Libyan government on the income from these facilities led many observers to describe the Idris regime as pro-Western. In many respects, this was a misnomer as it implied a widespread commitment to Western traditions, ideals and policies which simply did not exist, except perhaps in the minds of a few senior government officials. While the monarchy agreed to the Western bases in exchange for desperately needed financial and diplomatic support, it tried to minimize the impact of the West on Libya's socio-political values and structures, and emphasized its political non-alignment in the United Nations, the Organization of African Unity and elsewhere. The close association of the monarchy's Western orientation to its need for military-base revenues became clear once petroleum sales began to reduce its dependence on this income. In 1964 the Libyan government formally asked the United States and Britain to reconsider the future status of the bases. The United States accepted the principle of withdrawal from Wheelus base, and Britain began evacuating troops from the Tripoli area in 1965.

In addition to enriching the government, oil revenues also awakened the Libyan populace in the 1960s. Dissatisfaction with the slow rate of economic and political development since 1951 mounted as it became obvious that the Libyan government, as well as the society and economy, were unprepared to absorb and make good use of the new oil wealth. As a revolution of rising expectations occurred, the monarchy's entrance into pragmatic agreements for economic and technical co-operation with Libya's North African neighbours simply could not match the romantic appeal of the pan-Arabism offered by Egypt.[8]

In January 1964 student demonstrations broke out in both Tripoli and Benghazi in support of an Arab summit meeting in Cairo and to protest at an Israeli plan to divert water from the Jordan River to irrigate the Negev Desert. The demonstrations intensified after Nasser called for the liquidation of foreign bases in Libya. Demonstrations broke out again in 1965 over the issue of retaining diplomatic relations with West Germany after it had established relations with Israel. While Libya withdrew its ambassador in protest, it was one of the few Arab states not to break diplomatic relations.[9] Radical Arab ideologies in the 1960s, like the issues of foreign bases and foreign aid in the 1950s, increasingly exposed the consistent weakness of the monarchy's foreign policy — its vulnerability to decisions taken by others.

The year 1967 proved to be pivotal for the Libyan monarchy, since its response to the June 1967 Arab-Israeli war provided a catalyst for the 1969 coup d'état.[10] Popular reaction to the war was both widespread and violent as the Libyan citizenry exploded in a surprisingly emotional frenzy of Arab nationalism. Popular opinion was further inflamed when President Nasser unjustly charged that the swift defeat of Arab forces was due to British and American air support for Israel, in part originating from their air bases in Libya. While the Libyan government threatened to close down the bases and did shut down oil production briefly, disappointment over the Arab defeat turned to increased hostility towards the government for its tolerance of the bases and its alleged lack of conviction in the struggle against Israel.

At the subsequent Arab summit meeting in Khartoum in August 1967, the Libyan government joined the leading oil producers in agreeing to subsidize the losses of Egypt and Jordan in the Six-Day War; but it refused to take more stringent measures potentially detrimental to its own interests, such as cutting oil exports to the West.[11] Thereafter, the Libyan government continued to support Arab causes, but it did not seek a more aggressive role in the arena of Arab politics in general or the Palestinian issue in particular.

National identity

At independence, a low level of national consciousness or national identity had existed in Libya. Despite a series of revolts in the nineteenth century, nationalist tendencies under Turkish rule were largely latent while the role of the Sanusiya order in Cyrenaica remained predominantly religious. Resistance to Italian colonial rule accelerated the transformation of the order into a more political movement, but there was little evidence to suggest the Italo-Libyan struggle fostered a growing sense of national political identity. Consequently, it was hardly surprising that a lively debate occurred in the years immediately prior to independence as to whether to form a united Libya or to partition the territory into two or possibly three entities, each under a distinct political regime.[12]

The advent of independence unified Libya's three provinces but failed to forge a deep-rooted sense of national identity as did the bitter war of independence in Algeria. For the most part, Libyans continued to think of themselves as Tripolitanian, Cyrenaican or Fezzanese, not as Libyan. Moreover, the rise to statehood coincided with the rising tide of Arab nationalism in the Middle East and anti-colonial agitation in neighbouring North African states. The monarchy viewed Arab nationalism as a competing ideology inimical to its interests and sought to contain and direct its growth and influence in the kingdom. On the other hand, many Libyan nationalists, like Arab nationalists elsewhere, regarded the regime established under the federal union as simply another artificial structure imposed upon them by foreign powers.[13]

The absence of a historical sense of unity between the disparate components of the new state was reinforced by geographical and cultural differences. Geographically, the political division of the country into three provinces mirrored its basic physiographical character, as the three territories were separated by severe geographical barriers. The Sanusiya order, strong in Cyrenaica but much weaker in Tripolitania, was a divisive force. In addition, the Cyrenaicans had opposed Italian domination at considerable economic and human cost, while the Tripolitanians, despite the determined resistance of a few, had a far higher incidence of non-resistance or active collaboration. After 1951 the monarchy made major efforts to promote a cohesive national community; but with existing levels of inter-provincial rivalry and enmity, early results proved inconclusive.[14]

In the second decade of independence, analysts and observers were still highlighting the limited level of national identity or national consciousness in Libya.[15] In response to the public outcry caused by the June 1967 war, the monarchy intensified its efforts in this regard by stressing the existence of a Libyan identity with deep roots in pre-independence history. As a result, national consciousness continued to grow under the leadership of King Idris, albeit not fast enough to preserve the monarchy from the stronger pan-Arab ideology from further east.

Especially after oil revenues had begun coursing through the Libyan economy, younger Libyans were eager for change and sought a comprehensive ideology which would both explain and satisfy their yearning. To a large extent, the monarchy underestimated their need for ideological fulfilment and concentrated instead on material benefits. Consequently, nascent Libyan nationalism was only sometimes vital enough to satisfy their total needs.[16] In the final analysis, it proved unable to overcome the negative impact of tribal, provincial and religious loyalties and the positive appeal of a vibrant pan-Arabism.

Early statements of the RCC

The early statements of the RCC, beginning with the Proclamation of the Republic issued on 1 September 1969, the morning the coup d'état took place, invoked the traditional past, denounced the corruption of the monarchy and promised a thorough transformation of Libyan society.[17] Colonel Qaddafi's first major address was delivered on 16 September 1969, the 38th anniversary of the martyrdom of Umar al-Mukhtar, the Sanusiya sheikh and resistance leader hanged by the Italians in 1931. Qaddafi vigorously attacked the existing social order, calling for radical change in the socio-economic and political system. In the process, he outlined the major themes of the ideology which he and other RCC members were to expand and develop in coming months.[18]

Qaddafi described the events which had transpired on 1 September, not simply as a coup but as the beginning of a long, broad and deep revolution.

While the coup had been military in conception, planning, organization and execution, he described the armed forces as only the vanguard of the revolutionary process and called on the Libyan people to assume the leadership role. The enemies of the revolution were what he termed retrogression, the forces of backwardness and the forces of evil as well as imperialism and Zionism. Qaddafi used the slogan 'freedom, socialism and unity' to indicate the direction foreign and domestic policy would take. He defined freedom in a generic sense, declaring that every individual had the natural right to economic, social and political freedom. Socialism assumed an Islamic hue, as Qaddafi tied collective participation in production and consumption to Libya's Islamic tradition. The need for both national and Arab unity was repeatedly emphasized throughout the address, with the Palestinian issue highlighted as the major obstacle to Arab unity.[19] In the autumn of 1969, Qaddafi and other RCC members reiterated these themes in interviews and speeches throughout Libya.

Like many revolutionary theorists, Qaddafi used rhetoric and imagery which stressed originality; however, his early actions and statements contained much that was old as well as new. For example, it has been commonplace for revolutionary movements to attack the past to justify the present. It was also ordinary for them to invoke traditional values and a historical heritage in support of the new regime. The Egyptian Free Officers' movement, for example, portrayed the 1952 revolution as the culmination of a popular movement originating with the struggle against France in 1798. The sensitivity of the RCC to the relatively low level of national identity in Libya as late as 1969 was noteworthy, as it was careful to refer to both Cyrenaican and Tripolitanian martyrs.

Like the Libyan RCC, most revolutionary regimes have also tended to overemphasize the dependence and corruption of the monarchy. The familiar revolutionary trinity of unity, freedom and socialism was a theme of the Baath Party in 1946, and was later adopted — albeit in the revised order of freedom, socialism and unity — by the Egyptian government after 1952. The movement for Arab unity originated in Syria well before World War I, and the theme of pan-Arabism or Arab unity was constant in Baath Party literature by 1945. Taken as a whole, the early statements of Qaddafi and the other members of the RCC bore an uncanny resemblance to those of earlier revolutionary movements or governments. This harmony of views was especially significant as the Libyan revolutionaries were talking two or three decades after their precursors had first articulated such views; and in some cases, years after certain policies had been generally discredited elsewhere in the Arab world.[20]

The nascent ideology of the revolution was given legal expression in the temporary constitutional proclamation issued by the RCC on 11 December 1969. The preamble reiterated the regime's intention to fight reactionary forces and colonialism and to eliminate the obstacles to Arab unity. The revolution's goals were again summarized under the trinity of freedom, socialism and unity. Article One described Libya as a part of the Arab nation and repeated its commitment to comprehensive Arab unity. It also described Libya as a part of Africa, a concept which assumed new importance in the 1970s when Libyan foreign policy began to emphasize pan-Islamic or pan-African unity. Article Two described Islam as the religion of the state but did not signal the strong emphasis on Islam which would characterize the Libyan revolution and help differentiate it from those in Algeria, Egypt, Iraq, Syria and Tunisia. Eight of the remaining fifteen articles in the first chapter dealt with aspects of Libyan socialism, while the second half of the proclamation outlined the operative governmental structure. Thereafter, the direction and emphasis of Libyan foreign policy changed periodically, but its ideological foundation remained largely intact.

2

Arab Nationalism and the Third Universal Theory

> *The Arab Nation is apt to play the role of the bearer of a third theory because it is a nation of age-old civilization and is endowed with a heavenly and universal message, namely Islam.*
>
> ### Muammar al-Qaddafi

The Arab nationalist movement originated in the nineteenth century and reached its apogee in the 1960s. After the June 1967 war, Arab nationalism was a largely discredited idea whose time had apparently passed. Muammar al-Qaddafi revived both Arab nationalism and Islam as a component of Arab nationalism. Articulating a fiery, uncompromising form of Arab nationalism reminiscent of Gamal Abdel Nasser in his heyday, Qaddafi assigned it a central role in Libyan foreign policy.

Arab nationalism was undoubtedly Qaddafi's primordial value, and nationalism joined religion as a pillar of the Third Universal Theory. While Qaddafi's contributions to the theoretical foundations of Arab nationalism were questionable, he advocated significant modifications to traditional views of Islam. To evaluate his strain of Arab nationalism and the role he assigned to Islam, it is first necessary to examine briefly the sources and early history of the Arab nationalist movement.

Sources of Arab nationalism

The disparate currents which coalesced into an Arab nationalist movement cannot be identified as having a single, common origin. Both loyalty and hostility to the Ottoman Empire, as well as religious intensity and rational secularism, helped generate the sentiments which led to the development of Arab nationalism. At the same time, it was generally recognized that the three most dominant currents in the early years of the twentieth century were Islamism, Ottomanism and a growing sense of Turkish and Arab cultural distinctness which eventually developed into two separate nationalisms.[1]

By the turn of the century, an active Islamic reformist movement was well under way in the Middle East. Centred in Cairo, it had proponents in the major Arab cities of the Ottoman Empire. In the broadest sense, the movement aimed at stimulating a political and intellectual revitalization of Islam. Described by one historian as the 'defence of an injured self-view', the movement was in part a response to the political and cultural threat posed by Christian Europe. It was also 'an affirmation of the validity of the entire Islamic historical experience, an effort to assert the worthiness of a way of life and cultural tradition'.[2]

Islamic reformism and Ottoman patriotism, in both British-occupied Egypt and the Syrian provinces of the Ottoman Empire, fused into a vision of an independent Ottoman caliphate as vital to both the preservation of Islamic solidarity and the defence of Islamic territories from European imperialism. Ottomanism thus represented an attempt to evolve a sentiment of Ottoman nationalism which would embrace all the subject peoples of a multinational empire. While this vision was altered with the collapse of the Ottoman Empire, it served as an animating force for the majority of politically aware Arabs through the first two decades of the twentieth century. Before World War I, most Arab leaders simply did not see Arab nationalism as politically necessary; and it was for this reason that the Arabs found themselves without a nationalist ideology in the crucial decade after the war. In the early 1920s, many Arab leaders, for example the prominent Islamic nationalist Shakib Arslan, found it difficult to adapt to the changed circumstances, continued to hope for an Ottoman restoration, and thus refused to commit themselves to a purely Arab political movement.[3]

Nevertheless, the debates on Islamic reform and the nature of Ottomanism gave rise to sentiments which later developed into theories of nationalism. Two distinct sources of nationalist feeling were discernible in the period before World War I, one historically consistent and the other seemingly paradoxical. Both Islamic reformism and secular constitutionalism were of long-term significance because they raised questions that no Arab leader, including Muammar al-Qaddafi, could ignore.

Beginning in the late 1840s, American and European missionaries engaged in a sustained educational effort in Syria which encouraged the formation of a small but active Christian intelligentsia and professional class. These Syrian Christians demonstrated a receptivity to certain European attitudes which was not shown by their Muslim peers. For them, Europe was more a model to copy than a threat to ward off. In particular, members of the movement perceived secular constitutionalism as a major reason for European success and sought to transfer the idea to their own society. In turn, this led them to disparage Islamic institutions and to formulate in their place a doctrine of Arab secularism which viewed Islam as only one of several components of the Arab cultural heritage. This emphasis on Arab elements external to Islam was part of a broader effort to end the marginality of Arab Christians in Islamic lands. It reflected their desire to formulate a new society in which a divinely ordained social order was replaced by a rational, secular one which offered Christian Arabs a full political role. Members of this budding Christian intelligentsia pioneered the rediscovery of the classical Arabic literary heritage, experimented with new literary forms and helped shape an era, through their enthusiasm and practical intellectualism, which has been termed *al-nahdah*, or the awakening.[4]

The second formulation of a distinctly Arab component of cultural identity came from an unexpected source. The Islamic reformist movement understandably raised many questions about the reasons for the contemporary weakness of the Islamic world, and it was only a matter of time before political as well as theological answers were found. It was in the works of a Syrian journalist and administrator, Abdel-Rahman al-Kawakibi, that the nationalist possibilities inherent in Islamic reformism were probably first expressed. In addressing the problems of Islam in his day, al-Kawakibi concluded that the strength of an earlier Islam was its close identification with the Arabs and that it was the Turkish management of the religion which had corrupted it. His emphasis on the Arab role in Islam led al-Kawakibi to denigrate the Ottoman-Turkish contribution and eventually to move from simply praising the Arabs' role in Islam to glorifying the virtues of all Arabs, both Muslim and Christian.[5]

Development of Arab nationalism
Islamism and Ottomanism served as the principal factors of Arab political solidarity before World War I; but by the early 1920s Ottomanism was irrelevant, while Islamism was suffering ever deeper humiliation at the secularizing hands of the Turkish reformer Mustafa Kemal (Atatürk) and through the presence of European occupiers in the major cities of Arab Islam. Consequently, Arab attention focused on obtaining political independence from European control, as opposed to broader discussions of social reform or the adoption of particular political systems. In this milieu, budding Arab nationalism and vague formulations of Arab unity became increasingly interwoven with support for Palestinian Arabs in their opposition to Jewish land purchase and immigration.[6]

The Libyan case was not untypical. In the 1920s and 1930s, many of the surviving Libyan leaders opposed to Italian rule sought exile elsewhere in the Arab world where they conducted an active, if ineffective, war of words against the Italian occupation. A Tripolitania-Cyrenaica Defence Committee was established in Damascus under the leadership of Bashir al-Sadawi, a former member of a Tripolitanian delegation to the Sanusi leader Idris in 1922. Other groups of emigrés established themselves in Tunisia, Saudi Arabia, the Gulf and Egypt. In 1922 Idris established himself in Cairo, where he enjoyed cordial relations with the British authorities throughout the inter-war period.[7]

As Arab leadership organized to resist foreign occupation, it fostered an ongoing debate over what elements of the Arab heritage could best be employed as national symbols around which to organize the resistance and shape the image of independent Arab states. The debate over a secular versus an Islamic ideology was of particular importance. While some Arab writers continued to assert the primacy of Islamic bonds in the formation of an Arab political unit, others, such as the ideologue and educator Sati al-Husri, rejected Islamic sentiments in favour of a unified Arab nation bound by ties of Arab culture. Al-Husri provided probably the clearest exposition of a secular pan-Arab nationalism when he argued that the Arab nation consisted of all who spoke Arabic as their mother tongue. His emphasis was on the secular components of the Arab cultural heritage, and he insisted that one consequence of recognizing these components was to admit the existence of an Arab nation, including Egypt and North Africa, which was similar to the nations of Europe and, like them, should be unified politically.[8]

As late as World War II, Arab nationalism in the sense of a cosmic movement aimed at unifying the Arab nation still centred on Syria, Iraq and the Arabian peninsula. Neither Egypt nor the Maghreb played a significant role in the Arab nationalist movement until after the end of the war. In Egypt attention focused on the development of Egyptian nationalism in the inter-war period. In the Maghreb evidence of nationalistic feeling was visible, especially in Tunisia; but the nationalist movements lacked unity and direction. As the allies and other interested parties worked to determine the post-war future of Libya, for example, nationalist expressions repeatedly surfaced. On 7 October 1944, so-called extremist elements led a crowd of several thousand through the streets of Tripoli tearing down Italian street signs and replacing them with new ones in Arabic. At one point in 1945, demonstrations became almost a daily occurrence in Tripoli, with Jewish residents the subject of several mob outbursts. As events moved towards a partition of Palestine in 1947 and the proclamation of the state of Israel in 1948, ugly demonstrations again broke out in Libya and elsewhere in the Middle East. Arabs unable to express their growing anger over Palestine directly against the distant Palestine community often vented it locally upon Jews who in most cases had little or no connection with Zionism.[9]

Pan-Arabism

The 1950s have been aptly characterized as the decade of revolution in the Middle East. The period began with the Syrian coup in 1949 and ended with the coups in Iraq and Sudan in 1958. In the interim, every independent state in the Mashrek experienced at least one coup, whether successful or unsuccessful. At the same time, the states of the Maghreb rebelled against French domination; and the United Nations granted Libya independence. The policies pursued by many of these Arab revolutionary governments, particularly the one which came to power in Egypt, deeply influenced Qaddafi's approach to Arab nationalism. [10]

In Egypt, the Free Officers' movement inherited the Egyptian nationalism which had developed in the inter-war period. However, the nationalist ideology which had been the motive force behind the Egyptian nation-building process had become outmoded in terms of mid-twentieth-century Egyptian political and social conditions. After the overthrow of King Farouk, a shift in revolutionary action from the domestic to the international stage was accompanied by a redirection of ideological development in which Egyptian nationalism evolved into pan-Arabism. The conditions necessary to effect this evolution existed in the Egypt of late 1954, but the final and official adoption of pan-Arabism was due to President Gamal Abdel Nasser's subsequent diplomatic success. [11]

While the 1956 Suez crisis irrevocably confirmed Nasser in his role as an all-Arab leader, he began to assume the role in early 1955 when he launched a vigorous diplomatic offensive against the Baghdad Pact, a Western-sponsored regional defence organization. His subsequent trip to the Bandung Afro-Asian conference in April 1955, his arms deal with Czechoslovakia in September 1955 and his nationalization of the Suez Canal in July 1956 constituted further steps on the road to Arabism. By the end of 1956, his pan-Arab policy was fully crystallized. [12]

The peak of both Nasser's popularity and Arab nationalism occurred between 1956 and the June 1967 war. Nasser was immensely popular throughout the Arab world where his attraction cut across class and group lines. In late 1957, leading Syrian Baathists began pressing for a speedy union with Egypt, which was consummated on 1 February 1958, with the proclamation of the United Arab Republic (UAR). Backward Yemen soon joined the UAR in a loose federation termed the United Arab States; and in the early days of the July 1958 revolution, Iraq was also expected to join. Thereafter, the momentum was gradually lost. The Iraqi government decided to remain independent; Syria withdrew from the UAR in 1961; and Yemen was eventually expelled from its associate status. In 1962 civil war broke out in Yemen; and Nasser committed Egyptian troops to a prolonged struggle which tied up over one-third of the Egyptian army and proved a heavy burden on the Egyptian economy. [13]

After Syria's cession from the UAR, the Egyptian leadership introduced the new element of Arab socialism into its revolutionary ideology. Unity among the various Arab states was now seen as insufficient or impossible unless preceded by a socialist revolution. Thus the fundamental principle of Arab nationalism — the unification of all the Arab states from the Atlantic Ocean to the Gulf — lost its primacy and became conditional upon the success of the socialist revolution in each Arab state. This shift in policy was signalled when Nasser replaced the National Union with the Arab Socialist

Union as Egypt's sole political party. The socialist trend in the Arab world was further strengthened by the success of the extremist wing of the Algerian revolution and the subsequent declaration of a socialist democratic state in an independent Algeria.[14]

The Arab defeat in the June 1967 war dealt a severe psychological blow to the confidence and prestige of Arab leaders and the Arab people. As Fouad Ajami has perceptively observed, 'Pan-Arabism's retreat began in 1967 after the Six-Day War, which marked the Waterloo of Pan-Arabism.'[15] The 1967 defeat undermined the legitimacy of key revolutionary regimes, especially the pan-Arabists in Cairo and Damascus. But most especially, it discredited the Nasser regime and devalued its policies. A number of key events after 1967 symbolized the change which had occurred. In Egypt, Anwar Sadat replaced Nasser in 1970; and after the October 1973 war established Sadat's legitimacy, the Egyptian government pursued an increasingly independent foreign policy in which pan-Arabism was subordinated to Egyptian interests and concerns. To the Palestinians, one lesson of the 1967 war was that the state of Israel could not be destroyed by conventional armies led by existing Arab regimes. Therefore, the Palestinians in the guise of Palestinian nationalism resolved to do more for themselves. In Syria, the rise to power of Hafez al-Assad in 1970 marked the decline of the Baathist commitment to Arab unity, in favour of a more pragmatic ideology.[16]

Qaddafi's approach
While evidence of Arab nationalism and anti-Western feeling surfaced in Libya under King Idris, especially in the latter days of the monarchy, it fell to Qaddafi to articulate an Arab nationalist ideology. In the early years of the revolution, Qaddafi was the Arab nationalist par excellence, paying little more than lip service to the Arab socialist component of Nasserism. Freely acknowledging his debt to Nasser, Qaddafi described the Libyan revolution as a continuation of the Arab revolution best epitomized by the Egyptian revolution of 1952.[17] Faced with a relatively low level of national identity, Qaddafi also viewed the promotion of Arab nationalism as one means to overcome the regional, tribal and clan divisions which plagued Libyan society.[18]

Like al-Kawakibi, Qaddafi founded his Arab nationalism on a glorification of Arab history and culture which conceived of the Arabic-speaking world as the Arab nation. He saw Libya as the heart, the vanguard and the hope of the Arab nation, and thus as the custodian of Arab nationalism. In a theme common to Arab nationalists, Qaddafi blamed the backwardness of the Arab nation on four centuries of stagnation under Ottoman rule, the subjugation and exploitation of first European colonialism and then imperialism, and the corruption and repression of reactionary, monarchical rule. For example, the preface to the constitutional proclamation issued by the RCC on 11 December 1969 argued that an 'alliance between reactionary forces and colonialism' was responsible for the 'backwardness' suffered by the Libyan people, as well as for the 'corruption' spreading in their governing structures. At the heart of this concept of Arab nationalism was the feeling that the Arab people had special qualities, values and distinctions which set them apart from outsiders and gave them the right and the duty to manage their own resources and shape their own destiny.[19] Especially in the early 1970s, Qaddafi was reminiscent of Ajami's 'nativist' in that it seemed to feel the whole world should be in the Arab world rather than the Arab world simply being a part of the whole world.[20]

As in most revolutions, the first stage of the Libyan revolution was strongly nationalistic. Philosophically, Qaddafi articulated a three-fold concept of freedom which stressed the liberation of the individual from poverty, ignorance and injustice; the liberation of the homeland (Libya) from imperialist and reactionary elements; and the political, economic and social emancipation of the entire Arab world. Given the consistent, closely integrated ideological values which governed policies in these areas, developments in them tended to be highly interrelated, with external relations equally important to internal affairs and vice versa.[21]

Practically speaking, Qaddafi focused on highly symbolic acts of national independence which were widely popular and thus increased the legitimacy of the revolutionary government. In mid-September 1969, for example, the RCC declared that all signs, cards and tickets in Libya should be written in the Arabic language only. Similar measures had been enacted under the monarchy, but they were now more strictly enforced. The declaration was soon supplemented by an order requiring the mandatory translation of foreign passports into Arabic and a campaign to increase the use of Arabic as an international language, officially recognized by the United Nations and other international bodies. The RCC also banned the consumption of alcohol in Libya and any public entertainment which might be considered pornographic, obscene or vulgar. Law 56, issued on 5 May 1970, declared that 'no pornographic, obscene or vulgar performances or performances intended for or involving erotic excitement may be permitted'. While many such acts were of little practical value, they had an enormous symbolic impact because they emphasized the revolutionary government's rejection of foreign values.[22]

The new regime also moved quickly to end the base agreements negotiated with the British and American governments in 1953 and 1954 respectively and scheduled to end in the coming decade. While the monarchy had indicated as early as 1964 that it did not intend to renew the agreements, the RCC in late October 1969 pressured Britain and the United States to withdraw immediately, returning the facilities to Libyan control. After the

Western powers had complied with the Libyan request, the dates of their withdrawals were designated official public holidays by the RCC and celebrated annually with popular festivities, normally capped by a strongly nationalistic address by Qaddafi. Similarly, the day on which Italian–owned assets were confiscated and the remaining Italians expelled was also declared a national holiday.[23]

In a further attempt to increase domestic support for the new regime, the RCC carefully created or re-created resistance symbols and ideals from earlier generations. In particular, the RCC used — and distorted — the Italo-Libyan struggle which began at the end of 1911 and only ended in late 1931 after the Sanusi resistance leader Umar al-Mukhtar was finally captured and hanged. In one of his first speeches, Qaddafi portrayed the 1969 revolution as the continuation of the struggle for which al-Mukhtar and hundreds before him had died. Thereafter, representatives of the revolutionary government continued to describe the success of the revolution as the embodiment of the Libyan people's struggle throughout the generations, often referring specifically to military battles and martyrs from the Italo–Libyan wars.[24]

Revolutionary regimes have often taken a distorted view of their predecessors, since few dictatorial or totalitarian governments could thrive if they were required to be objective in their interpretation of their socio-economic and political inheritance.[25] The RCC was no exception. It was stridently critical of the programmes and policies of the monarchy, which it dismissed as stagnant, corrupt and inefficient. Major participants in the old regime were branded enemies of the people and imprisoned or expelled. Further recognizing the low level of national identity, Qaddafi repeatedly stressed the need for national unity. Like most revolutionary leaders, Qaddafi saw unity as the most important form of allegiance, with no loyalty taking precedence over that to the state and its revolutionary government. All Libyans were expected to support the revolution and work to achieve its goals. In this respect, the domestic repression and control which became increasingly evident in Libya in the 1970s belied the government's alleged concern for the liberation of the individual.[26]

Third Universal Theory

By late 1972 Qaddafi had begun to give the tenets of his strain of Arab nationalism a theoretical foundation with the articulation of what came to be called the Third Universal (or Third International) Theory. The Third Universal Theory was an attempt to develop a practical alternative to communism and capitalism, both of which Qaddafi, like many Arab nationalists, found unsuitable for the local environment. Initially, the theory condemned both systems as monopolistic, communism as a state monopoly of ownership and capitalism as a monopoly of ownership by capitalists and companies. Later in the decade, the revolutionary government adopted a centrally controlled economy and pursued a path to socialism more fundamental and extreme than that of its Arab neighbours. In the beginning, Qaddafi also grouped the United States and the Soviet Union together as imperialist countries intent on expanding spheres of influence in the Middle East; but later he increasingly drew a distinction between the foreign policies of the superpowers. Qaddafi also denounced the atheistic character of the Soviet regime, rejecting communism as 'a political and economic concept void of the Word of the Almighty... '[27]

Downplaying economic interpretations of history, Qaddafi based the Third Universal Theory on the twin pillars of nationalism and religion, which he described as the paramount drives moving history and mankind.[28] Nationalism in general was a product of the world's racial and cultural diversity, and was thus viewed as both a necessary and a productive force. Arab nationalism in particular was considered to have rich and deep roots in the ancient past. Because the Arab nation was the product of an age-old civilization which was in turn based on a 'heavenly and universal' message, namely Islam, Qaddafi argued that the Arab nation had both the right and the duty to be the bearer of the Third Universal Theory to the world.[29]

The advocacy of an alternative path, or third road, between communism and capitalism was common to many Islamic reformers and Islamic ideologies in the twentieth century. While Qaddafi viewed his message as universal, his theory aroused very little interest outside Libya; and attempts to export it met with minimal success. Northern Chad, occupied by the Libyan armed forces for a number of years, remained the only area outside of Libya where the institutional aspects of the theory were applied to any large extent.[30]

While Qaddafi never produced a coherent, comprehensive discussion of religion, his thoughts in various statements and seminars focused on the centrality of Islam to religion and the Quran to Islam. Adopting a catholic concept of Islam reminiscent of the ideas of the founder of the Syrian Nationalist Party, Antun Saadah, and the Baath ideologue Zaki Arsuzi, he argued that 'There is nothing in real life... for which principles are not found in Islam.'[31] Islam was God's final utterance to man; therefore, 'Islam and the theories derived from it are the only path that can lead humanity out of darkness into the light.'[32] In April 1972, the first session of the Libyan Arab Socialist Union declared Islam the single source of human values and civilization and termed the struggle against the imperialist-Zionist alliance a holy war. In December 1978, the Libyan General People's Congress passed a resolution stating that one of the grounds for the abrogation of Libyan citizenship was the abandonment of Islam for another religion.[33]

For Qaddafi, the unity of God was the essence of religion; and thus he refused to distinguish among what he referred to as the followers of Muhammad, Jesus and Moses. For God, there was only one religion, and that was the religion of Islam; consequently, all monotheists must by definition be Muslims. Qaddafi referred to his contention that anyone who believed in God and his apostles was a Muslim as the 'divine concept of Islam'.[34]

In a 1980 discussion of the status of Christian Arabs, Qaddafi expanded his argument, clarifying his position on the interrelationship of Arab nationalism and Islam. He stated that every nation, especially the Arab nation, must have a religion, and that the religion of Arab nationalism was Islam. In his mind, Christian Arabs had simply adopted the wrong position and must convert to Islam if they were to become real Arabs. Qaddafi concluded that 'it is wrong to be an Arab and a Christian at the same time. The prophet of the Arabs is Muhammad, and the Quran came down in the Arabic language'.[35] In this manner, Qaddafi firmly rejected the doctrine of secular Arab nationalism developed by Syrian Christians over one hundred years earlier. Similarly, he adopted a position opposed to Michel Aflaq of the Syrian Baath Party, who had argued that Arab nationalism comprehended Islam but was superior to it. Baath leaders, for the most part, were either indifferent or hostile to Islam, because their movement was committed to destroying tradition and 'tradition in the Arab world was deeply and ultimately Islamic'.[36]

The Sanusiya order, like the Wahhabi movement of the Arabian peninsula, was a revivalist as opposed to a reformist movement, as it was essentially conservative if not reactionary. While the similarities can be overemphasized, there were some important continuities between the doctrines of the Sanusiya revival movement and the more fundamentalist elements of Qaddafi's early approach to Islam. In search of Islamic unity, the Sanusiya order accepted both the Quran and the *sunna* (the way of the Prophet) as the basis for Muslim life, while largely rejecting additional doctrinal sources like *ijma*, or general agreement, and *qiyas*, or analogy. Seeking to return to an earlier, simpler form of Islam, the order also downplayed the role of the various schools of Islamic jurisprudence, although it tended to follow the Maliki rite dominant throughout North Africa.[37] Qaddafi emphasized the order's fundamentalist elements in the early years of the revolution in large part to establish his own religious credentials and thus enhance the legitimacy of the regime. At the same time, he discouraged the formation or revival of religious lodges and brotherhoods, and pursued socio-economic and political policies which reduced the residual power and prestige of the Sanusi movement.[38]

Changing role of Islam

In the early, highly nationalistic phase of the revolution, Qaddafi initiated a programme to reinstate the *sharia*, or Islamic law. At the time, the legal system that prevailed in Libya was drawn largely from French models and was similar to that in Egypt, Syria and Iraq, although it also reflected Italian influence due to Libya's exposure to Italian law during the colonial era. In October 1971, a law was promulgated which established a commission to review existing Libyan law with a view towards eliminating rules that violated the *sharia* as well as devising projects for reinstating fundamental *sharia* principles. The commission's greatest impact was in the area of criminal law; however, not all the traditional features of the *sharia* in this area were revived. Some of the principles of *sharia* law regarding aleatory contracts and interest charges were also revived; but the new laws were drafted in such a way as to avoid conflict with Western commercial and investment practices. Minor changes in the law, for example making the state responsible for collecting the *zakat*, or Islamic alms tax, were also enacted.[39]

Not all of these early changes to the legal system enhanced the prestige and application of the *sharia*. The separate jurisdiction of *sharia* courts was abolished, leaving secular courts to sit on *sharia* matters; and the venerable Islamic institution of the family *waqf*, a form of trust established to provide income for family members, was abolished. Modest reforms to the law of marriage and divorce were also enacted which reduced the sway of the *sharia* and modified it in its remaining areas of application. Great publicity was given to the reinstatement of *sharia* law; but by 1974, when the trickle of enabling legislation had dried up, the Libyan legal system as a whole was not markedly more Islamic. Moreover, in some areas the Westernizing process continued.[40]

For the next few years, Qaddafi focused on publicizing and implementing the Third Universal Theory as outlined in the three volumes of *The Green Book* published after 1975. At the same time, his ideas on the foundation of Islam, Islamic jurisprudence and the role of religious leaders shifted in the direction of the transcendence of God, with Qaddafi himself becoming a new prophet of Islam. In two important speeches in 1978, he argued that the current state of Islam was God's punishment for a people whom he had intended to be the finest on earth but who had forsaken the teachings of Islam, deviated from the straight path drawn by the Islamic religion, and become backward and a target for all colonial powers. In particular, he moved to correct contemporary Islamic practices which he considered contrary to the faith. He rejected official interpretation of the Quran, with the exception of his own, as blasphemy and sin, contending that every Arab could read it and apply it without the help of others. As Qaddafi had emphasized earlier, 'the heavenly books rightly direct man and allow him to think, choose, study and deduce freely to conclude results; otherwise, what is man's role?'[41]

Similarly, he criticized emphasis on the *hadith*, the collected traditions or 'sayings' of the Prophet Muhammad as received through oral transmission, on the grounds that the Quran was the truest source of God's word. In response to claims that *ijma* had established that certain standard *hadith* were trustworthy, he insisted that Muslims had no assurance that false *hadith* had not been inserted even in standard collections. He also criticized the recognized schools of Islamic jurisprudence, such as the Hanafi, Maliki and Hanbali, alleging they were the product of struggles for political power and unconnected with either Islam or the Quran. Qaddafi emphasized that outside the sphere of what he defined as being the concern of religion, *The Green Book* should be applied. If religious scholars (*ulama*) and jurists (*fuqaha*) chose to oppose *The Green Book* on the grounds that it conflicted with Islam, he indicated they could expect the same fate that befell Turkish religious leaders when they opposed Atatürk's progressive reforms and stirred up opposition against him.[42]

Qaddafi's initial approach to Arab nationalism, Islam and government was primarily in terms of the use of Islamic precepts, as opposed to Islamic organizational structures, for state purposes.[43] Later, reformist elements of that approach — such as a progressive role for Islam, the rejection of the *hadith*, the transcendence of God and the purely human role of the Prophet — were employed to reduce the role of religious leadership and bring Islam under closer control of the revolution. When Libya's religious leadership criticized Qaddafi's policies, he purged them, explaining that mosques were intended to be places of worship and not arenas for the discussion of social, economic and political issues.

While some observers described Qaddafi's denial of political influence to religious leaders as secularism, it was really more than that, since the denial extended to every elite or popular body that might reduce the regime's power. Furthermore, religious bodies and religious leadership were denied not only political influence but even autonomy in religion itself. Secularism generally refers to the separation of church and state with the latter being supreme, but it does not necessitate or anticipate the state's control of the details of religious teaching or the harnessing of religion to the purpose of the state.[44]

While Qaddafi's concept of Islam was increasingly divergent from that of Nasser, his use of the Islamic component of Arab nationalism had much in common with Nasser's. Shortly after coming to power, the Egyptian president began to use Islam to mobilize the masses for new internal goals, to neutralize potential opposition and to further the regime's foreign policy in Africa and the Middle East. This policy was strengthened over time as the regime recognized more and more that Islam remained the widest and most effective basis for consensus, despite efforts to promote alternatives like secularism, nationalism and socialism.[45] In the process, the Egyptian government tried to induce the masses to see beyond religion or to see it differently, that is to see it as the regime planned to use it — to buttress nationalism, socialism and popular democracy. In this context, Nasser's denial of political influence to the *ulama*, like Qaddafi's, was not truly secularist. Because strong religious beliefs and loyalties characterized their respective peoples, the avowedly secular leaders of both states were not content to remain simply secular. Both Qaddafi and Nasser went beyond secularism in an effort to make Islam an internal and external instrument in support of the revolution.[46]

In later years, the Islamic character of Qaddafi's Arab nationalism and the supposed universal elements of his Third Universal Theory became increasingly paradoxical. Qaddafi's response was to continue to emphasize the centrality of Islam to Arab nationalism while downplaying Islam's role in the Third Universal Theory. While his strategy remained vague, his downplaying of Islam appeared designed to give the Third Universal Theory wider appeal outside Libya. In any case, his argument that the Third Universal Theory was the basis for a new world order centred on the Arab nation logically resulted in Islam having a central role.[47]

Islam and Arab nationalism

Qaddafi modelled his approach to Arab nationalism on a wide range of Arab and Islamic thinkers, but the influence of Nasser was paramount. His model was Nasser's fiery Arab nationalism of the 1950s and not the more subdued version of the late 1960s. While Qaddafi revived Arab nationalism, he did very little to change its philosophical approach or content. His early speeches were modelled closely on those delivered by Nasser some two decades earlier; and the emphasis of such speeches changed very little after 1969. Speeches delivered by Qaddafi in the second half of the 1980s contained the same references to Palestine, the Italo–Libyan war, Zionist forces and imperialism as those delivered almost two decades earlier. The level of continuity was doubly remarkable given the socio–economic and political changes which occurred in the Middle East in the intervening period, and highlighted the anachronistic character of Qaddafi's approach to Arab nationalism.

Qaddafi also revived Islam as a key component of Arab nationalism. While it would be an overstatement to claim that the September 1969 coup marked the beginning of the Islamic revival in the Middle East, it played a role in that revival. Islam quickly assumed a dominant role in the symbols and vocabulary of the Libyan revolutionary government. Rooted in the Sanusi tradition, Qaddafi's concept of Islam soon transcended that tradition as he imposed on Libya a brand of Islam which increasingly bore little relationship to the mainstream religion. Qaddafi believed the Arab and Islamic identities were inextricably linked; therefore, he felt the Arab revolution must also be an Islamic one. From this, it followed that the leader of Arab nationalism must also be the leader of Arab Islam and offer revolutionary programmes for both.

Qaddafi saw himself as a revolutionary thinker as well as a revolutionary leader. He courted dialogue with intellectuals inside and outside the Muslim world; and his writings, especially *The Green Book*, were translated and disseminated widely. His public statements frequently referred to his ideological ascendancy and reiterated his conviction that the Third Universal Theory would eventually guide the world. In the interim, the revolutionary ideology developed under the umbrella of Arab nationalism, and encapsulated in the Third Universal Theory, provided the framework for Libyan foreign policy after 1969.

3
Qaddafi's Holy War

The third theory is based on the concept of launching a holy war for the sake of God, the Almighty, and the propagation of God's religion and establishing His precepts on earth.

Muammar al-Qaddafi

The Palestinian question did not contribute to the early development of Arab nationalism; however, it became the principal catalyst for the rise of the movement after World War I when the growth of the Zionist movement culminated in the creation of the state of Israel. The common Arab nationalist viewpoint, based on the notion of a conspiracy against the Arab world, was that Palestine remained an integral part of the Arab nation which must be liberated. The enemy was Zionism, a European political movement, and not the Jews as such. The hostile forces of imperialism were Israel, the seldom-named Zionist invader state, and the colonial powers in Western Europe and North America responsible for imposing this indignity on the Arab people. In the eyes of Arab nationalists, the imperialist powers, motivated by greed and a hatred of Islam and the Arabs, created Zionist Israel in a deliberate conspiracy to divide the Arab people and exploit Arab resources. Conservative Arab states which aligned themselves with the West were viewed not only as reactionary and corrupt but also as collaborators with imperialism and Zionism.

Arab solutions to the Palestinian problem varied over the years; but they often centred on a *jihad*, or holy war, whose objective was nothing less than the total liberation of Palestine. Qaddafi accepted enthusiastically the common Arab nationalist viewpoint towards the Palestinian issue, and seized on *jihad* as the only solution to the problem. Ideologically, his approach to *jihad* was based, first, on the Islamic components of his definition of Arab nationalism, and later on the Third Universal Theory. Over the years, he expanded both the scope and application of *jihad*; and in the process, he found himself increasingly at odds with the mainstream leadership of the Palestinian movement.

Reorientation
While the Libyan monarchy had sympathized with the Palestinians, the

35

Revolutionary Command Council moved from sympathy to active support. The Palestinian cause was placed in the forefront of all Arab causes, with the road to Palestine described as the path to the liberation of Arabs everywhere. Palestine was seen to be an integral part of the Arab nation, which could never be truly free and united until Palestine was liberated. The Zionist presence in Palestine was dismissed as nothing more than the latest bridgehead or military base to protect the interests of imperialism and neo-colonialism in the Middle East. The revolutionary government pledged all its material and moral capabilities to the Palestinian cause, and declared that its diplomatic relations with other states would be strongly influenced by their position on the Palestinian issue. In later years, it often made good on this threat, especially in Africa where Libyan largesse was largely predicated on a state's termination of diplomatic relations with Israel.[1]

Arab unity became a pivotal part of the early Libyan position on the Palestinian issue. As Palestinian nationalism emerged under the mandate, Palestinian leaders concluded they must involve the rest of the Arab world in their struggle if they were to achieve the desired diplomatic result. By the late 1940s, Palestine had become an Arab problem; and it remained at the centre of inter-Arab politics for the next two decades. In this period, Palestinian organizations, parties and leadership were generally secondary to a plethora of Arab political movements, especially Nasserism and Baathism. Qaddafi and the other members of the RCC adopted the old slogan that Arab unity was the road to Palestine. They argued that Palestine was lost when the Arabs were divided and that they must unite before they could hope to free it.[2]

Qaddafi saw *jihad* as the action element of Arab nationalism. *Jihad* was the requisite tool to achieve social justice inside and outside Libya. Initially, both imperialism and communism were considered equal threats; however, as the revolution unfolded, imperialism was increasingly identified as the prime target for *jihad*. As Qaddafi emphasized in 1973, 'any contribution to liberate the world from imperialism should be considered an integral part of *jihad*.'[3]

The RCC soon gave practical expression to Qaddafi's emphasis on *jihad*. In January 1970, a Jihad Fund was created to establish a strong Libyan armed force 'to support the armed struggle for the liberation of usurped Arab territories from Zionist control'.[4] Funded initially from public and private contributions including the *zakat* (Islamic alms tax), a *jihad* tax on profits and income was later imposed to increase the financial strength of the fund. An Association for the Propagation of Islam was also founded in 1970 to train Muslim missionaries. By 1977, the association reportedly had deployed 350 missionaries, only two of whom were Libyans.[5] In May 1979 at an Islamic conference in Morocco, the Libyan foreign minister expressed support for the creation of a pan-Islamic military force; and at the end of the decade, an Islamic Legion, partially composed of mercenaries from the Sahel and the

Sahara, appeared in public for the first time. Its official aim was to buttress the Palestinian struggle as well as to support Islamic movements struggling against oppression. More recently, Qaddafi announced in March 1985 the formation of a National Command of the Revolutionary Forces of the Arab World, or Pan-Arab Command, a shadowy group which seemed destined to combat American influence in the Arab world.[6]

Fatah

The concept of *jihad* found its most practical expression in Qaddafi's support for Palestinian groups. In particular, the RCC endorsed and supported with money and facilities the mainstream Fatah wing of the Palestine Liberation Organization, whose leader Yasser Arafat was a frequent visitor to Libya after 1 September 1969. Given the background and experience of RCC members as intense, early Nasser-style Arab nationalists, this policy direction was to be expected and would have been remarkable only if it had not occurred. Other Palestinian factions were disapproved of, if not purged or expelled. Members of the Marxist Popular Front for the Liberation of Palestine (PFLP), for example, were condemned by Qaddafi as 'neither fighters nor liberators' but rather 'lackeys of philosophy'. Because 'their pamphlets contained more on Marxism than on the Palestinian cause', Qaddafi expelled them from Libya. For the Libyan regime as for many Arab regimes, there was no battle-cry more indispensable than the Palestinian one, but the Palestine liberation movements had to be creatures of Arab regimes. Qaddafi, in particular, remained concerned that the Palestinian issue complement and not obstruct the move towards Arab unity.[7]

Qaddafi eagerly endorsed the concept of a war of liberation as the appropriate combat instrument against Israel. In the beginning, he advocated direct military action against Israel. He maintained this emphasis even after the October 1973 war strengthened the PLO, and the oil weapon proved a much more effective instrument in support of Palestinian goals.[8] In theory, Qaddafi's maximalist position left no room for negotiation or compromise; but in practice, his emphasis on the 'totality of the battle' was open to interpretation in different contexts and times. For example, Libya did not join in the October 1973 war, arguing that conditions were not right for a total Arab victory. While Libya supplied oil, money and weapons, Qaddafi claimed that protracted conflict, guerrilla operations and trading space for time were the best ways to overcome Israel's power. His policy of standing aside when the battle was joined increased Libya's estrangement from Syria and Egypt.[9] Nevertheless, Qaddafi continued to argue that the real issue was the survival of the Arab nation. Its existence was incompatible with the Zionist state, and only one of the two could survive. From this perspective, it was hardly surprising that Qaddafi's objective remained the complete, total liberation of Palestine and the expulsion of all Jews who had settled there after 1948.[10]

In support of his rhetoric, Qaddafi frequently called for direct action. As early as 1972, several hundred Libyans, with job tenure and associated rights guaranteed by the RCC, were believed to be serving with Arab guerrilla forces in Syria or Lebanon. In July 1972, the First Nasserite Volunteers' Camp, a base for equipping and training *fedayeen* (guerrilla fighters) for the conflict with Israel, was opened east of Tripoli near Misurata. Qaddafi continued to advocate the use of armed force to liberate Palestine long after his peers had shifted to other means. In the second half of the 1970s, the formation of ad hoc, surrogate groups made it possible for the leaders of governments and political movements to pursue the liberation struggle while dissociating themselves from acts of violence. In this changing milieu, Qaddafi literally stuck to his guns, although he began to differentiate between revolutionary violence, which he strongly supported, and terrorism, which he claimed to oppose.[11]

In addition to Palestinian groups, Qaddafi also extended Libyan support to a wide variety of other groups engaged in so-called wars of national liberation. In June 1972 at ceremonies marking the second anniversary of the United States' withdrawal from Wheelus air base, Qaddafi made broad statements of Libyan intent to provide material support to minority Muslims in the Philippines, the Irish Republican Army (IRA) in Ireland and militant black groups in the United States. The resulting diplomatic furore later caused Libyan to tone down its proposed aid to the level of moral support; nevertheless, evidence of Libyan material support for guerrilla-cum-terrorist groups mounted over the years. Such efforts focused on Africa and the Middle East but included movements in Central and South America, Europe and Asia. At a time when state-sponsored terrorism became, in effect, surrogate warfare between governments, Qaddafi played an active role because the provision of support for and shelter to terrorists enhanced the international status of an otherwise not very important state.[12] Qaddafi's support also exposed his befuddled thinking on the social context of the Libyan revolution. Convinced the Third Universal Theory was applicable beyond Libya's shores, he mistakenly believed he could tie acceptance of Libyan financial, material and moral support to the adoption of his theoretical formulations.

Palestine before unity
As Qaddafi refined his policy on *jihad*, the Palestinians themselves, especially the members of Fatah, were moving in new directions which made the content and direction of Qaddafi's policy increasingly irrelevant. After 1961, some Palestinians became convinced that the Arab governments, if left to themselves, could not be relied upon to bring about the desired confrontation with Israel. These Palestinians concluded they must take the lead in seeking to redress their grievances. The June 1967 war accelerated this

process as it shattered the prestige and moral leadership of conservative and revolutionary Arab regimes alike, fundamentally altering the terms of the relationship that had previously existed between the Palestinian guerrillas and the Arab states.[13]

With the leadership of the Arab world disoriented, it seemed even less likely that it could or would do much to help the Palestinians. Consequently, Palestinian leaders, many of whom had for years subordinated their political activities to the cause of Arab unity, began to call for the creation of Palestinian political organizations independent of the Arab states. In the process, they reversed the old slogan that Arab unity was the path to the liberation of Palestine, arguing that the liberation of Palestine would become the road to Arab unity. This heightened sense of Palestinian self-respect and determined activism contrasted sharply with the low morale in the Arab states after the June defeat, and provided a focus for political activity, especially among Palestinians in Jordan and Lebanon. By February 1969, when the leadership of the PLO was taken over by Fatah, and the guerrilla movement thus became the official representative of the Palestinian people, the PLO became a major political force in the Middle East with a distinctive ideology, a set strategy, a programme of action and both the political and military means for their execution.[14]

Key events in 1970–75 reinforced the determination of the Palestinians to chart their own future. When the Jordanian government moved against the Palestinian guerrillas in Jordan in September 1970, for example, Syria was the only Arab government to come to the Palestinians' aid. The lesson the guerrillas drew from the so-called Black September was that they could rely on no Arab regime, however friendly, to put its commitment to them above a more pressing *raison d'état*.[15] Paradoxically, the PLO, whose military role in the October 1973 war had been marginal, emerged strengthened from the conflict. Meeting in Algeria in November 1973, Arab heads of state designated the PLO as 'the sole legitimate representative of the Palestinian people', although the decision was not publicized at first to avoid embarrassing King Hussein of Jordan. The resolution was officially confirmed in October 1974 at an Arab summit meeting in Rabat, Morocco.[16]

As the political visibility and viability of the PLO increased, it moderated its stand on the use of terrorism as a political tactic. In part, this was due to the success with which Arab states had manipulated oil deliveries and prices during the 1973 war. As the oil weapon proved to be a more effective tool than terrorism in achieving Arab goals, several Arab states evidenced their increasing disillusionment with Palestinian terrorism. In December 1973, for example, when Palestinian terrorists massacred 33 airline passengers in Rome and Athens, the terrorists were refused permission to land by every Arab country, including Libya. In addition, the achievements of Palestinian terrorists proved increasingly counterproductive. Operations like the terrorist attack on the Israeli Olympic team in September 1972, and the kidnapping of Opec ministers in December 1975, risked alienating world opinion as well as the very Arab governments in a position to manipulate the oil weapon. PLO recognition of its vulnerability in this regard surfaced in January 1975 in response to a terrorist attack at Orly airport near Paris. After suggestions were made that the pro-Arab policy of the French government should be reviewed because it failed to prevent the incident, the PLO issued a strong condemnation of the attack, announcing that in future it would treat hijacking of airplanes, ships or trains as crimes, and would impose death penalties on hijackers if their actions led to loss of life.[17] Whether or not the PLO faithfully followed this policy after 1975 is, in this context, less important than the fact that its issuance suggested a realization that public reaction to terrorist activity could retard rather than advance the movement's objectives.

The unregenerate rejectionist

While the strategy and tactics of the PLO underwent considerable change in the 1970s, there was little perceptible movement in Qaddafi's approach to the Arab-Israeli conflict. Libya remained an unregenerate rejectionist, arguing that the crux of the problem was the Israeli presence in the Middle East. Support for liberation and radical movements increased as Libyan foreign policy generally moved towards the left. Qaddafi expressed support for the Dhofar revolutionaries in Oman, supported Algeria on the Western Sahara question and expanded ties with the more radical Palestinian movements, boasting that only Libya stood behind the rejectionists in the Arab world.[18]

The Libyan government had termed the 1972 attack on the Israeli Olympic squad at Munich a 'heroic action', and the bodies of the five Arab guerrillas killed in the action were later flown to Tripoli, where they were buried as 'hero martyrs'.[19] Qaddafi denied involvement in the 1975 kidnap of Opec ministers; but inconclusive evidence suggested Libyan complicity. Throughout the Lebanese civil war which broke out in April 1975, Libya continued its support of Palestinian as well as leftist groups, apparently in the hope that the struggle would end Lebanon's confessional-sectarian divisions of political and military power, especially the dominant position of the Maronite Christians. In particular, Qaddafi's lieutenant, Abdel-Salam Jallud, worked hard and courageously, albeit unsuccessfully, during this stage of the conflict to save the Palestinians from political and military humiliation. Despite a short-lived participation in the largely Syrian-manned Arab Deterrent Force, Libya was basically opposed to Syria's intervention in Lebanon in 1976, as this probably saved the main rightist Christian forces from total defeat.[20]

During the civil war, Libya also bolstered the political standing of Lebanon's largest sectarian minority, the Muslim Shiite sect led by the Iranian-born Imam Musa al-Sadr. Musa al-Sadr disappeared in August 1978 while on a visit to Libya to obtain material support for his movement Amal. Qaddafi subsequently referred to Musa al-Sadr as an 'agent' of the Shah of Iran; and although Qaddafi denied any knowledge of his whereabouts, the Imam's fate remained a mystery which continued to plague subsequent Libyan relations with Lebanon, Iran and Shiite communities elsewhere.[21]

In particular, the government of Ayatollah Khomeini long refused to establish close official ties with Libya until Qaddafi had satisfactorily explained the disappearance of Khomeini's friend Musa al-Sadr. Nevertheless, Libya remained for several years a consistent supporter of Iran in its war with Iraq. In June 1985, Libya and Iran issued a joint communiqué announcing what amounted to a strategic alliance. This caused Iraq to break diplomatic relations with Libya. Later, Qaddafi distanced himself from Iran in an apparent effort to win Muslim support for his intervention in Chad. In early 1987, he commented that it was not important who won the Gulf war as long as it was brought to an end. At about the same time, articles appeared in the Libyan press which condemned Iran as un-Islamic because the Iran-contra fiasco had revealed it was dealing with both Israel and the United States.[22]

The visit of Egyptian President Anwar Sadat to Jerusalem on 19 November 1977 led to the formation in Libya in December 1977 of the Steadfastness and Confrontation Front. Founding members included Syria, Algeria, Libya, South Yemen and the PLO. Iraq participated in the conference but refused to sign the final declaration after disagreeing with Syria. Libya played an instrumental role in the formation of the Steadfastness Front, whose creation fulfilled a long-standing Libyan objective of establishing an anti-Egyptian alliance. While the Steadfastness Front expressed support for a variety of revolutionary and liberation movements in the Arab world, its major purpose was to co-ordinate Arab opposition to Sadat's peace initiative.[23]

Opposition to Sadat's initiative, the 1978 Camp David accords and the 1979 Egypt-Israel peace treaty went beyond the confines of the Steadfastness and Confrontation Front. This fact pressured Qaddafi to modify Libyan foreign policy in two significant ways. To gain greater support against Sadat, Libya had first to mend its fences with as many Arab states as possible, most particularly influential Arab powers like Saudi Arabia, Iraq and Morocco who were not members of the Steadfastness Front. To advance this objective, Qaddafi in June 1979 visited Syria, Jordan, Iraq, Kuwait, Bahrain, Qatar, the United Arab Emirates, Saudi Arabia, North Yemen and South Yemen. Second, Qaddafi had to moderate his rejectionist stance on the Arab-Israeli conflict. Opposition to the Egypt-Israel peace treaty in the Arab

League, and to a lesser degree within selected governments in the Steadfastness Front, was not the same as Qaddafi's opposition to a peaceful settlement of the Arab–Israeli conflict. What key Arab states objected to was the idea of a separate peace treaty, and the way in which the Egypt–Israel pact ignored the national rights of the Palestinian people and their desire to establish an independent sovereign state.[24]

Qaddafi's move towards moderation was fleeting. At the end of 1979, an ongoing feud with the PLO, particularly with the mainstream Fatah wing, became public knowledge and led Libya to break relations with and end support for Fatah. The central issue in the dispute was PLO commitment to and capability for armed struggle. The dispute came to a head in December 1979, when Qaddafi attempted to organize the Palestinians living in Libya into his unique governmental system of congresses and committees. The PLO saw this move as a challenge to its position as the sole legitimate representative of the Palestinian people. On 16 December 1979 the PLO office in Benghazi was closed; and on 6 January 1980 the Libyan General People's Congress, the national legislative body, announced it was breaking relations with Fatah because of the policies of the Fatah leadership towards Palestine, its move towards 'capitulationist' settlements and its refusal to adopt Libya's congress-committee system. In the interim, representatives of five radical member groups of the PLO — the Popular Front for the Liberation of Palestine, the Popular Front for the Liberation of Palestine – General Command, the Democratic Front for the Liberation of Palestine, the Popular Struggle Front and Al-Saiqa — had met in Libya on 25–29 December 1979, and expressed their support for Libya's position on the use of armed struggle and a prolonged, popular liberation war as the correct means to liberate Palestine. A joint statement issued by the Palestinians termed armed struggle the path to the liberation of Palestine and rejected as false any belief that Palestine could be liberated through diplomatic efforts alone. While these radical groups agreed with Qaddafi on the place of armed struggle, it was also significant that they saw fit to remind him in their joint statement that the unity of the Palestinian people 'should be maintained within the framework of the PLO, the sole legitimate representative of the Palestinian people'.[25]

Beirut, 1982
The impact on the PLO of the summer 1982 war with Israel in Lebanon was not unlike the impact of the 1967 war on Nasser. The defeat of the PLO knocked it down from unprecedented heights of power, international recognition and prestige. Moreover, the loss of Beirut rendered the PLO a homeless organization, one increasingly the prisoner of its own internal divisions and of several antagonistic Arab regimes. The war also provoked a diaspora of Palestinian leadership — undoubtedly the most devastating blow

in the history of the PLO and the most crippling setback to Palestinian nationalism since 1948. After 1982, the Palestinians were unable to exploit those aspects of life in Beirut which had enabled the PLO to develop into a sophisticated organization, conditions non-existent elsewhere in the Arab world. In their new locations, the Palestinians often found their leadership on a short leash, with the refugees generally confined to camps. In a few cases, the host countries even claimed the right to represent and speak for the Palestinians.[26]

The 1982 war also demonstrated the obsolescence of pan-Arabism and the belief in a common Arab destiny. While the Arab states condemned Israel's expansionism, for the most part they sought to confine the damage to the Palestinians as they themselves wanted no part of the defeat. This Arab attitude was partly understandable as the Palestinians had traditionally shared only their setbacks with the Arabs while achievements and victories were treated as exclusively Palestinian. Both Beirut and the Palestinians had become a heavy burden on Arab regimes, and the latter showed little interest in sharing the humiliation of a PLO which many had come to dislike and which they supported only reluctantly. In addition, many Arab states had other priorities clearly more pressing than the liberation of Palestine, especially after Egypt had come to the peace table with Israel; Iraq and Iran had become embroiled in the Gulf war; and 'the Palestinians themselves had become deeply divided, corrupt, and more bureaucratic than revolutionary'.[27]

Increasingly isolated in the Arab world and preoccupied with events in Africa, Qaddafi played a secondary role in the 1982 war, as he had done in the 1973 war. His most memorable contribution to the fighting was a call for Yasser Arafat to commit suicide rather than accept disgrace and leave Beirut, a suggestion motivated more by self-interest than sound strategy. In a speech on 1 September 1982, which marked the 13th anniversary of the Libyan revolution, he termed the dispersal of the Palestinians 'the highest treason' and vowed to continue along a path of 'battle and confrontation' while other Arab states, with the exception of Syria, 'knelt before the enemy'.[28] Qaddafi clearly had no desire to become involved in Arab or Western discussions on the Palestinian issue; and later in the month, he boycotted an Arab summit in Fez, Morocco, dismissing its resolutions on the issue as 'high treason'.[29]

In January 1983, talks between Yasser Arafat and Jordan's King Hussein on a joint approach to the peace process precipitated a week-long meeting in Libya between Qaddafi and representatives of the same five radical member groups of the PLO which had come to Tripoli in December 1979. All five groups had relatively close ties with Syria, which was reportedly suspicious of Arafat's growing ties with Hussein. At the end of the meeting, the group issued a statement which rejected the Middle East peace plan adopted at the Arab summit in September, especially any formula which permitted the

Jordanian government to represent the Palestinian people. This move countered Arafat's attempt to forge a joint negotiating position with King Hussein along the lines suggested by President Reagan in September 1982. In a separate statement, Qaddafi added without elaboration that the Libyan government had developed with the five radical Palestinian groups a political and military action programme.[30]

Earlier, Libya had called for a summit meeting of the Steadfastness Front, although Iraq had recently blessed the PLO-Jordanian dialogue while Algeria had always supported whatever policy was acceptable to the PLO. During the first week of February 1983, Libya hosted a conference of dissident organizations and movements in Tripoli. Both Qaddafi's keynote address and the subsequent conference resolution charted a course of defiance and military opposition to Israel, the United States and Arab regimes friendly with the United States. After the Lebanese disaster, Qaddafi argued that the Arab nation was struggling for its very existence. Concrete Libyan actions in support of this renewed emphasis on radical solutions included an alleged plot against the Sudanese government, increased co-ordination of policy and resupply arrangements with the Soviet Union, arms shipments to Nicaragua and deeper involvement in Chad.[31]

Events over the next 12 months merely confirmed the extent to which Libya and Syria (with their ally Iran) had become the major radical elements in the Middle East. In Lebanon, Libya consistently espoused the Syrian position, rejecting the Lebanon-Israel accord of 13 May 1983 as an insult to the Arab homeland and demanding the withdrawal of the multinational peace-keeping force. Denouncing the Zionist enemy, Qaddafi continued to stress his absolute support for the Palestinian people and for resistance based on armed struggle. There was to be no negotiating with or recognition of the Zionist enemy.[32] Reacting to a French raid against Shiite positions in Lebanon, Qaddafi said the Arab nations and other Islamic states must be prepared for a new holy war against the Western nations. He termed the liberation of Lebanon a national, pan-Arab and Islamic duty.[33] In February 1984, the Jordanian government severed diplomatic relations with Libya after the Jordanian embassy in Tripoli was attacked and burned to the ground. At issue was Qaddafi's opposition to King Hussein's rapprochement with the Arafat wing of the PLO and the recall of the Jordanian National Assembly as part of Hussein's strategy on the Palestine issue. Qaddafi was predictably delighted when the Lebanese cabinet abrogated the 1983 accord with Israel in the spring of 1984. Libya resumed diplomatic relations with Lebanon in early May.[34]

In the coming months, Qaddafi was preoccupied with a proposed union with Morocco; however, neither his rhetoric nor his policies changed appreciably. In June 1984, he stated that Arab states which had not joined his fight against American imperialism and Israel by the 15th anniversary of the

Libyan revolution would be considered hostile to the Libyan people. On 1 September he returned to the old slogan that Arab unity was the path to the liberation of Palestine. He called upon Arab nations to join his political union with Morocco, so that a unified Arab force could march towards Palestine and destroy what he termed the 'so-called' state of Israel. In the interim, Qaddafi was charged with involvement in mining the approaches to the Suez Canal and with complicity in a plot to seize the Grand Mosque in Mecca. In August 1984, the Saudi Arabian government expelled several hundred Libyan pilgrims, many of whom were armed, because they allegedly planned to establish a People's Congress in the Grand Mosque. Towards the end of the year, Qaddafi signalled a willingness to reopen relations with Yasser Arafat; however, little progress was made after the PLO insisted that negotiations take place outside Libya and include a guarantee of non-interference in PLO affairs.[35]

Libyan relations with the PLO later improved. As the PLO appeared to give armed struggle against Israel priority over the peace process, Libya fostered PLO attempts to re-establish a military presence in southern Lebanon. In November 1986, Abdel-Salam Jallud travelled to Damascus with a message from Qaddafi to President Assad which reportedly supported the PLO's return to Lebanon. Jallud remained there until February 1987 in an attempt to mediate a solution to the fighting around the Palestinian camps in Beirut. In December 1986, Qaddafi urged the Palestinians to continue fighting Muslim Shiite forces in southern Lebanon and called for other Lebanese Muslim groups to support the Palestinians. At about the same time, a PLO envoy travelled to Libya. His arrival marked a resumption of official relations between Libya and the PLO and followed an offer by Qaddafi to host a session of the Palestine National Council to promote PLO unity. Relations between Libya and the PLO continued to improve, at least temporarily, in the spring of 1987; and two PLO officials attended Libyan ceremonies in March 1987 which marked the 10th anniversary of the proclamation of the Jamahiriya political system.[36]

Qaddafi and terrorism

Qaddafi's prolonged association with terrorism — defined here as the use by a group for political ends of covert violence which is usually directed against a government but may be against another group, class or party — led to much adverse publicity.[37] In recognition of this fact, Qaddafi unsuccessfully attempted to differentiate between terrorism, which he claimed to reject, and revolutionary violence, which he openly advocated. In March 1985, for example, he told the General People's Congress that Libya had the right to liquidate the opponents of the revolution inside or outside Libya in the full light of day. At the same time, Qaddafi compared Libyan dissidents in Europe to members of the Red Army Fraction, the Red Brigades and the

Irish Republican Army, and threatened further backing of such groups if European governments continued to protect opponents of his regime. He also reiterated support for black and Indian separatist groups in the United States, and announced the formation of a new Arab organization to confront Israel and the United States.[38]

The contradictions inherent in the Libyan position on terrorism were evident in the aftermath of the December 1985 terrorist attacks on the Vienna and Rome airports. The Libyan news agency, Jana, first described the attacks, generally credited to an extremist Palestinian faction headed by Abu Nidal, as 'heroic', saying they were fully justified because the international community was ignoring the plight of the Palestinians, thus causing them to adopt violent methods. The next day, the Libyan People's Bureau in Vienna sought to distance itself from the Jana statement by saying that the Libyan government understood the attackers' motives but neither sponsored nor supported terrorism. Four days later, Qaddafi himself denied direct or indirect involvement in the attacks, asserting that there were no Palestinian training camps in Libya. At the same time, he emphasized his support for the Palestinian cause, arguing that such attacks were part of the Palestinian people's struggle to liberate their homeland. He added that such attacks would not be legal if conducted by Libya or another sovereign state, which amounted to implicit agreement that they were legitimate weapons in the hands of Palestinian extremists. Qaddafi warned that if Israel or the United States retaliated for the attacks by attacking Libya, this could plunge the Mediterranean region into war. On the same day, PLO chairman Yasser Arafat charged that Syria and Libya were behind the recent rash of terrorist attacks in Europe and were supporting them to discredit the PLO and hinder Arab negotiations with Israel.[39]

Over the next two months, Qaddafi continued to contradict himself; and in the process he further blurred the difference between terrorism and wars of national liberation. On 10 January 1986, he reportedly condemned the terrorists who attacked the Rome and Vienna airports as madmen, and said he was trying to discourage Palestinians from attacking targets outside Israel or Israeli-occupied territories. A week later, Qaddafi told a cheering crowd in Libya that his government would equip and train guerrillas for terrorist and suicide missions. Admitting complicity with the more radical Palestinian groups, he described Libya as a base for the liberation of Palestine. Qaddafi then informed the Italian government, in a message which contrasted sharply with earlier statements, that he was willing to stop Arab terrorist operations in Europe if the United States promised not to attack Libya. Given Libya's limited influence on most terrorist groups, Palestinian or otherwise, this was an idle promise which Qaddafi was not in position to honour. In any case, Palestinian officials were quoted within the week as saying that Qaddafi had recently proposed to militant Arab leaders a new wave of violence in Europe and the United States.[40]

With the spotlight on Qaddafi's policy of *jihad*, public debate for the remainder of 1986 focused on the extent and effectiveness of Libya's support for wars of national liberation. In a January 1986 white paper, the US Department of State had charged that Libya provided money and military training to the Kanak Socialist National Liberation Front, the main political movement seeking independence for the French Pacific territory of New Caledonia, as part of Libyan opposition to French policy in Chad. While a Kanak delegation visited Libya in March 1986, the front later distanced itself from Libya as well as from other liberation movements. Similarly, the Libyan People's Bureau in Kuala Lumpur denied any links with a Malaysian Muslim fundamentalist known locally as Ibrahim Libya after his followers clashed with police leaving several dead.

In March 1986, the General People's Congress announced the creation of suicide commandos to attack Israeli and American interests worldwide; and later in the same month, Libya hosted an International Conference for Combating Imperialism, Zionism, Racism and Fascism. The conference was attended by some 700 organizations, parties and movements. On cue, Qaddafi was elected leader of the world revolution of progressive forces; and the conference called for the creation of an international revolutionary force. Later in the spring, South Africa linked African National Congress (ANC) activities to Libyan terrorism; and India became the first state to rebuke Libya publicly for local recruitment for the Islamic Legion. On 1 September 1986, Qaddafi, in an outburst of rhetoric, threatened to resign his position as Guide of the Jamahiriya and become commanding officer of a revolutionary army which would liberate the entire world.[41]

After the spring 1987 débâcle in northern Chad, the Libyan government stepped up its support for wars of national liberation. Qaddafi's attention focused on the South Pacific in apparent retaliation for French and US assistance to the Chadian government. The Libyan government was again reported to be supplying arms to Muslim guerrillas in the southern Philippines, as well as offering financial support, training and military assistance to a number of radical groups on South Pacific islands. In April 1987 Libya hosted a conference on anti-colonialism in the South Pacific. According to the Libyan news agency, it was attended by representatives from Australia, Fiji, Indonesia, Japan, New Caledonia, New Zealand, Papua New Guinea, the Philippines, the Solomon Islands, Thailand and Vanuatu. Addressing the meeting, Qaddafi accused the Western nations of turning the South Pacific into a region of strife and conflict, and called on revolutionary groups there to fight for freedom.

Greater Libyan interest in the South Pacific was disturbing to a number of states, in particular New Zealand and Australia. Both governments repeatedly expressed their concern, which centred on Libyan involvement in the small island nation of Vanuatu. Libya was active in establishing a diplomatic mission on the island, and a group from Vanuatu had reportedly travelled to Libya for paramilitary training. Although leaders of the Kanak Socialist National Liberation Front continued to downplay their ties with Libya, both New Zealand and Australia remained concerned that Libya would use Vanuatu to aid radical Kanak rebels in their fight against French rule in New Caledonia.[42]

Policy failure

The Palestinian issue was a focal point of Libyan foreign policy after 1969. Libya's bilateral and multilateral relations were largely defined in terms of how other states approached the issue and its resolution. The importance of the Palestinian question to Libyan foreign policy stemmed from its central role in the ideology of the Libyan revolution. Qaddafi's rejection of the state of Israel was symptomatic of a broader rejection of the existing international system. While his holy war aimed at a radical solution to the Palestinian question, its wider objective was the achievement of a new world order based on the ideas encapsulated in the Third Universal Theory.

Palestine was central to Qaddafi's ideology, but he was not a major actor in Palestinian politics. He remained the committed rejectionist when individual Palestinians, as well as Palestinian groups, began to accept in different degrees the need for a compromise solution to the Palestinian problem. Increasingly isolated from the mainstream leadership of the Palestine Liberation Organization, his role was reduced to that of the spoiler. He would not contribute to a negotiated settlement to the problem, but he laboured endlessly to prevent others from achieving a viable solution.

State-sponsored terrorism has often been the instrument of political leaders with ambitions in excess of their power base. This was true in Libya's case, since its commitment to violence as an instrument of state policy served to distinguish it from such minor states as Mali or Mauritania. Frustrated abroad, the Libyan government exported the violence which came to be used almost routinely as a weapon of internal repression and social control. As Qaddafi increased his rhetorical and material support for state-sponsored terrorism, his return on investment plummeted. The resultant publicity heightened political isolation rather than political clout, and retarded rather than advanced the policies he advocated.

4

The Quest for Arab Unity

Arab unity is an inevitable necessity, a vital necessity.

Muammar al-Qaddafi

Arab nationalism and the quest for Arab unity have marched hand in hand for more than half a century. Both movements were largely the product of the post-World War I period, and both were catalysed by Zionist activities in Palestine which eventually led to the creation of the state of Israel. Arab nationalism would have come into being regardless of the drive for a Jewish national home in Palestine; but the creation of Israel provided a common focus of shared discontent, a galvanizing force that overrode other considerations. As Arab nationalism focused on opposition to the new Jewish state, Arab rhetoric centred on Arab unity as the solution to this most perplexing Arab problem.[1]

Pan-Arabism has dominated recent Arab political life, especially in the 1950s and 1960s; but the practical prospect of union was never great. The ideal of Arab unity remained a chimera unable to overcome the reality of inter-Arab subterfuge and bickering. Practical attempts at union, such as the United Arab Republic, the United Arab States and the Arab Federation, were short-lived and monuments to a failed idea rather than milestones along the road to greater Arab unity. The pan-Arab movement was simply unable to transcend the political realities of the Arab world; and after the 1967 defeat, most Arab leaders abandoned the objective of comprehensive Arab unity and adopted a more pragmatic approach to regional relations.

The new pan-Arab leader
Muammar al-Qaddafi, the Arab nationalist par excellence, was also the consummate Arab unionist. He approached both ideals with a purist fanaticism which refused to acknowledge the real obstacles in their path. For Qaddafi, the quest for Arab unity was a 'pressing necessity' which had been on the minds of the Arab people 'since time immemorial'.[2] At his first press conference in February 1970, he produced a formula for Arab unity. His

theme was the past failure of Arab unity, which he attributed to Byzantine philosophies and sterile ideological disputes. His solution was a unified movement which grouped all Arabs together.[3]

Initially, Qaddafi's approach to Arab unity focused eastward on the pan-Arab core. Apart from his admiration for President Nasser, he considered Egypt to be the essential nucleus of an Arab union. With the cause of Palestinian liberation as the focus of Arab interest, the Maghreb was simply too remote from the Arab heartland to absorb Qaddafi's attention. At the same time, he condemned the Libyan monarchy's equivocal stand on Maghreb unity, which he variously decried as provincialism or regionalism, as a diversionary tactic designed to camouflage its opposition to total Arab unity. Regionalism was abhorrent because it was 'an innovation of imperialism which has been perpetuated by its agents', as well as being 'ineffective in the face of imperialist challenges and Zionism'. Regionalism resulted in 'the frittering away of the Arab homeland and the division of the Arab people', and 'failed to defend the Holy Land, protect Palestine, or extinguish the Aqsa Mosque fire', which occurred in Jerusalem in 1969. Qaddafi also downplayed the role of the Arab League, arguing it had too often been a mere platform for demonstrating enthusiasm and verbal support for unity as opposed to being an effective vehicle for the promotion of comprehensive unity.[4]

Intertwined with the Palestinian issue, the quest for Arab unity was closely tied to Qaddafi's call for *jihad*. Qaddafi argued that Arab unity would precede the liberation of Palestine and was in fact a prerequisite for its liberation. In his mind, the Holy Land was lost when the Arab world was divided, and it could be regained only after the Arabs had joined together.

> 'We will arrive at Palestine, Brethren, when we have pulled down the walls which impede the fusion of the Arab people in the battle. We will reach the Holy Land when we have removed the borders and partitions... We shall liberate Palestine when the Arab land has become one solid front. What is going on in the occupied land of Palestine affirms the necessity of unity... Arab unity, therefore, will serve as a strong and decisive answer to the challenge of both imperialism and world Zionism... '[5]

In addition to Zionism and imperialism, the real obstacles to Arab unity were, in Qaddafi's view, the occupants of palaces and thrones, enemies of Arabism and Islam, and those motivated by selfish interests.[6] The monarchical governments of Morocco and Jordan, in particular, were considered obstacles to unity. In addition to being monarchies, which was a painful reminder of the Libyan and Egyptian experiences, both Morocco and Jordan maintained relatively close relations with the United States. Libya soon figured in foiled coup and assassination attempts against both states.

Qaddafi openly supported an abortive assassination attempt against King Hassan of Morocco in July 1971, and Libya was later implicated in a plot to kill Jordan's King Hussein in November 1972.

Qaddafi's involvement in the domestic politics of neighbouring states exemplified the extent to which the pan-Arab movement in general, and Qaddafi's approach to union in particular, weakened the traditional distinction between foreign and domestic politics, encouraging the interference by one state in the internal affairs of another. Arab leaders like Qaddafi felt they had the right, even the duty, to become involved in the politics of other Arab states. In this context, it was noteworthy that while Arabs might deplore such interference they seldom protested at it.[7]

Related to this heightened propensity for domestic intervention was the growing tendency of Qaddafi, and other Arab and Islamic revolutionary leaders, to distinguish between the governments and peoples of a given state. Qaddafi frequently expressed friendship and affection for the people of the United States, for example, while harshly criticizing the policies of its government. The reduced distinction between external and internal affairs, and between peoples and governments, helped explain Qaddafi's early emphasis on national unity as a first step towards Arab unity. Faced with nascent levels of national identity and domestic political support, Qaddafi emphasized the importance of consensus and national unity both to secure the Libyan revolution and to advance Arab unity.[8]

The Tripoli Charter
Qaddafi's early emphasis on Arab unity was quickly rewarded with practical results. At the end of an inconclusive Arab summit meeting in Rabat, Morocco, in December 1969, the heads of state of Libya, Egypt and Sudan removed their discussions to Libya. Further talks resulted in a tripartite agreement, dated 27 December 1969 and known as the Tripoli Charter. Consolidating the three progressive revolutions into a so-called Arab Revolutionary Front, the charter established a supreme planning committee and a common security system. The remainder of the communiqué was circumspect, making no reference to an eventual political union and limiting itself to the establishment of joint ministerial commissions to pursue co-ordinated policies. The three Arab leaders agreed to meet at regular intervals, but the Egyptian government insisted that attempts at economic integration be limited to concrete initiatives such as joint agricultural projects and the formation of a joint development bank. Shortly after the Tripoli Charter was signed, Qaddafi pressed for the full constitutional union of the three states; but the other signatories, especially Egypt, made clear their reservations. The ensuing year was punctuated by a series of ministerial-level meetings which produced agreements for technical co-operation, the relaxation of customs duties and a freer flow of labour between the neighbouring states.[9]

On 8 November 1970, the heads of state of Libya, Egypt and Sudan met in Cairo, where they formed a tripartite federal union. President Nasser had died of a heart attack on 28 September 1970; and his place in the talks was taken by his successor, President Anwar Sadat. The Syrian government, at the request of its new head of state, General Hafez al-Assad, joined the federal plan on 27 November. After further negotiations, the governments of Libya, Egypt and Syria announced on 17 April 1971 the formation of a tripartite federation. The Sudanese government, due to internal problems, did not formally accede, but the way was left open for its subsequent membership.[10]

The talks which led to the announcement of the Federation of Arab Republics, also known as the Confederation of Arab Republics or Union of Arab Republics, were tense. Qaddafi pressed for an integrative type of unity, while Syria favoured a loose federation as a first stage towards union. Egypt's leaders were divided, with President Sadat later charging that pro-Soviet political opponents had tried to sabotage his efforts at pan-Arab unity as part of an effort to oust him and seize power.[11] Significant policy differences also separated Libya, Egypt and Syria. Ignoring Egypt's recent peace moves in response to American initiatives (the Rogers plan), the federation was founded on the principles of no negotiated peace agreement with Israel and no slackening of support for the Palestinian cause. Egypt and Libya also followed opposing policies on the Pakistan-India-Bangladesh issue. Apparently, Qaddafi thought he could use the legacy of Nasser's pan-Arab policies to ensnare the new Egyptian leadership in binding alliances. But the Sadat government increasingly considered Egypt's interests first and those of the Arab world second.[12]

The statutes of the Federation of Arab Republics placed it somewhere between a federal and confederal system. While the new structure was directed to lay the groundwork for a common foreign policy and a combined military command, the member states retained their own armed forces and the power to maintain their own diplomatic relations with other states. The supreme authority was a council of the three presidents, each of whom would serve a two-year term as federal president. Initially, this supreme body of three was to function on the basis of a majority vote, but Egyptian concern that it would be dominated by the more radical policies of Libya and Syria led this to be changed to the principle of unanimous vote. There was to be a federal parliament composed of an equal number of representatives from each member state and entrusted with federal legislative functions. Pending the establishment of a single political structure, each state was responsible for organizing its own political system, although political groups in one state were prohibited from operating in another except through the recognized political front command. For Qaddafi and the other members of the RCC, the formation of the Federation of Arab Republics was a significant step on the road to Arab unity; but when compared to the United Arab Republic, the 1958-61 union between Egypt and Syria, it was a modest undertaking.[13]

Sudan's removal from union plans in 1971 had both short-term and long-term consequences for Libya's quest for Arab unity. Jafar al-Numairi came to power in May 1969, when a small group of army officers, subsequently supported by the Sudanese Communist Party, executed a successful coup d'état. Thereafter, a power struggle developed within the ruling revolutionary council between Numairi and left-wing elements allied to the Communist Party. Sudanese Communists opposed a union with Egypt and Libya because they considered their neighbours reactionary. They were especially critical of Libya's new leaders because the latter forebade the organization of political parties, particularly the Communist Party, and because they had not yet granted diplomatic recognition to the People's Republic of China, the Democratic People's Republic of Korea or the German Democratic Republic. In addition, Numairi faced a determined secessionist movement in southern Sudan. The northern two-thirds of the country was largely Arab and Muslim, while the southern one-third was composed of heterogeneous ethnic groups more African than Arab in culture and religion. Qaddafi consistently underestimated the impact of minority groups on union efforts, but Numairi was determined to resolve his constitutional problems before committing himself to Arab unity.[14]

President Numairi's attitude infuriated Qaddafi, who accused him of betraying the Arab nationalist cause. But he came to Numairi's aid a few months later when leftist forces attempted to overthrow him in July 1971. Firmly opposed to communism, Qaddafi forced down a British airliner carrying two of the leaders of the coup from London to Khartoum, and delivered them to Numairi, who executed them. Ironically, the consolidation of Numairi's rule, far from consummating Sudan's membership in the Federation of Arab Republics, moved it towards the Arab axis being formed by Saudi Arabia and the Gulf states under US protection. In particular, diplomatic relations with Libya deteriorated after September 1972, when the Sudanese government, seeking to defuse the political crisis in central Africa, forced five Libyan planes carrying military equipment to Idi Amin's Uganda to land in Khartoum. Relations improved at the end of 1974 when Numairi visited Libya, but deteriorated again in July 1976 when Libya was implicated in an abortive Sudanese coup.[15]

While Qaddafi sparred with Numairi, the momentum for Arab unity stalled as the feebleness of the Federation of Arab Republics, and the policy disorientation of its constituent parts, became increasingly evident. The three heads of state signed the draft constitution of the federation in Damascus in August 1971, and the document received the customary near-unanimous approval of the electorates of the three countries in referendums on 1 September 1971. Sadat was named the first president of the presidential council in October 1971; and after a federal cabinet was formed, the new federal entity was declared officially in existence on 1 January 1972. Thereafter, new federal structures worked closely with the three governments to initiate a series of gradual measures aimed at slowly amending existing rules and regulations to promote unity through increased individual interchange.[16]

The Benghazi Declaration

Frustrated with the slow progress towards Arab unity, Qaddafi seized the initiative in February 1972 in a confidential proposal to President Sadat for immediate, total union. Sadat was granted time to consider; but when he failed to respond, Qaddafi repeated his proposal in a public statement six months later. He asserted that the unification of the Arab world into a single nation state was an absolute necessity, and then proceeded to detail and analyze the various methods by which unification could be achieved. He concluded that those Arab states which refused to unite voluntarily should and would be conquered and forced to unite.[17]

At the beginning of August 1972, Sadat travelled to Benghazi, Libya, where he found Qaddafi prepared for immediate union. According to Qaddafi's plan, Sadat would become president of the joint state and Qaddafi would become vice-president and commander-in-chief of the armed forces. Sadat opposed immediate union for two reasons. Based on Egypt's bad experience of politicians holding military posts, he insisted that the position of commander-in-chief be held by a professional military man and be removed from politics. Second, he argued that immediate union would impose economic difficulties on Libya for which Egypt would be responsible as there were more than 10 Egyptians for every one Libyan. Sadat's counter-proposal was that the two states proceed gradually towards union, to which Qaddafi agreed.[18]

In the Benghazi Declaration, dated 2 August 1972, Qaddafi and Sadat announced plans to merge their respective states on or before 1 September 1973. A unified political command was established, with seven joint committees to lay the foundations for unity in areas such as constitutional matters; political organizations; legislation and the judiciary; administration and finance; and education, science, culture and public information. At a subsequent meeting the following month, the defence and national security committee was subdivided into defence, security and foreign-affairs committees, thereby increasing the total to nine. Cairo was declared the capital of the new state, whose form of government was opaquely described as a consultative, democratic republican system. Thereafter, the machinery to promote unification met frequently, but real decision-making power remained in the hands of Qaddafi and Sadat. Consequently, until a few months before the merger deadline, practically nothing was known about the details of the proposed union.[19]

On the surface, a merger of Libya and Egypt offered both states tangible benefits. Union would bring Egyptian technical expertise, administrative training, experience and prestige to underdeveloped, underpopulated Libya. In turn, overcrowded Egypt would obtain new resources and room for expansion, as well as access to Libya's oil wealth. Above all, the merger would be a concrete step towards Qaddafi's supreme goal, total union of the Arab people. A successful merger with Egypt would lay the foundation for the subsequent incorporation of surrounding Arab states.

Despite these inducements, the two states gradually moved apart after August 1972. First of all, the joint committees formed to advance union proved to be bureaucratic in operation, and the abilities of many of their members were limited. Second, many aspects of the societies of Egypt and Libya were fundamentally different, and xenophobia was rife. Many Egyptians viewed their neighbours to the east as crude and rustic, while the Libyans complained the Egyptians were rude and overbearing. Egyptian concern about Libyan society intensified after Qaddafi launched his popular revolution in April 1973 and insisted on the *sharia* as the source of future joint legislation.

Major foreign-policy differences also existed. Sadat pursued a broad policy of Arab solidarity and reconciliation, while Qaddafi was more selective in his friends and openly hostile to several governments which he considered unacceptable. On the Palestinian issue, Sadat had begun to take a more bellicose public stand in the latter half of 1972; but in general, his more sophisticated approach to negotiation and settlement stood in marked contrast to Qaddafi's fixation with a war of liberation.

Finally, and probably most important, the temperaments of the two leaders proved incompatible. Accounts differ as to exactly when Sadat reached the conclusion that Qaddafi was mentally unbalanced, if not insane, but it was no later than the end of 1973. Qaddafi, on the other hand, became convinced that Sadat was not a true revolutionary in the Nasser mould and was not sincerely concerned about the liberation of Palestine.[20]

With union discussions progressing so slowly, they were soon overtaken by political events in the region. In February 1973, a Libyan plane violated Sinai air space and was shot down by Israeli fighter planes, with a loss of life of 108 people. Qaddafi blamed Egypt for not intervening and orchestrated anti-Egyptian demonstrations in Libya. The Egyptian consulate in Benghazi was attacked, and Egyptian citizens working in Libya were charged with being a fifth column. In April, Sadat had to intervene to prevent Qaddafi from retaliating for the incident by torpedoing the liner *Queen Elizabeth II* on a special voyage to celebrate Israeli independence.

In June, Qaddafi arrived in Cairo for a prolonged, unscheduled visit during which he was deeply critical of Egyptian society. His erratic, uncompromising behaviour confirmed the doubts of many Egyptians opposed to union. Qaddafi's next step was to organize a motorcade of some 20,000 vehicles to drive from the Libyan-Tunisian border to Cairo in support of immediate union with Egypt. This so-called Green March was probably the first public manifestation in Libya of the new governing concept of the masses and certainly the last official attempt to export the cultural revolution to Egypt. Qaddafi's pressure was counter-productive as the Egyptian authorities stopped the motorcade and Sadat shelved the plans for a merger.[21]

At the same time, Sadat did allow Qaddafi to preserve appearances. On 29 August 1973, the unified political command announced a series of unification measures scheduled to take effect on 1 September 1973. The official declaration established a joint constitutional assembly and created a free economic zone on the border between the two republics. On 10 September, a supreme planning council was established, with resident ministers replacing the ambassadors of the two states in Cairo and Tripoli.[22]

While the plan for union by stages appeared to preserve the principle of Arab unity, the breach was drastic. Qaddafi did not participate in the decision to launch the October 1973 war one month later, a conflict which deeply estranged him from the leadership of Egypt and Syria as well as other Arab states. Qaddafi rightly felt he had been slighted and was being treated as a junior partner in the Federation of Arab Republics, which called for a consensus on decisions involving war or peace. Emphasizing that he had not been consulted, he termed the clash a 'comic-opera war' and declared himself opposed to its timing and limited objectives. He preferred the total annihilation of Israel. Qaddafi's conduct during the war left him isolated from the Arab world in general and Egypt in particular. Intent on pursuing a strategy of moderation and co-operation with the United States, a strategy with which other Arab states were in broad agreement, President Sadat showed no patience with Libyan extremism. He accused Qaddafi of organizing sabotage attacks inside Egypt. In retaliation, Libya stopped its economic subsidies to Egypt, and Egyptian labourers working in Libya began to return home. Qaddafi refused to attend the November 1973 Arab summit in Algeria; and on 1 December 1973, Libya broke off diplomatic relations with Egypt.[23]

For the remainder of the decade, Libya's breach with Egypt was a major obstacle in the path of Qaddafi's quest for greater Arab unity. Divergent stands on the Palestine issue were one problem, but to a certain extent, these differences masked the broader questions which separated Qaddafi and Sadat. Quite simply, Qaddafi aspired to play a greater role in Arab politics than Libya's military, political and demographic capabilities would justify or allow. In pursuit of this objective, Qaddafi sought to establish a special relationship with Sadat's Egypt similar to the one he had enjoyed, or thought he had enjoyed, with Nasser's Egypt. Sadat, on the other hand, did not take

Qaddafi or his aspirations seriously. Faced with an impossible situation, Qaddafi joined Arab critics of Sadat's gradual move away from the twin pillars of Nasserism—socialism at home and pan-Arabism abroad.[24]

Swing to the Maghreb

It has occasionally been suggested that Libya had no Maghreb policy before 1972; this was far from true.[25] Less than three months after the September 1969 coup, Qaddafi removed Libya from the Permanent Consultative Committee for the Maghreb which King Idris had joined. The move reflected his concern that involvement with the traditional bloc of North African states might be harmful to his plans for greater Arab unity. Nevertheless, Libya did not ignore its Arab neighbours to the west. As mentioned earlier, relations with Morocco were especially tense in the early years when both states engaged in hostile propaganda. The Moroccan government resented Libya's support for Moroccan dissident groups, while the Libyan RCC criticized King Hassan's regime as corrupt, feudal and reactionary. Morocco was a natural target for the RCC because the monarchy's ties to the West and lack of commitment to the recovery of Palestine were strongly reminiscent of the policies of the Idris regime.[26]

On the other hand, Libyan relations with Algeria's revolutionary government were generally good. Qaddafi even prompted Algeria to join the Federation of Arab Republics, but Algeria declined, reportedly because it felt federation plans were too much dominated by Egypt. While bilateral co-operation increased, there was little question of formal union. Algeria preferred to devote its attention to internal matters and Maghreb affairs, adopting a less militant stand than Libya on the Arab-Israeli conflict. Algeria's preferred approach to unity was to build from the bottom up through concrete projects, as evidenced by a February 1973 agreement for enhanced Libyan-Algerian economic co-operation. Rivalry between the two states centred on a border dispute dating back to a 1955 agreement with France, and on natural competition for political influence in both the Maghreb and the Sahel.[27]

Early relations with the Tunisian government were poor, in large part because Qaddafi tended to accept at face value the anti-Bourguiba opinion prevalent in pan-Arab circles. Relations improved in the summer of 1970 when Qaddafi was received in Tunisia with great honours and had an opportunity to familiarize himself with the practical problems of the country. At the same time, the new friendship was slow to move beyond good-neighbour relations as the Tunisian government maintained a moderate position on the Arab-Israeli issue and retained close political ties with the West.[28]

Qaddafi returned to Tunisia on an official visit in December 1972. Frustrated with the slow progress in union talks with Egypt, he unexpectedly offered Tunisia an immediate union. The suddenness of the offer caught the Tunisian government completely off guard, but it quickly rejected the proposal. President Bourguiba explained that his government had no disagreement with the distant target of Arab unity but preferred to work towards it gradually through increased economic and political co-operation. To this end, Libya and Tunisia signed a joint communiqué on 17 December 1972, which focused on specific projects such as joint exploitation of the continental shelf; increased co-operation in the areas of education, information and defence; and the expansion of agreements through which Tunisians could freely enter Libya to work. Agreement was also reached for quarterly meetings at the prime minister level to advance co-ordination and co-operation. The first such meeting was held in Tripoli on 29 January 1973. Eight years later, the Tunisian secretary general for foreign affairs stated that his government had signed some 15 accords with Libya in 1972-74; and if all of them had been fulfilled, the two states would have been over 50 per cent unified by 1981.[29]

Qaddafi did make one more attempt at total union with Tunisia. In January 1974 he visited the Tunisian island of Djerba, where he and an ailing Bourguiba agreed in a single session to create an Arab Islamic Republic with a single constitution, a single president, a single army, and the same legislative, executive and judicial powers. Since Qaddafi had been frustrated in the Mashrek (the Arab East), the proposal looked uncommonly like an act of pique on his part.[30] Moreover, it evidenced even less planning than his 1972 proposal for immediate union with Egypt. Senior members of the Tunisian government were stunned by Bourguiba's acceptance; and after the Tunisian prime minister returned from abroad and the Tunisian foreign minister was dismissed, cooler heads prevailed. Tunisia allowed the pact to lapse, and it soon became a dead letter. The Algerian government also actively opposed the union as it neither wanted to unite with its neighbours nor see them unite with each other. In November 1974, a Libyan delegation visited Tunisia to breathe life into the union, but its efforts were to no avail.[31]

Arab disunity, 1975–80

With the death of Nasser, Qaddafi had tried unsuccessfully to assume the mantle of pan-Arabism and achieve practical results where his mentor had experienced agonizing failure. By 1974 he had actively pursued union with at least five Arab states, including all of those contiguous with Libya. For a wide variety of internal and external reasons, none of them were interested in the immediate, total union he advocated. As this first phase in his quest for Arab unity ended, Qaddafi's enthusiasm was surely dampened; but he did not abandon the pursuit. For the next five years, he continued to discuss Arab unity, but more as a long-term goal than an immediately achievable objective. In the interim, he appeared to recognize more clearly the divisions blocking Arab unity; but he refused to accept them.

By 1975 the Arab political landscape was dotted with rivalries and conflicts. Many of these were long-standing and not directly connected with the Arab-Israeli conflict. Egypt and Libya shared almost no common ideological or political ground. Algeria and Morocco were in deep conflict over the Western Sahara issue. Iraq and Kuwait disputed rival territorial claims. Iraq and the United Arab Emirates were on opposite sides over the Oman revolt. Syria quarrelled with Iraq over protracted ideological disputes as well as the sharing of the waters of the Euphrates River. The Palestinians were at loggerheads with Jordan in a conflict which had led to heated battle in 1970. Moreover, many of these bilateral disputes had multilateral dimensions, as individual states sought diplomatic support for their respective positions and policies. The Lebanese civil war, which began in 1975, highlighted the multilateral character of many issues as well as the full extent to which political, ideological, social and economic rivalries permeated the Arab world.[32]

A number of fundamental factors contributed to heightened inter-state conflict and the reduction in pan-Arabism in this period. First, the universalism of pan-Arabism had derived to a considerable extent from the universalism of the Ottoman Empire. Six decades after the collapse of the Ottoman system, whatever unity was lent to Arab society by Ottoman universalism was becoming a faded memory. Second, Arab nationalism had been conceived and propagated by Arab intellectuals; but as practical politicians and a development-oriented élite increasingly dominated Arab politics in the independence era, the power and prestige of intellectuals waned.

Third, the anti-colonialism which developed after World War I had lent a great deal of unity to the Arab system; but its power declined after independence, when it was only partially replaced by anti-imperialism. Arab success during the October war in 1973 contributed to a growing maturation of the Arab world outlook. Fourth, before independence, a relatively mobile élite existed in the Arab world, disseminating pan-Arab ideas as it moved from one state to another. This group disappeared in the modern era as more parochial élites focused on the bureaucratic interests which developed in each Arab state.

Fifth, from Suez to Nasser's death, the power of pan-Arabism derived from the power of the Egyptian President's charismatic leadership. After 1970, no Arab leader, including Qaddafi, was able to provide similar inspiration and guidance. Finally, the Arab world initially viewed the creation of the state of Israel as a traumatizing experience which demanded a common Arab solution. Sadat's diplomacy after the October war changed this familiar perspective, focusing on Israel's boundaries rather than Israel's existence. In short, the Sadat government rejected the inter-Arab division of labour which for over two decades had assigned Egypt the principal obligation for upholding a pan-Arab cause.[33]

While Egyptian diplomacy in the latter half of the 1970s was hardly responsible for all Arab problems, it certainly exacerbated inter-Arab divisions. If the October war marked the zenith of pan-Arab solidarity in the post-Nasser period, the Sinai II accord concluded in September 1975 represented its ebb. The accord brought Arab rivalries and differences into the open and confirmed the deep divisions in Arab ranks. The details of the diplomacy which led first to the September 1978 Camp David accords, and then to the March 1979 Egypt-Israel peace treaty, have been examined in detail elsewhere and need not be repeated here. The agreements exemplified the extent to which Sadat had transformed Egypt from the symbol of Arab unity to the focal-point of Arab divisions. As diplomatic manoeuvring between the United States, Egypt and Israel had intensified, the ambivalence of Saudi Arabia and Jordan, the militancy of the Steadfastness and Confrontation Front (consisting of Libya, Algeria, South Yemen, Syria and the PLO) and the open hostility of Iraq all contributed to the state of uncertainty prevailing in the Middle East.[34]

Qaddafi aspired to a leadership role in Arab politics throughout this period but was largely shunted aside. In 1976 Libya was implicated in an abortive attempt to overthrow President Numairi while the governments of Egypt, Saudi Arabia and Sudan were reportedly undertaking a co-ordinated effort to topple Qaddafi's regime. In 1977 Egypt attacked Libya in a brief, punitive war after Israeli intelligence reportedly provided Egypt with limited information suggesting that Qaddafi planned to assassinate Sadat. Relations between the two states remained tense for the remainder of the decade.[35] The previous year, the heads of state of Algeria, Libya and Niger initiated a series of meetings which appeared to signal a new phase of Saharan co-operation; however, practical achievements were slow to accumulate. Libya and Algeria had signed a mutual defence pact (Treaty of Hassi Messoud) in 1975, in which they pledged to come to each other's aid if attacked. Nevertheless, Algeria did not provide military assistance to Libya in the 1977 border war with Egypt, although Algerian diplomacy helped bring the fighting to an end. For a variety of reasons, which included differing concepts of regional integration and the growing Soviet role in Libya, Algeria intended to keep Libya at arm's length.[36] A similar situation existed in Tunisia, with which Libya again proposed union in February 1978 after both states agreed to submit a heated dispute over offshore oil rights to the International Court of Justice (ICJ) at The Hague. The Tunisian government rejected Qaddafi's latest overture because of what it described as differing political orientations, as well as its preference for promoting unity by concentrating on functional issues such as health and education.[37]

Phase two

Towards the end of 1980, Qaddafi initiated a second major phase in his search for Arab unity. In a 1 September 1980 speech marking the 11th anniversary of the revolution, he proposed that Libya merge with Syria. In a characteristic pose, he then threatened to resign from office and enlist as a *fedayeen* in Palestine if his proposal was rejected. Syrian President Hafez al-Assad immediately accepted the proposal; and the following day, the two governments declared their intention to work towards a unified government. A 13-point joint statement, issued on 10 September 1980, indicated that a unitary state with 'a single identity on the international level' would be formed between Libya and Syria. The form of government was not outlined, but the declaration stated that it would have 'democratic popular institutions that will enable the masses to practise their full role in building their society and future'. Hostile to Zionism, imperialism and reaction, the new state was described as 'a base for the Arab revolutionary movement' and 'a nucleus for all-out Arab unity'. It was made clear that other Arab states wishing to join the Libya-Syria union would be welcome.[38]

The merger came at a time when both Syria and Libya were somewhat isolated in the Arab world. Syria was increasingly at odds with Iraq, ruled by a rival wing of the Baath Party, which had been making a strong bid for regional leadership as well as attempting to build ties with Saudi Arabia and the Gulf states. Syria was also becoming increasingly estranged from Jordan, which it accused of harbouring members of the fundamentalist Muslim Brotherhood. In October 1980 Libya had declared its support for Iran in the Gulf war, causing Iraq to sever diplomatic relations. Relations were also broken off with Saudi Arabia during this period. Finally, Libya's deep involvement in Chad in the autumn of 1980, an intervention which led to the announcement in January 1981 of union between Libya and Chad, provoked considerable opposition inside and outside Africa.[39]

Twelve months after its announcement, details of the proposed Libya-Syria union remained unclear. Apparently, union plans lapsed because the two states could not agree on operative governmental institutions for the unified state. Syria preferred a loose federation, while Libya insisted that its own political system be adopted. In August 1981 Qaddafi visited Syria in an effort to give the union some substance. His visit followed a week in which Libya had clashed militarily with the United States, had been expelled from Somalia and had formed a new alliance with South Yemen and Ethiopia.[40] Qaddafi's visit to Syria coincided with a meeting in Egypt between the leaders of Egypt and Israel to discuss means to accelerate the peace process outlined in the Camp David accords. In Damascus, Qaddafi and Assad agreed to resume talks aimed at merger; but one week later, on the first anniversary of the announcement of the union, Qaddafi admitted his disappointment that it had not been consummated. He blamed this failure on regional and separatist factors, as well as the bureaucrats left to implement the union. A more realistic appraisal would have focused on the difficulty of uniting two disparate cultures and economies with single-minded political leaders which were separated geographically by a distance of several hundred miles. Union talks between Syria and Libya continued over the years but little substantive progress was achieved.[41]

Elsewhere in the Mashrek, prospects for enhanced Arab co-operation were slim. Qaddafi's radical policies alienated him from the governments of Jordan, Saudi Arabia and the Gulf states, while Libya's support for Iran in the Gulf war alienated Iraq. The assassination of President Sadat appeared to offer at least the potential for improved relations with Egypt, but Qaddafi's radical policies torpedoed the prospect. In March 1983 Libya called for Egypt's suspension from the non-aligned movement; and in January 1984 it openly resisted readmitting Egypt to the Islamic Conference Organization. Two months later, Qaddafi declared union between Libya, Syria and Egypt to be essential, and announced he was reviving the 1971 tripartite federation. He then threatened to stage a second unity march on Egypt to force unification.[42]

In the coming months, Libya was implicated in a plot to mine the Red Sea; a defecting Libyan pilot claimed his government had plans to bomb Egypt's Aswan Dam; Libya was strongly critical of Jordan's re-establishment of diplomatic relations with Egypt; and Egypt foiled a Libyan plot to assassinate a former Libyan prime minister. It was hardly a scenario for increased Arab unity. Relations between Libya and Egypt remained understandably tense, especially after Libya suddenly expelled tens of thousands of Egyptian workers in the autumn of 1985. President Mubarak termed the expulsions 'inhumane' and added that those responsible would pay a high price.[43]

Qaddafi and Numairi meanwhile remained implacable enemies. The Sudanese government laboured determinedly to thwart Libyan objectives in Chad and elsewhere, while the Libyan government called periodically for Numairi's overthrow. To achieve that objective, Qaddafi openly supported the rebel Sudanese People's Liberation Movement (SPLM), established by Colonel John Garang de Mabior in the south in 1983. Such support was ironic. Qaddafi had earlier refused to acknowledge the importance of minority groups in the Arab world — and the SPLM represented non-Muslim minority interests in Sudan. Weeks before Numairi's overthrow, the Libyan and Sudanese governments reportedly held secret talks; and at the beginning of April 1985, Numairi announced he had recently rejected a Libyan offer of $5 million to sign a unity agreement.[44]

Nevertheless Qaddafi welcomed the overthrow of Numairi with the words 'Sudan is ours'; and on 24 April 1985, diplomatic relations were restored after a four-year break. A statement issued in both capitals at the time spoke of the need to confront the dangers which imperialism and Zionism posed for the Arab nation. Qaddafi was the first head of state to visit Sudan after Numairi's overthrow; and during his visit he called for other Arab armies to follow Sudan's example and overthrow reactionary Arab regimes. In July 1985 the two governments agreed to a military co-operation pact, an agreement which effectively ended Libyan assistance to the SPLM. Libya pressed the rebels to lay down their arms and open negotiations with the government. Sensitive to Egyptian and US concerns about the military co-operation pact, the Sudanese government denied it was tantamount to a strategic alliance, and insisted that improved relations with Libya would not be at the expense of ties with traditional allies.[45]

Throughout 1986 economic and military co-operation between Libya and Sudan increased, although the limits to closer political ties became apparent. In addition to Libyan crude-oil deliveries, a Libyan–Sudanese agricultural company was reactivated; and a multi-million-dollar joint venture was established to increase investment in Sudan. In September 1985 the Sudanese government had announced it would take delivery of Libyan supplies of light weapons, ammunition and military spare parts; and in March 1986 it accepted additional military aid, including training assistance. The Sudanese government denounced the US air raid on Libya in April 1986, but emphasized that it hoped to maintain its relations with the United States while strengthening those with Libya. In a surprise visit to Sudan in September 1986, Qaddafi again suggested a union between the two states. At the same time, he called on Ethiopia to stop supporting the SPLM.

Two months later, the United States announced it was rescinding a seven-month-old order which had called for the evacuation of US personnel from Sudan and had put much of the USAID programme on hold. The decision was based in part on the US perception that the Sudanese government had distanced itself a little from the Qaddafi regime. Within two weeks, Egypt said it viewed with scepticism Sudanese claims that several hundred Libyans in Darfur province were agricultural as opposed to military advisers, and that Sudan had severed its military ties with Libya. The exchange highlighted the difficult position of the Sudanese government, as both the Egyptian and US governments viewed stronger Sudanese ties with Libya as inimical to their own strategic interests.[46]

Return to the Maghreb
As Qaddafi fumbled for the key to greater Mashrek unity, he again stepped up the level of Libyan diplomatic activity in the Maghreb. The major impediment to greater union remained the position of Tunisia, which both Libya and Algeria viewed as basic to the security of their respective regimes. Qaddafi's policy towards Tunisia at this time oscillated from offers of union

to intervention, and thus heightened the sense of insecurity felt by both Tunisia and Algeria.

At the beginning of 1980 Tunisian dissidents, calling themselves the Tunisian Armed Resistance, crossed from Algeria into Tunisia and attacked the Tunisian mining town of Gafsa. Proof of Libyan support for the attack was inconclusive, but the Tunisian government accused Libya of intervention and broke off diplomatic relations. While Tunisia later moved to restore official relations, they remained tense. In 1981, the two states failed to reach agreement over offshore rights to the oil-rich continental shelf; and Libya inexplicably vetoed Tunisia's bid to join the Organization of Arab Petroleum Exporting Countries and expelled several thousand Tunisian workers.[47]

While border altercations and charges of Libyan intervention continued, relations between Libya and Tunisia promised to improve when the International Court of Justice delivered its February 1982 verdict on the offshore boundary dispute. The judgement was a compromise which fully satisfied neither party, although Libya gained more than Tunisia and certainly more than it had expected.[48] The decision of the ICJ coincided with the first meeting since 1974 between Qaddafi and President Bourguiba of Tunisia. At the end of a five-day visit, the two heads of state signed an agreement providing for renewed co-operation in a variety of areas. The Libyan foreign minister later claimed the agreement provided for the permanent co-ordination of the foreign policies of the two states. Subsequent ministerial-level meetings were held later in 1982 to implement the broad outline for economic, social and cultural integration contained in the February 1982 agreement.[49]

In March 1983 the Tunisian foreign minister was quoted as saying that Libya should be part of moves towards greater Maghreb unity; and in August 1983 Qaddafi returned to Tunisia for additional talks aimed at increasing co-operation in the Maghreb. In the course of the discussions, Qaddafi reaffirmed his recently adopted view that regional unity could promote the wider quest for Arab unity. At the end of the year, a joint Libyan-Tunisian economic affairs committee met and agreed upon increased socio-economic co-operation in a variety of areas from budget preparation to desertification.[50]

Qaddafi's new approach to regional unity marked a significant change in Libyan foreign policy. Since 1969 he had strongly opposed regional groupings, arguing repeatedly that they hindered progress towards greater Arab unity. The full reasons for this policy reversal remained unclear, but it appeared to be motivated by the complete failure of earlier attempts to promote broader Arab unity. In any case, Qaddafi spent much of the next two years advocating a step-by-step approach to Arab unity in the Maghreb. 'Let every regime remain as it is — the monarchist a monarchist and the republican a republican. But let there be periodic bilateral meetings between officials — say between Libya and Tunisia, for example.' Eventually, the bilateral meetings would become trilateral and so forth, so that a number of ministers from different countries would be meeting and taking decisions. 'This will gradually remove differences and unity will ultimately be achieved.'[51] At the same time, he was careful to leave the door open to a wider, faster approach. 'If unity is not achieved between Libya and Tunisia with the step-by-step approach, by economic integration, then there will be no excuse for those who oppose revolutionary unity, unity by revolution, integration-type unity.'[52]

Qaddafi's emphasis on the step-by-step approach to Arab unity reached a high point in the summer of 1985. In May he asked an unidentified group of Arab lawyers to draft proposals aimed at achieving Arab unity while allowing each state to retain its own system of government and control over its economic policies. In June Qaddafi addressed a message to all Arab heads of state which proposed closer ties among the Arab people. Libyan envoys dispatched to explain his plan variously described it as being inspired by the European Economic Community or by a federation similar to the Soviet Union or the United States. While Qaddafi implied that his plan for union did not require even conservative Arab states to make major policy changes, his proposals were generally greeted with silence.[53]

As part of his efforts to promote Maghreb unity, Qaddafi had also moved to improve diplomatic relations with Algeria. He travelled to Algeria in January 1982; and after the visit Radio Tripoli announced the two states had agreed to unite. The Algerian government quickly denied a merger was in the making, but did agree to a wide-ranging co-operation agreement in April 1982.

While joint statements of support for a greater Arab Maghreb followed the 1982 agreement, policy differences thwarted closer co-operation. In particular, the Algerian government remained wary of Qaddafi's interventionist policies and his predilection towards destabilizing actions both in North Africa and in Africa south of the Sahara. It had very mixed feelings about Libyan interventions in Chad in 1980–81 and 1983; and it was adamantly opposed to Qaddafi's desire to unite the Saharan and Sahelian states into some kind of Islamic Republic. A greater Saharan entity, especially one dominated by Libya, was totally unacceptable to Algeria, as it represented an explicit challenge to Algeria's intent to be the dominant power in North Africa.[54]

Libyan relations with both Algeria and Tunisia began to deteriorate at the end of 1983, when Libya made a formal application to join the Algerian–Tunisian treaty of fraternity and concord signed on 19 March 1983. Although Mauritania had already joined the treaty as a co-opted member, Algeria adamantly opposed Libyan membership because of the policy differences already mentioned and the ongoing border dispute. Thereafter, Libyan relations with Algeria showed little improvement, while its relations with Tunisia cooled as the two states traded charges and countercharges over border incidents and alleged support for dissidents. In October 1984 Libya announced it was naming a former Tunisian foreign minister to be its ambassador to the United Nations. To many, this was seen as a sign of Libya's displeasure at Tunisia's policies — its opposition to improved Libyan relations with Morocco, its insistence that the ICJ reconsider its 1982 award on the offshore boundary dispute, and its unwillingness to consider a Libyan unity agreement outside the framework of the Algerian-Tunisian treaty. Libya increased further the diplomatic pressure on Tunisia by suggesting that the large Tunisian labour force in Libya might soon be forced to leave.[55]

The Treaty of Oujda

Compared to Tunisia or Algeria, the prospects for sustained co-operation between Libya and Morocco in the early 1980s appeared remote, for reasons discussed earlier. Nevertheless, relations began to improve after a tactical rapprochement in mid-1981. At this point, Libya wanted to resume full diplomatic relations but was unwilling to meet Morocco's condition that it end its support for the Polisario Front. In any case, Libya considerably moderated its support for Polisario at OAU meetings in the summer of 1981, while Morocco refrained from condemning Libyan involvement in Chad. This mutual restraint suggested a tactical compromise had been reached; however, in January 1982 Libya apparently reneged on its pledge to end military support for Polisario. A second tactical reconciliation developed in mid-1983 which went beyond the earlier rapprochement. After shifting responsibility for the Western Sahara conflict onto the OAU, Qaddafi declared that Libya no longer had problems or differences with Morocco, and followed up this declaration with his first visit to the Moroccan capital since 1969.[56]

Libya agreed to suspend aid to Polisario in return for a Moroccan pledge not to condemn Libyan involvement in Chad. King Hassan also promised to help improve Libya's strained relations with Egypt and Saudi Arabia. A new element in the 1983 rapprochement was Morocco's willingness to turn Libyan dissidents over to Qaddafi. Once diplomatic relations were resumed, a joint Moroccan-Libyan commission met in January 1984 and agreed to increase trade relations and co-operation in the industrial sphere, to form a joint bank and to explore opportunities for Moroccan construction companies in Libya. The Libyan government also promised to encourage Moroccan labour migration to Libya.[57]

Shock waves reverberated through Arab and Western capitals when Libya and Morocco subsequently signed a treaty of union in August 1984. Proposed by King Hassan, the Treaty of Oujda, dated 13 August 1984, provided for considerably less than Qaddafi's oft-stated goal of full and integral Arab unity. The treaty called for a federation, known as the Arab-African Union, in which both signatories retained their sovereignty. It established a joint presidency which alone had decision-making powers, a rotating permanent secretariat, a joint legislature, a court of justice and advisory councils at various levels. The accord also called for common approaches in foreign policy and close co-operation in economic, social and political matters; but it permitted either party to enter into treaties with third countries without the prior approval of the other. An article stipulating that an act of aggression against one party would be regarded as an act of aggression against the other was in effect a mutual defence pact. The official objective of the union was greater Maghreb and Arab unity, and it provided for third states to join — subject to the approval of both signatories. A Libyan diplomat later suggested that likely candidates to join the union included Senegal, Mauritania, Mali, Niger, Chad and Sudan. Referendums in Morocco and Libya on 31 August and 1 September respectively approved the treaty by massive majorities.[58]

Both parties gained from the 1984 treaty. It reduced the diplomatic isolation that previous policy initiatives had created for Libya, while striking a blow for the sacred cause of Arab unity. It also helped cut through the isolation Morocco had suffered as the result of the war in Western Sahara and the Algerian-Tunisian-Mauritanian entente of 1983. Morocco later said one benefit of the accord was that it implied Libyan recognition of Morocco's claim to the Sahara which, even if true, greatly overestimated the political value of such recognition. According to many analysts, other benefits of the treaty included Libyan agreement to end support for the Polisario Front in return for Moroccan agreement not to interfere in Chad. Such interpretations were not strictly accurate. In the private agreement in June 1983, Qaddafi had already agreed to end aid to Polisario in return for Morocco turning a blind eye to Libyan policy in Chad; and Qaddafi had largely kept his promise. Hence, the treaty really only formalized Qaddafi's earlier promise to end Libyan support for Polisario. As Morocco considered the Western Sahara issue an internal affair, it no doubt viewed the pledge of non-interference in each other's internal affairs as a kind of insurance policy. Morocco also received promises of Libyan financial support, as well as assurances that Libya would no longer aid opponents of the monarchy. Finally, the accord helped demonstrate Moroccan independence from the United States.[59]

A wide variety of states, especially Algeria and the United States, condemned the Treaty of Oujda. Algeria had long argued that a major obstacle to North African unity was Morocco's stand on the Western Sahara; in this light, it condemned the treaty as another example of Moroccan expansionism. Algeria responded to the treaty by encouraging neighbouring states such as Mali, Mauritania and Tunisia to condemn it, and by increasing its assistance to Polisario.

The United States viewed the accord as signalling a sudden alteration in the balance of forces in North Africa. It had been co-operating closely with the Moroccan government, while working to confront and isolate the Libyan government as a major source of terrorism in the world. It was especially concerned about the treaty's stipulation that an act of aggression against one party would be considered an act of aggression against the other, since many members of the US government viewed the possibility of a confrontation with Libya as not unlikely. Towards the end of 1984, the United States asked Morocco for assurances that military goods sent to it would not go to Libya.[60]

The long-term prospects for the Arab-African Union were never bright. The political positions of the signatories were diametrically opposed, with Morocco being essentially a status-quo power interested in evolutionary change, while Libya remained a centre for dynamic, revolutionary change. This basic incompatibility became increasingly obvious over the next two years as the bilateral commissions moved laboriously to translate treaty clauses into functioning administrative bodies. After the accord had been in jeopardy for some time, King Hassan finally abrogated it on 29 August 1986, declaring it null and void. As a pretext, he cited the joint Libyan-Syrian communiqué issued earlier that week which had called Hassan's recent meeting with Israeli Prime Minister Shimon Peres an act of treason. King Hassan was the first Arab head of state since President Sadat to meet publicly with an Israeli prime minister. Qaddafi responded to Hassan's abrogation of the treaty by declaring it illegal and asking the ICJ to investigate the affair.[61]

Seldom concerned with legal niceties, Qaddafi then mobilized Libyan diplomacy against Morocco. Polisario's President Muhammad Abdelaziz was the only head of state to attend the 1 September ceremonies held in Tripoli two days later. At the same time, Qaddafi made fresh overtures to Algeria and Tunisia. Relations with Algeria had already begun to improve after a meeting between President Chadli Benjedid and Qaddafi in the southern Algerian town of In Amenas in January 1986. Increased economic co-operation and unity talks followed, and Algeria strongly condemned the US air raids on Libya in April 1986. Pleased with Libya's break with Morocco, Algeria responded to Qaddafi's overtures by expressing its solidarity with Libya against further US aggression; however, it showed little enthusiasm for new talks aimed at union with Libya.[62]

Libyan relations with Tunisia had not improved to the extent they had with Algeria. Libya's expulsion of Tunisian workers had led to a break in diplomatic relations in September 1985; and at the end of the year, the ICJ rejected Tunisia's application for a fresh judgement on its disputed maritime boundary with Libya. Several Arab and African states promoted a reconciliation between the two countries in early 1986, but little progress was achieved. Consequently, it was not altogether surprising that the Tunisian government responded to Qaddafi's August 1986 overture by refusing to grant landing rights to a Libyan envoy.[63] Diplomatic relations promised to improve at the end of 1986 when the Algerian government sponsored attempts to bring Tunisia and Libya together in a tripartite regional alliance; but the durability of any new bonds remained suspect.[64]

Assessment

Qaddafi's recent statements on Arab unity contained much that was old and little that was new. Comprehensive Arab unity remained the ultimate objective, as the means for the Arab people to realize their potential. 'The solutions to all problems — those of oil, education, health, culture, science, scientific research, backwardness, housing, communications — all these can only be solved by unity.'[65] Despite the flirtation with a gradualist, step-by-step approach, complete integration remained the preferred path to the ultimate objective. Regionalism was a serious threat to pan-Arabism because it threatened to distract the attention of the Arab people from greater Arab unity. 'To God, the ideal, of course, is to achieve comprehensive Arab unity without blocs or axes. What is happening is totally different. Groupings are forming due to the deteriorating situation and fear that the Arab nation will disappear and fall apart.'[66] Qaddafi remained concerned that regional co-operation should advance and should not be a substitute for comprehensive Arab unity. The enemies of Arab unity were imperialism and Zionism, and the road to the liberation of Palestine continued to be the unification of the Arab nation.

If anything had changed, it was the exaggerated role accorded Libya in the Arab world and beyond. In the context of its unique governing system, Qaddafi claimed that Libya offered 'a universal model for all the Arab peoples'. As the conflict with the United States intensified, he claimed, 'a new internationalism at world level had been established; its centre is in Libya, its headquarters in Libya, its leadership in Libya in order to struggle with the Libyan people for the Gulf of Sidra and for Palestine and against the United States and Zionism'.[67] Qaddafi continued to search for a formula which grouped all Arabs into one movement, but it was to be a movement under his control and leadership.

With the death of Nasser, Qaddafi remained the only serious proponent of Arab unity. His message of pan-Arab dreams and ideological designs found few followers in a world which knew their failures all too well. Libya was the first Arab state to combine pan-Arabism and oil wealth, two forces often at odds in recent Arab history; but Libyan foreign policy offered no new gambits or perspectives to policies outworn in the Middle East. Qaddafi repeated Nasser's policies and Nasser's errors. Only gradually did he begin to see the significant differences that separated the Arab people, and recognize the weighty problems of tactics and strategy which faced the Arab states. In the process, neither the passion of the Libyan revolution nor its money were enough to reverse history and revive an exhausted idea.

Moreover, Qaddafi's strategy compounded the problems arising from an anachronistic policy. His continuing reliance on socio-economic and political destabilization created division, not union, in the Arab world, as the evidence of direct and indirect Libyan involvement in the internal affairs of neighbouring states became irrefutable. His policies were also contradictory. Libya's migrant-labour policies, its support for the non-Arab side (Ethiopia) in the Eritrean conflict and its assistance to Iran in the Gulf war belied his emphasis on pan-Arabism. While Qaddafi continued to emphasize Arab unity, Libyan foreign policy often put practical interests of state ahead of the nebulous concerns of the Arab nation.

5
Positive Neutrality

> *With regard to foreign policy, we will follow a policy of absolute neutrality without partiality to East or West.*
>
> **Muammar al-Qaddafi**

Libyan relations with the East and West power blocs underwent a dramatic shift in the first decade of the revolution. At first Libya proclaimed a policy of non-alignment and refused to espouse the causes of non-Arab states, especially the policies of the two superpowers. Later, diplomatic relations with the West deteriorated; and long-standing economic ties were subjected to growing strains. In the process, both economic and political ties with the West were gradually supplanted by those with the East. By late 1978, Qaddafi was threatening to join the Warsaw Pact.

Early expression of positive neutrality
The doctrine of positive neutrality did not originate with Qaddafi nor with the Libyan revolution. In the context of the anti-Western movement, its roots were found in the historic Muslim resentment of the emerging power of western Europe. Such resentment was manifest in the disparate currents which coalesced into an Arab nationalist movement in the early twentieth century. Confronted with a world dominated by alien ideologies, the common reaction of Arab states was to pursue an independent policy which emphasized Arab solutions to Arab problems.

In recent times, positive neutrality has also been a response to the bipolarization of international power. After World War II, the Arabs tended to reject both the Eastern and Western blocs on the grounds that they followed different but equally misguided ideologies. The United States was seen as the major opponent of Arab nationalist goals, while the Soviet Union's recognition of Arab neutrality was dismissed as a largely tactical device. Nevertheless, the Arab concept of neutrality was seldom balanced evenly between the two power blocs. The basic neutralist position was revisionist in that it challenged the status quo supported by long-established Western assumptions and positions. In this light, the essence of positive neutrality was anti-imperialism in the classical sense of the term.[1]

Egyptian foreign policy under Nasser epitomized the contemporary Arab approach to positive neutrality. In effect, he played one power bloc off against the other in an effort to reap the maximum advantage from both sides. Egypt expected to receive levels of economic and military aid the West had given only to its closest allies, and to do so without undertaking the responsibilities of the Western alliance system. At the same time, Egyptian policy assumed a growing pro-Soviet orientation as the Soviet Union extended increasing amounts of military, diplomatic and economic assistance. Positive neutrality eventually became a doctrine of Egyptian foreign policy and an integral part of Nasser's ideology. It also gained widespread application outside Egypt. It was adopted throughout the Third World and contributed to the philosophical make-up of organizations such as the Afro-Asian movement, the Non-Aligned Movement and the economic Group of Seventy-Seven.[2]

Qaddafi's initial exposition of positive neutrality was very much in line with the approach taken by Nasser in the mid-1950s. He professed a belief in the unity of Third World causes and proclaimed a policy of absolute neutrality between East and West. 'The foreign policy of my country in the revolutionary era,' he stated on 12 October 1969, 'is, in brief, positive neutrality, non-alignment and support for all liberation causes and for freedom in the whole world.' The following month, he re-emphasized his commitment to positive neutrality and peaceful coexistence as touchstones of Libyan foreign policy.[3] Later, Qaddafi described positive neutrality, non-alignment and peaceful coexistence as the 'central concepts' of his Third Universal Theory. He argued that his new theory was necessary to defend the nations of the Third World from the designs of the superpowers, who were conspiring to divide the world between them.[4]

Nevertheless, Qaddafi's neutralism was never uniformly neutral. His basic external commitment was to fight imperialism, defined in terms of Western colonialism and political intervention. He rejected foreign control of any type and promised vigorous ideological and operational hostility to imperialism wherever it was found. Generally, his approach was to befriend states with a similar viewpoint while confronting those opposed to it. Like Nasser, Qaddafi also sought a leadership role in the Non-Aligned Movement, an ambition he was not able to satisfy.[5]

The development and practical application of Qaddafi's doctrine of positive neutrality is best examined through a review of Libyan policy towards the Soviet Union, the United States and western Europe. Stridently critical of both communism and capitalism, Qaddafi initially dismissed both as two sides of the same coin. Thereafter, early Libyan policy towards East and West followed a divergent pattern. As its criticism of American foreign policy intensified, Libya maintained close commercial ties with the West.

Libya exported most of its oil to western Europe and used oil revenues to import large amounts of Western technology. Qaddafi also criticized the foreign policy of the Soviet Union, especially the emigration of Soviet Jews to Israel; but events inside and outside the Middle East fostered a deepening Libyan-Soviet relationship, especially in the area of arms transfers.[6]

Early Soviet contacts

During the post-war debate over the future of Italy's former colonies, the Soviet Union hoped to increase its military presence in the Mediterranean and its political influence throughout the Middle East. Recognizing the strategic value of Libya, the Soviet Union proposed at the 1945 Potsdam conference that it assume a trusteeship over Tripolitania. When the United States, Britain and France rejected the proposal, the Soviet Union, alert to a possible communist victory in the Italian general elections, promoted an Italian trusteeship over Libya. In 1948 the Russians abandoned their support for Italy and began to advocate a collective trusteeship, an idea supported at one time or another by the remaining members of the Big Four. The Soviet proposal was later rejected; and with no solution in sight, the Big Four referred the problem to the United Nations. In the General Assembly a final proposal for a trusteeship dividing Libya between Italy, France and Britain was defeated by the Arab-Asian and Soviet blocs. On 21 November 1949, the UN adopted a resolution providing for a united, independent Libya.[7]

During the reign of King Idris, contact between Libya and the Soviet Union was minimal. Full diplomatic ties were not established until 1955, and diplomatic and commercial interchange developed slowly. The Soviet Union took part in the annual Tripoli trade fair, and a few Libyan students studied in the USSR. Libyan parliamentary delegations visited the Soviet Union in 1961 and 1968, and a delegation from the Supreme Soviet visited Libya in 1966. A Libyan-Soviet trade agreement was signed in 1961, but no trade was recorded until 1963.[8]

The Soviet Union moved quickly to recognize the revolutionary government; and on 4 September 1969 the Soviet chargé d'affaires in Tripoli stated that his government supported Libya and was ready to provide any necessary assistance. The previous day, Tripoli Radio had broadcast a report that the British government had decided not to intervene to restore the monarchy because of the presence of the Soviet fleet in the Mediterranean. The radio report was significant as it implied the RCC was concerned about such a threat and hoped the Soviet Union might come to its aid; however, there was no evidence of a Soviet show of force on the morrow of the coup.[9] Comments on the new regime in the 6 September and 14 September issues of the Soviet newspaper *Pravda* were friendly but included no specific commitments or promises of Soviet friendship. The Russians were waiting to see what direction the new regime would take.[10]

While the revolutionary government hoped for early Soviet diplomatic support as it consolidated the revolution, it soon showed considerable suspicion and distrust for the Soviet government. Members of the RCC emphasized that they did not intend to imitate any foreign system, whether that of the Soviet Union or elsewhere. In particular, Qaddafi feared that communist ideology might have some appeal to uneducated Libyans, as well as the handful of Libyan intellectuals educated in the Soviet Union. He was also strongly critical of Soviet support for the partition of Palestine and Soviet willingness to allow Soviet Jews to emigrate to Israel.

As the decade progressed, Qaddafi occasionally increased his anti-Soviet rhetoric. He grouped the Soviet Union and the United States together as 'policemen' of the world, and adamantly rejected the patronage of either. Well after the October 1973 war, Libya's media engaged in a campaign of abuse and recrimination against the Soviet Union, depicting it as a 'godless' and 'perfidious' power which could be more hostile towards the Arab people than the United States. Hence it was clear from the beginning that emerging Libyan-Soviet ties were based more on a common interest in preventing the spread of US influence in the Middle East than on sentiment or ideological conviction.[11]

Arms build-up

The Soviet government maintained a low profile in Libya during the early years of the revolution. It welcomed the closure of British and American bases and largely ignored the Libyan decision in 1970 to buy French Mirage fighter planes. On 9 November 1969, *Pravda* published an interview with Qaddafi in which he reportedly said he considered the Soviet Union to be the best friend of the Arabs, and viewed Soviet aid to Egypt and other Arab states as aid to Libya. The Soviet military equipment sought by Libya was not long in coming. An initial delivery of 30 medium tanks and 100 armoured personnel carriers and other vehicles arrived in July 1970.[12]

The next few years witnessed an unprecedented build-up of Soviet arms in Libya. In early 1974 the Libyan government sought unsuccessfully to diversify by purchasing more arms in western Europe. Its efforts were to no avail, in part because of Libyan support for European dissident groups; and despite Qaddafi's antipathy towards the Russians, Libya turned again to Moscow. In May 1974 during Prime Minister Jallud's first visit to the Soviet Union, the two governments concluded general trade and industrial co-operation agreements which included the supply of Soviet arms in exchange for Libyan oil. Details were completed in a subsequent agreement at the end of the year.[13]

This agreement was facilitated by the strains in Soviet-Egyptian relations. A joint communiqué issued by Libya and the Soviet Union called for the withdrawal of Israeli troops from occupied Arab lands and pledged additional support for the Palestinian movement. On the other hand, the

Soviet Union refused to endorse Libya's radical stand on the use of force against Israel; and Soviet leader Brezhnev reportedly wrote to President Sadat of Egypt expressing a conciliatory view of future Soviet-Egyptian relations. Willing to sell arms to the Libyans, the Russians were careful not to become embroiled in the vendetta between Qaddafi and Sadat. Soviet Premier Kosygin visited Libya in May 1975; shortly after his departure, another large arms deal was reported which appeared to be a multi-million-dollar addition to the 1974 agreements.[14] By 1976 Libya was thought to have one of the highest per capita ratios of military equipment in the world. Most of this vast new arsenal remained in storage, since the Libyan armed forces lacked the trained manpower to maintain and operate it.

Qaddafi embarked on this major armaments programme because he had concluded that Libya's limited military capability was one of the major reasons it was not involved in the October 1973 war. Ironically, it was the October war which caused the dramatic increase in the price of oil and thus gave Libya the oil revenues necessary to purchase sophisticated arms. By assembling a vast arsenal, Qaddafi hoped to end his isolation from the Arab confrontation states and regain the limelight he had enjoyed in the Arab world in the early 1970s. He referred to his weapons as an 'arsenal for Islam', although it remained unlikely that either Libya or the other Arab states could provide the trained manpower to use it. Libya's performance in the brief border war with Egypt in July 1977 confirmed its limited capacity to wage even a short conventional war.[15]

In the context of the long-standing Soviet interest in increasing its Middle East presence, Libya offered the Soviet Union some compensation for the loss of its position in Egypt, as well as a possible base from which to undermine the Sadat regime. Libya also offered attractive financial terms, as it paid promptly in the early years of the relationship in hard currency and oil, both scarce in the Comecon countries. Finally, both Libya and the Soviet Union had a mutual interest in undermining Western positions in Africa and the Middle East, although the ultimate geopolitical objectives of the two states were dissimilar. In this regard, the early Soviet arms relationship with Libya was a gamble, since any resemblance between Soviet and Libyan aims was largely coincidental.[16]

Deepening Soviet relationship

After 1976 Soviet-Libyan relations continued to develop, particularly on the technical level. Shortly after the Kosygin visit in May 1975, the two governments had announced that the Soviet Union would provide Libya with its first nuclear reactor. The Libyan news agency said the 10-megawatt facility would be used for peaceful purposes only, and Western experts later confirmed that its small size would confine it to research activities. In late 1977 it was reported that Libya had also contracted with the Russians for the construction of a 440-megawatt nuclear power plant similar to those already provided by the Soviet Union in eastern Europe and Finland. This indication of expanding co-operation in the nuclear field caused deep concern in the West, as Qaddafi was also widely believed to be involved in funding nuclear-energy projects in Pakistan that were thought to reflect his desire to obtain nuclear weapons.

In the area of arms transfers, the July 1977 clash with Egypt prompted Libya to engage in another military build-up. A new agreement with the Russians brought the delivery of MiG-25s to Libya in 1978. Libya was the first country to import these sophisticated fighter planes, and Qaddafi later boasted that Libya owned Soviet weaponry not yet provided to Warsaw Pact members.[17]

When Qaddafi visited the Soviet Union for the first time in December 1976, political relations between the two states were complicated by Soviet support for a Geneva conference on the Middle East. Qaddafi feared the conference would lead to a sell-out of Palestinian interests. The Russians were also encouraging Egyptian interest in the Geneva meeting at a time when Qaddafi was thoroughly disenchanted with Sadat. President Sadat's visit to Jerusalem in November 1977 strengthened political ties between Libya and the Soviet Union, as it provided the latter with a rationale for supporting the rejectionist Steadfastness and Confrontation Front formed in Tripoli in December 1977. In February 1978 the second summit of the Steadfastness Front called for closer ties between the Arab states and the Soviet Union; and Libyan relations with the latter expanded in the course of the year.[18]

With the conclusion of the September 1978 Camp David Accords, Qaddafi publicly departed from his earlier commitment to non-alignment. In October 1978, for example, he first made his preposterous threat to join the Warsaw Pact. Few observers took the comment seriously, least of all the members of the Warsaw Pact; but it symbolized the extent to which Qaddafi had departed from his initial position on positive neutrality. In addition to reflecting his deteriorating relations with the West, the statement also betrayed a growing impatience as his ambitions to shape world affairs were thwarted at every turn. Qaddafi was still not enamoured of the Soviet system, but the political interests of Libya and the Soviet Union appeared to be converging.[19]

Libyan co-operation with the Soviet Union increased in most areas over the next few years. Libya did not condemn the Soviet invasion of Afghanistan in 1979, and Kabul Radio later reported Libyan agreement to finance several Afghan development projects. Another major arms deal was concluded in 1980; and by 1981 Libya was reported to have the highest ratio of military equipment to manpower in the Third World. Nato planners were increasingly concerned about the possibility that Soviet forces might obtain the use of Libyan bases in the event of a crisis in the Mediterranean. Such concern was heightened by the visit of two Soviet frigates to Tripoli in July 1981, the first such visit since Qaddafi had come to power. In turn, the Russians supported the 1981 treaty of friendship and co-operation between Libya, Ethiopia and South Yemen as a means to challenge Western policy in the Indian Ocean and the Gulf. Economic co-operation also increased, with the emphasis on joint projects to expand Libya's power production, including the oil and gas industries. Qaddafi continued to stress nuclear research and to emphasize the right of small states to use nuclear energy for peaceful purposes. Periodically, Qaddafi also expressed interest in concluding a treaty of friendship and co-operation with the Soviet Union; and after several false starts, it was announced in April 1983 that the two states had reached an agreement in principle to sign such a pact.[20]

Strains in the Soviet–Libyan relationship

On the surface, Libya's diplomatic relationship with the Soviet Union was characterized by cautious co-operation; however, considerable tension strained the relationship. Periodically, the strain arising from a lack of ideological compatibility, compounded by the unorthodox nature of Libyan foreign policy, came to the surface to disturb existing relations. At the end of 1981 Qaddafi, acting also as a representative of the Steadfastness Front, made his second official visit to the Soviet Union. During the visit, he antagonized his hosts by insisting on prayers at the closed Grand Mosque in Moscow and by visiting Muslim cemeteries where he read Quranic verses. At an official dinner in Qaddafi's honour, Brezhnev underlined the importance of the visit but also alluded to the ideological differences separating the two states. Qaddafi made the same point in an interview given while he was in Moscow. Emphasizing the need to strengthen relations between the Arab states and the Soviet Union, he pointed out that the policies of the Steadfastness Front and the Soviet Union were not identical on key issues. In Chad the Soviet Union had declined to support Libyan aid to the Goukouni Oueddei government. With regard to the Camp David accords and the Egypt-Israel peace treaty, Qaddafi emphasized that the Russians had rejected them only because they had led to a separate settlement between Egypt and the 'Zionist entity', while Libya rejected any kind of settlement. Qaddafi explained these policy differences as largely due to the fact that the Soviet Union was one of the superpowers; and Libya could not expect to have policies identical to a superpower.[21]

Soviet reluctance to move too close to the Qaddafi regime strengthened as the decade progressed. When the United States shot down two Libyan planes in August 1981, the Soviet press reported both the US and the Libyan version of the incident and contented itself with calling for Third World countries to respond to American provocations. Similarly, the Russians encouraged closer Libyan ties with their East European allies, as a way to maintain the economic and military benefits of the overall relationship without committing the Soviet Union to a closer identification with a leader in whom it did not have full confidence. Qaddafi visited Hungary, Romania and Yugoslavia in 1981; and Libya concluded pacts with Czechoslovakia, Bulgaria, Romania and Yugoslavia in 1982-83.[22]

In 1984–85 Soviet concern with the direction and emphasis of Libyan policy increased. The reported Libyan bombing of Omdurman, a suburb of the Sudanese capital Khartoum, in March 1984, and the alleged Libyan involvement in the mining of the Red Sea and the Gulf of Suez in mid-1984, were harmful to Soviet objectives. By increasing tensions in the Middle East, such actions served to bring more US military forces, at Arab request, onto the scene. Qaddafi's growing association with state-sponsored terrorism was also viewed by the Russians as counterproductive. Moreover, as oil revenues declined, the economic benefits of the Libyan connection decreased. While the Libyans had purchased $15-$20 billion worth of Soviet weapons by the end of 1986, the Libyan government was estimated to owe the Russians $5-$7 billion of the total in outstanding payments.[23]

Reluctant allies

In October 1985 Qaddafi paid his third official visit to the Soviet Union. His objectives included Soviet assistance in the construction of a nuclear reactor convertible to military uses, additional weapons and military equipment, a doubling of Soviet daily purchases of Libyan crude oil and the conclusion of a treaty of friendship and co-operation. The Soviet news agency Tass described the discussions in Moscow between Qaddafi and Gorbachev as having taken place in an atmosphere of friendship and mutual understanding. But Qaddafi left Moscow with considerably less than he wanted.[24]

The Russians agreed to help with a nuclear reactor, but one that could be used for power generation only and would not be convertible to military purposes. They referred Libyan arms requests to a commission and pressed for payment for earlier purchases. Later, Libya confirmed it was acquiring Soviet Sam-5 anti-aircraft missiles. A deal was also struck for the purchase of additional oil for export to Yugoslavia. A long-term agreement expanding economic, trade, scientific and technical co-operation to the year 2000 was negotiated; but the communiqué announcing the agreement made no mention of the friendship and co-operation treaty agreed to in principle in 1983. Five months later, after Qaddafi had ruled out the possibility of Soviet bases in Libya, a Soviet official indicated that plans to sign a friendship treaty had been shelved. Somewhat disingenuously, the official explained that both states considered the existing level of relations to be satisfactory and in no need of strengthening by legal acts or formal pacts.[25]

A number of key issues continued to separate the Soviet and Libyan governments. In Moscow, Qaddafi and Gorbachev had reportedly had a spirited argument over Libya's virulent anti-Israeli line at a time when the Soviet Union was exploring a renewal of diplomatic relations with Israel as part of a general broadening of options in the Middle East. Soviet ties to Libya were also strained by the latter's support for Iran in the Gulf war, including the supply of Soviet weapons, while the Soviet Union tended to support Iraq. As oil prices began to fall, the Libyans also pressed the Russians to take larger amounts of oil, rather than hard currency, in exchange for arms.[26]

The April 1986 bombing attack by the United States on targets around Tripoli and Benghazi strained a Soviet-Libyan relationship which could already be described as testy. In the build-up to the raids, the United States reportedly kept the Russians regularly informed as to its manoeuvres; nevertheless, the latter made no apparent effort to intervene on Libya's behalf.[27] Shortly afterwards, Qaddafi again repeated his threat to join the Warsaw Pact; however, he received no further encouragement from Moscow. While the Russians denounced the raids, using them as a pretext to cancel a scheduled meeting between Secretary of State Shultz and Foreign Minister Shevardnadze, they were content to promise Libya only that they would help rebuild its defensive capability. When Jallud returned to Moscow in May 1986, the Russians were reluctant to extend additional credits for arms, rejected a mutual defence treaty and differed with Libya about its distinction between supporting revolution and supporting terrorism.[28] The Soviet Union remained an ally of Libya; but it was an aloof, reluctant ally. It was unlikely to modify that stance and enter into a closer alliance with the Qaddafi regime until it was sure that important foreign policy decisions would not be made in Tripoli without extensive prior consultation.

Early relations with the United States
Diplomatic relations between Libya and the United States were not good at any time after 1969. The two states held such diametrically opposed views on world issues in general and Middle Eastern questions in particular that there was little opportunity for a rapprochement to develop. Qaddafi was adamantly opposed to the international status quo, while the United States was its primary proponent and buttress. When the Libyan revolutionary government tied its bilateral relations with other states to their position on the Palestine issue, the United States was a target for special criticism. Moreover, what Libya saw as justifiable support for national liberation movements, the United States viewed as blatant interference in the domestic affairs of other states, if not active support for international terrorism.[29]

At the same time, the two states were bound by a web of common economic interests that both were reluctant to forgo. Historically, US foreign policy in the Middle East aimed to protect the flow of oil to the United States economy and the economies of its Western allies on terms that maximized volume, minimized price and avoided interruptions of supply. Closely related to this objective, the United States sought to recycle as large a share of petrodollars as possible through the US economy, largely in the form of US exports to the region. Libyan oil was especially prized, as it was high-quality, low-sulphur crude which was well-suited to American refining needs. Consequently, a primary commercial objective of the United States throughout the 1970s was to preserve the dominant position of American oil companies in Libya.

A secondary objective which grew from the presence of the oil companies was the obligation to safeguard the American community of several thousand people living and working in Libya. On its side, the Libyan government, in particular Qaddafi, respected American expertise and desired continued access to American technology. Libyan students were enrolled in American colleges and universities in large numbers, and Libyan co-operation with the private sector in the United States remained at a high level, despite the precarious nature of official relations.[30]

In large part because of this important economic relationship, early US policy towards revolutionary Libya could be termed one of conciliation. As it had done with Egypt in the early days of Nasser's revolution, the US government focused primarily on Libya's external orientation, as opposed to its internal evolution, and stressed the long-term compatibility of US-Libyan interests. In any case, there was little evidence to support the conspiracy theories which surfaced later to suggest that the United States had installed Qaddafi in power and shielded him during the early years of the revolution. As discussed earlier, Qaddafi's early anti-communist, anti-Soviet policies, often cited in support of conspiracy theories, were consistent with deep-seated ideological convictions. In fact, it would have been surprising for Qaddafi to articulate any other position. At most, the US government, through its Central Intelligence Agency, probably alerted the Libyan government on one or more occasions to potential coup attempts.[31]

After 1972, US policy moved from one of conciliation to one of constraint. With the withdrawal of the US ambassador to Libya in 1972, diplomatic representation at the ambassadorial level ended to the present time (1987). For the remainder of the decade, various American administrations tried to pay as little attention to Libya as possible. They imposed additional restraints on commercial dealings, in particular blocking delivery of several million dollars' worth of transport equipment deemed to have potential military uses; but the thrust of American policy in the region was to ignore Libya. The general feeling in Washington was that provoking Qaddafi or precipitating an economic or military showdown with Libya would run counter to the step-by-step peace process pursued by the United

States in the region in 1973–75, as well as the Camp David diplomacy of the Carter administration later in the decade.[32]

Not surprisingly, the United States policy of constraint in 1972–80 was largely a failure. Qaddafi continued to oppose the chief Middle Eastern goals of the United States because they were antithetical to his own. He adamantly opposed every US plan for an Arab-Israeli settlement; and as his personal relationship with Sadat deteriorated, he became the most shrill Arab critic of Egyptian peace initiatives. The Libyan government was a founding member of the Steadfastness and Confrontation Front and subsidized radical Palestinian factions opposed to any form of peace settlement with Israel. Libyan purchases of Soviet weapons continued; and during periods of regional tension, Qaddafi could be counted on to urge Arab oil producers to use the oil weapon against the United States.[33]

During the Carter administration, bilateral diplomatic relations became increasingly strained. This was especially true after the Libyan government did little to protect the US embassy in Tripoli when it was stormed by Libyan students in the early days of the hostage crisis in Iran. Concerned for their safety, the United States had recalled all its diplomatic personnel from Libya by May 1980. At the same time, reports increased of Qaddafi agents planning to assassinate Libyan dissidents outside Libya, including some residing in the United States.

In early 1980, Libya was linked to an abortive coup in Tunisia which was launched from the southern mining town of Gafsa. The United States, together with France, responded to the incident with an emergency shipment of military equipment to Tunisia. Thereafter, the threat of Libyan intervention continued, especially in countries with close political ties to the United States. In the summer of 1980, Libya and Egypt again experienced a brief border confrontation; and later in the year, Qaddafi roundly denounced a military co-operation agreement negotiated by the United States with the governments of Egypt, Somalia and Oman under the guise of the Carter Doctrine, which called for the protection of the Gulf. Nevertheless both governments still seemed willing to coexist with a mutually unsatisfactory diplomatic relationship which neither was able to improve but both were unwilling to rupture, in part because of the economic considerations referred to earlier.[34]

The redirection of US policy
The election of Ronald Reagan to the US presidency at the end of 1980 produced a dramatic shift in the Libyan–US relationship. Once in office, the Reagan administration systematically increased the military, diplomatic and economic pressure on Libya in an effort to isolate it internationally and promote the downfall of the Qaddafi government. Qaddafi, inaccurately labelled a Soviet puppet, was characterized as an international rogue who had

to be corralled if not replaced. In a little over a year, US foreign policy towards Libya had been fundamentally altered. The US government had come to recognize Qaddafi, not as simply an irritant or a nuisance, but as an enemy.[35]

The first concrete public step taken by the Reagan administration was to close the Libyan People's Bureau (embassy) in Washington in May 1981. The official statement accompanying the closure cited a wide range of Libyan provocations and misconduct, including support for international terrorism, which were deemed contrary to internationally accepted standards of behaviour. Related steps taken at the same time included a decision to subject all Libyan visa applications to a mandatory security advisory opinion, and advice to American oil companies active in Libya to initiate an orderly reduction of Americans working there. Other elements of the widening American campaign included increased assistance to neighbouring states opposed to Libya such as Tunisia and Sudan, improved co-ordination of US policy with its European allies and a calculated threat of military intervention. Nato allies were asked to reject state visits by Qaddafi and to maintain or expand existing embargoes on arms deliveries and oil exploration. Military force was first employed in August 1981 when the United States, in the process of challenging Libyan maritime claims to the Gulf of Sirte, shot down two Libyan aircraft. There were also reliable reports of greater clandestine activity by the United States which included disinformation, propaganda dissemination, sabotage and support for dissident groups.[36]

Over the next two years, the Reagan administration continued to pressure Qaddafi's regime, with much of the focus on bilateral economic relations. In March 1982 it announced an embargo on Libyan oil and imposed an export-licence requirement for all American goods bound for Libya except food, medicine and medical supplies. Arguing that Libya was still actively supporting subversive and terrorist activities, it also urged its allies in western Europe to support wider economic sanctions; but for a variety of reasons, all of them politely declined. In fact, Qaddafi was on a visit to Austria, his first official visit to a European state, when the American sanctions were announced. In early 1983, the US government dispatched Awacs surveillance aircraft to Egypt in response to an alleged Libyan threat to the Sudanese government. While the crisis quickly passed, the aggressive American response embarrassed the Egyptian government and thus underscored, not for the last time, the difficulty of putting pressure on any Arab government without incurring the wrath of other Arab or African states. At the end of 1983 the Reagan administration again publicly urged its European allies to join in curbing exports to Libya.[37]

The increased pressure of the Reagan administration came at a time when Qaddafi's policies in the Middle East and Africa were suffering an unprecedented series of setbacks. Libyan armed forces had intervened in Chad in the winter of 1980-81, but were forced to withdraw under Western and African pressure some 10 months later. The débâcle in Chad was only the first of a series of foreign-policy defeats suffered by Qaddafi over the next 18 months. The shooting down of two Libyan aircraft in the autumn of 1981, and the March 1982 embargo on Libyan oil imports, have already been mentioned. In the autumn of 1982, attempts to convene a summit meeting of the Organization of African Unity (OAU) in Tripoli, with Qaddafi as chairman, broke down, in large part because of opposition to Libyan policies in sub-Saharan Africa. American diplomats were reportedly active in lobbying OAU members to shift the venue of the OAU summit, as well as its presidency, from Libya. At the same time, Qaddafi isolated himself from many Arab leaders by refusing to attend an Arab summit in Fez, Morocco, and then attacking as treason the peace proposals adopted there. The OAU summit finally opened in Addis Ababa in June 1983, where it was chaired by the Ethiopian head of state. Qaddafi briefly attended the meeting but quickly departed after suffering the double indignity of being denied the chairmanship and seeing his protégé, the Polisario Front, effectively barred from the meeting.[38]

Throughout 1984-85, the Reagan administration maintained its pressure on the Libyan government. Large-scale sales of American grain were permitted for the first time since 1982; however, the movements of Libyan diplomats accredited to the United Nations were curtailed under the toughest regulations applied to any government delegation. In October 1985 Qaddafi cancelled plans to visit the United Nations to participate in ceremonies marking its fortieth anniversary, supposedly because its headquarters were located in a country which he considered to be an enemy of humanity and a leader of international terrorism. He called for the removal of the world body to a country where it would not be handicapped by the policies of the United States.

In November 1985 the American government, under the influence of congressional representatives from oil-producing regions of the US, banned the import of all Libyan oil products. In response to the December 1985 terrorist attacks on Rome and Vienna airports, it also terminated direct economic activities with Libya, froze Libyan assets in the United States and called on the 1,000-1,500 Americans still working in Libya to return home. The Reagan administration urged the governments of western Europe to join it in imposing new economic and political sanctions against Libya, but again it received a tepid reply. At this point, President Reagan also examined, for the third time since taking office, the option of a military strike against Libya, but chose to limit the American reaction to economic and diplomatic measures. A major factor in his decision was said to be his concern for the safety of American citizens still resident in Libya. At the same time, covert action designed to undermine Qaddafi was reportedly stepped up.[39]

Dénouement

In the spring of 1986, events in the Mediterranean region moved inexorably towards armed conflict. The *casus belli* proved to be US resolve to challenge Libya's claim to sovereignty over the Gulf of Sirte, a gulf which is some 275 miles wide. The United States based its legal position on a 1958 convention on the territorial sea and contiguous zone which only allowed nations to claim coastal embayments less than 24 miles wide. The Libyan government was not a party to the 1958 convention. In response to fresh manoeuvres in the disputed waters in mid–March 1986, Libyan missiles and ships attacked the US flotilla without inflicting any damage; and US forces responded by sinking several Libyan craft and damaging Libyan missile sites.[40]

In public, Qaddafi responded to the worsening crisis with rhetoric and bombast. Pledging to defend what he termed the 'line of death' across the mouth of the Gulf of Sirte, he threatened to broaden his struggle against the United States, and boasted he had plans to confront the United States militarily. In private, he attempted to open a dialogue with Washington using various European and Arab governments, including Saudi Arabia, as intermediaries. The Reagan administration's response to such overtures was that it had no interest in developing a direct or indirect dialogue with the Qaddafi regime.

After three more terrorist attacks in early April 1986, including a West Berlin discotheque bombing linked by radio intercepts to Libya, the Reagan administration resolved upon the tough response it had been wanting to make for months. On 15 April 1986, US bombers attacked five targets near Tripoli and Benghazi. The Reagan administration described the raid as a justified retaliation for the Berlin bombing as well as dozens of other terrorist attacks planned by Libya. A week later, President Reagan warned Libya to change its policies or face further military action.[41]

World reaction to the raid, especially in the Arab, African and Islamic worlds, was generally hostile. The Non–Aligned Movement condemned the attack as a blatant, unprovoked act of aggression; and as a demonstration of support, it sent a delegation to Libya on 20 April. The Opec member states also condemned the attack but rejected a Libyan demand for an immediate oil embargo against the United States. Moderate Arab states, such as Egypt and Jordan, were trapped between traditional ties of Arab solidarity and uneasiness over United States actions. While many had decided Washington should either take decisive action or leave Qaddafi alone, they all recognized that no Arab leader could endorse an armed attack on another Arab state, especially one by a superpower, without undermining his own domestic political position. Hence most Arab as well as Islamic states extended Libya various degrees of rhetorical support in the name of Arab or Islamic unity.

For example, a United Arab Emirates trade delegation cancelled a scheduled visit to Britain in protest at British involvement in the raid; and an Afghan resistance leader cancelled a scheduled trip to the United States to make clear his organization's opposition to an armed attack on a Muslim brother. Saudi Arabia and the Gulf states, placed in a compromising position because of their close political ties with the United States, roundly condemned the attack.[42] While the general condemnation of the attack inside and outside the Middle East could not be taken as an endorsement of Libyan foreign policy, it did suggest the United States had underestimated the negative political fall-out from the raid.

The April raids did not have a significant impact on Libyan-American relations. After a period of seclusion, Qaddafi returned to the world stage with his radical, rejectionist policies wholly intact. While his support for state-sponsored terrorism might be more circumspect, he remained opposed to the international status quo and determined to employ all of Libya's resources to overturn it. The Reagan administration, on the other hand, stepped up its programme of diplomatic, economic and military pressure designed to precipitate the downfall of the Qaddafi regime.

While the evidence suggested that the Reagan policy of calculated hostility and stern retribution was hardly more successful in redirecting Libyan foreign policy than were less bellicose policies of earlier American administrations, it did focus attention on a major irony in the US-Libyan relationship. Probably because of his own esteem for American power and prestige, Muammar al-Qaddafi had often betrayed a need for US recognition of his position and importance. Hence the foreign policy of the Reagan administration encouraged as well as discouraged the Libyan policies it was designed to check, since US foreign policy helped generate the international recognition craved by Qaddafi.

Qaddafi and Europe

In 1969 Qaddafi approached the industrialized states of western Europe with the same ideological framework applied elsewhere. Preferring to operate on a bilateral basis, he condemned their earlier support for imperialism and emphasized that good relations would depend on their stand on Middle East issues, especially the Palestine question. The character and extent of subsequent relations varied considerably from state to state, but the common focus was commercial. The states of western Europe, to a greater or lesser degree, relied on supplies of Libyan crude oil, while Libya desired European goods and technology. As investment and commercial ties expanded, the European allies of the United States became less and less interested in supporting a policy of isolating Libya because they had their own growing economic interests to protect. Equally important, many of these states felt

US policy towards Libya was misguided if not dangerous.

Early Libyan relations with Italy were strongly influenced by the Italo-Libyan struggle and the bitter heritage of the colonial period. When the RCC seized power, a large, economically important Italian community existed in Libya; but it tended to live apart with its own schools, churches and customs. In June 1970 Qaddafi announced that the time had come to avenge the Italian occupation, and he warned that the large Italian community would be compelled to leave unless it abandoned its imperialist attitude. A few days later, the RCC issued a decree confiscating all Italian property in the country.

Diplomatic relations between Libya and Italy began to improve after 1975, however, when an agreement was reached regarding compensation for the property confiscated in 1970. A major commercial transaction was concluded at the end of 1976, when the Libyan government purchased a sizeable stake in Fiat, an investment it retained until late 1986. In October 1978 Qaddafi remarked that present-day Italy was not the imperialist power of the past and that the general bilateral relationship was positive. By the mid-1980s, Italy had become Libya's main commercial partner, as well as one of Europe's strongest advocates of an ongoing dialogue with the Libyan government.[43]

Qaddafi was highly critical of British policy in the Middle East dating as far back as the Balfour Declaration (1917), and he especially condemned Britain's close political, economic and military relationship with the Idris regime. While the British government had agreed to an expeditious withdrawal from its Libyan base facilities, a number of issues combined to strain bilateral relations in the early years of the revolution. After Britain suspended military equipment agreements negotiated with the monarchy and refused to fulfil subsequent Libyan orders, the Libyan government nationalized British Petroleum's interests in Libya, officially in retaliation for alleged British complicity in the Iranian occupation of three disputed islands in the Gulf. Other sources of disagreement included Libya's intervention in Maltese negotiations with Britain over base leases on the island, and alleged Libyan support for elements of the Irish Republican Army (IRA). The Libyan government also opposed a British decision in March 1977 to supply a large quantity of tanks to Iran.[44]

Once its North Sea oilfields began producing high-quality crude, Britain became something of an exception in western Europe as it had no further need for Libyan oil. Partly for this reason, diplomatic relations with Libya remained circumspect even as commercial relations expanded. As increasing numbers of Libyan exiles in Europe were attacked in the spring of 1980, for example, the British government was one of the few governments in Europe to take a reasonably firm stand against the mounting Libyan campaign of political terrorism. In April 1984, Britain broke diplomatic relations with Libya after demonstrations in front of the Libyan embassy in London culminated in the death of a policewoman and the closure of the embassy. In the course of talks in Rome in March 1985 aimed at improving relations, Qaddafi threatened to retaliate against European countries harbouring Libyan dissidents, while a Libyan representative at the talks commented publicly that Britain had not shed its colonial and imperialist mentality. No significant improvement in Libyan relations with Britain occurred in the succeeding 12 months prior to the departure in April 1986 of American bombers from British bases to attack Libya. Towards the end of the year, Britain banned Libyan Arab Airways flights, after evidence at a London trial implicated the airline in terrorist activities in Britain. In response to this decision and a related one breaking diplomatic relations with Syria, Libya closed its airspace to British aircraft. The decision had little practical effect as British carriers had not flown to Libya since the summer of 1986.[45]

After the Algerian war had ended in 1962, France had experienced a remarkable post-colonial recovery in the Middle East. By February 1970, President Nasser could comment that only France of the major Western powers had a Middle Eastern policy free of imperialist ambitions and thus acceptable to the Arabs. A turning-point in Franco-Libyan relations came in January 1970, when Libya contracted to buy from France 110 Mirage fighter aircraft. The agreement, the largest French arms sale in history to that date, was widely viewed as a major diplomatic coup for both signatories. The deal enhanced French standing in the Arab world while helping to offset the drain on the French balance of payments caused by Libyan oil imports. For Libya, it represented a successful break in Libya's traditional dependence on the United States and Britain for military equipment. It also provided tangible evidence of revolutionary Libya's commitment to an independent foreign policy and a position of non-alignment vis-à-vis the superpowers.[46]

The French government continued to make diplomatic and commercial gains in Libya; and in November 1973 President Pompidou received Qaddafi when the latter visited Paris to participate in a colloquium organized in his honour. In 1974 the two states signed an agreement under which Libya exchanged a guaranteed oil supply for technical assistance and financial co-operation. By 1976 diplomatic relations had begun to deteriorate as Libya criticized French willingness to sell arms to both sides in the Middle East conflict. Later, Qaddafi also criticized the sale of French weapons to Egypt. An even more serious source of dispute was Qaddafi's increasingly aggressive policies in sub-Saharan Africa. As the second decade of the Libyan revolution progressed, French and Libyan policies in Africa repeatedly clashed, especially in the Western Sahara, Zaire and Chad.[47]

As Libya clashed with its neighbours to the north, it moved to reduce the presence of Nato forces in the Mediterranean. As mentioned earlier, Libya intervened in 1971 in Maltese negotiations over the future status of British and Nato base facilities on the island. Libya reportedly promised the Maltese government a considerable amount of financial aid if it would reduce or eliminate existing Nato facilities. While Libyan intervention did not prevent Malta from eventually agreeing to a new, seven-year pact covering both British and Nato forces, the final agreements did represent something of a Libyan victory. The prolonged negotiations enabled Malta to obtain increased revenues for the base facilities, as well as to assert strong claims to national independence and neutrality. In addition, the final agreement included a clause which precluded the use of Maltese facilities for attacks against Arab states.[48]

Albeit not without controversy, diplomatic relations between Libya and Malta were generally cordial over the next few years. In 1976, for example, the two states agreed to refer an offshore oil dispute to the International Court of Justice (ICJ). As in a similar dispute with Tunisia, the question of offshore oil rights with Malta was an extremely sensitive one for Libya. Both disputes involved potential new oil discoveries likely to become operational in the 1990s, when Libya's onshore production would begin to decline.

While an opportunity for closer economic and military relations appeared to present itself in 1979, as Britain prepared to evacuate its forces from Malta, relations actually deteriorated after Libya failed to compensate Malta for the financial losses resulting from the British withdrawal. As with Libyan diplomacy in sub-Saharan Africa, a continuing source of strain in the relationship was the Maltese claim that Libya failed to provide the economic assistance or trade opportunities it had promised. In 1979–80 Libya closed broadcasting and educational facilities on Malta; and in August 1980 Malta looked to Italy, as opposed to Libya, to guarantee its neutrality. Diplomatic relations later improved; and in 1984 the two states signed a security and co-operation treaty. The ICJ finally ruled on the offshore oil dispute in June 1985; and at the end of that year, a demarcation agreement implementing the court decision was signed. At the same time, the 1984 treaty and two other trade agreements were ratified.[49]

Europe's response to Reagan

As the US government, especially after the election of Ronald Reagan, stepped up its diplomatic, economic and military pressure on Libya, it urged the governments of western Europe to co-operate in isolating Qaddafi. Their equivocal response to repeated American urgings was based on a variety of interrelated arguments. These will be discussed below; however, the policies of individual governments were often separated by subtle, albeit significant, differences in approach and emphasis. At the same time, several European governments adopted a policy towards Libya which largely depended on their interpretation of the impact of specific American or European actions on their individual interests. For example, the French government in April 1986 refused to allow American aircraft to use French air space on their way to bomb targets in Libya — exactly two months after French aircraft had bombed Libyan-backed opposition forces in Chad. Arguing initially that violence was not an effective way to combat terrorism, French officials later justified their opposition to the American punitive raids on the grounds that the French had favoured stronger action.[50]

Extensive commercial relations with Libya obviously affected European policy towards the latter. Italy and West Germany, in particular, had developed strong trading links with Libya; and with the exception of Britain, most of the other states in western Europe relied, to a greater or lesser extent, on steady supplies of Libyan crude oil. The impact of trade was complicated by the fact that most European states had a sizeable number of citizens living and working in Libya whose welfare was a constant concern. The British Foreign Office in late April 1986 succinctly described the position of all the European governments when it warned British residents in Libya that there was a distinct limitation on the consular protection which could be provided.[51]

Commercial activities became less of a restraint on European policy in the aftermath of the 1985-86 collapse in oil prices and the resulting cutbacks in Libyan development projects. As cheaper oil became available elsewhere, most European states substantially reduced their imports of Libyan crude. Libya's growing financial constraints, coupled with its poor payment record, also reduced the attractiveness of the few development projects still active. Nevertheless, European creditors such as Italy remained very concerned that European and American policies towards Libya should not provoke the latter into stopping all attempts to settle arrears. The Libyan government, in turn, was increasingly concerned at its creeping isolation. In 1984-85 it made several unsuccessful representations to the European Economic Community (EEC) for closer ties on the grounds that it was the only Mediterranean state, apart from Albania, which did not have an economic co-operation agreement with the EEC.[52]

Several European governments also argued that the United States was not serious in its application of sanctions and that sanctions, in any case, were seldom effective. France and Italy, in particular, were extremely reluctant to follow America's lead because they did not believe it was serious in its progressive application of economic sanctions. They questioned why they should risk their relatively greater investment for what they viewed as a largely symbolic American demonstration of disapproval of Libyan policy.[53] The strength of this argument gradually weakened as the United States increased its economic pressure; and it had largely disappeared by February 1986, when the United States appeared to terminate all commercial interaction between itself and Libya. Equally important, many European governments, especially the British, felt strongly that history had demonstrated that economic sanctions were seldom effective. They cited

British sanctions against Rhodesia in the 1960s as well as the ineffective sanctions applied more recently by the United States against the Soviet Union, Poland, Nicaragua and Iran.

While commercial relations affected European policy towards Libya, they were never the overriding factor sometimes implied by American officials and commentators. European governments also argued that the American approach to terrorism in general and to Libya in particular was only treating the symptoms of the disease and not the cause, which they believed to be deeper issues such as the Palestine question, the Iran-Iraq war and the Lebanese civil war. The governments of France, Italy and Greece, in particular, had supported the Palestinian cause, emphasizing the issue was a political one, not simply one of refugees, and maintaining that it must be resolved through negotiations.[54] In this context, the use of force by the US government produced dismay across much of the European political spectrum. With the exception of Britain, the European governments were generally critical of the April 1986 bombing raid, most of them arguing it was illegal under international law and more likely to promote terrorism than to prevent it. The feared reprisals commenced immediately with the execution of a kidnapped American and two Britons in Beirut, an attack on an American embassy employee in Sudan and a Libyan missile attack in the direction of a US installation on the Italian island of Lampedusa.[55]

At various times, a number of European states also emphasized the absence of explicit proof of Libyan support for terrorism, a connection frequently difficult to make with state-sponsored terrorism. The governments of Austria, Greece and Italy, in particular, attached great importance to this point. In early 1986, for example, the Italian government emphasized that it intended to maintain its privileged position with Libya until solid proof emerged that Qaddafi had been supporting terrorist groups. In the aftermath of the April bombing raid, the Greek government continued to emphasize that there was no hard proof of Libyan involvement in state-sponsored terrorism.[56]

Given the diversity of interests and opinions involved, it was hardly surprising that the governments of western Europe had a difficult time formulating a joint response to Libya's alleged links with international terrorism. While the European governments were unanimous in their condemnation of state-sponsored terrorism, they shared a general feeling that the Reagan administration was overestimating the Libyan threat and overreacting to it. They also worried that the aggressive policies of the United States could compound the Soviet threat to Nato by leading Libya to provide the Russians with a naval base at Tobruk or elsewhere on the Libyan coast. The Soviet Union's growing influence among members of the Gulf Co-operation Council (GCC) heightened related concerns about an increase in Soviet influence throughout the Middle East.[57]

The issue also tested broader relationships, including stronger European co-operation and joint European policies towards the United States and the Middle East. From this angle, the foreign-policy setbacks of the Reagan administration in late 1986-87, visible manifestations of deeper problems, only confirmed most European governments in the wisdom of pursuing a Libyan policy one step removed from that of the United States. An ill-conceived disinformation campaign against Libya in the autumn of 1986 damaged the credibility of the administration, directed attention away from Libya's own actions and exposed a schism in administration policy towards Libya. The Iran-contra fiasco was even more damaging, as it left the anti-terrorism policy of the United States in total disarray. The sale of arms to Iran, which with Libya and Syria was the state the United States had most frequently associated with terrorism, contradicted official US policy towards the Iran-Iraq war. More importantly, the United States appeared to be guilty of that ambiguity towards state-sponsored terrorism, in the sense of arranging secret bilateral deals with radical regimes, of which it had often criticized its European allies.[58] Hence America's attack on Libya, followed as it was by a series of setbacks for American foreign policy, contributed to a sharp debate within the Atlantic alliance about the Reagan administration's command of the foreign-policy agenda. The debate highlighted the extent to which Europeans and Americans often see the world differently, including the country dubbed by Qaddafi the Great Socialist People's Libyan Arab Jamahiriya.

6

The Third Circle

Libya, geographically, is an African country, and with the revolution therein and the progressive strides she has taken, she has a role and an obligation towards the continent to which she belongs.

Muammar al-Qaddafi

Colonel Qaddafi never formally adopted Nasser's three-circles strategy which had focused on the Arab, African and Islamic worlds; but, in effect, Africa became the third circle of Libyan foreign policy. Especially in the early 1970s, sub-Saharan Africa was the scene of intense Libyan diplomatic and propaganda activity and soon became one of the revolution's earliest, and most stunning, foreign-policy triumphs. Thereafter, Libyan diplomacy in the region atrophied and then collapsed, leaving Libyan policy virtually bankrupt.

Libya had enjoyed a prolonged relationship with sub-Saharan Africa, with the earliest bases of Libyan interaction and co-operation centred on trade and religion. Pre-colonial trade routes, one of which passed through Libya, ran from central Africa through the Sahel to the North African coast. These trade links, coupled with Libya's geographic location well into the Sahara desert, helped account for Libyan interest in the politics of central and eastern Africa. Commercial intercourse was reinforced by religious ties as Islam became a major social and political force in the area. Centuries ago, Muslim missionaries in the form of Sufi holy men and Muslim traders brought Islam to central and west-central Africa. In the last century, the Libyan-based Sanusi order buttressed this development by establishing religious lodges south of Chad and west to Senegal. The French government correctly viewed the spread of the Sanusi order as a threat to its influence in central Africa; after 1902, it waged war on the order, progressively destroying its Saharan centres.[1]

After Libya achieved independence, the African policy of the monarchy focused on Chad. Diplomatic relations with the remainder of the states in sub-Saharan Africa were of small consequence and generally constructed within the framework of the Organization of African Unity (OAU), of which Libya was a founding member. In 1955 Libyan motorized units penetrated the Aouzou strip in northern Chad, considered by the Ottoman Empire to be an integral part of its North African province; but they were repulsed by French troops. With the outbreak of the Chadian rebellion in 1965, Libya provided support to the *Front de Libération National Tchadien* (Frolinat), the major rebel group. Relations on a government-to-government level later improved; and a few months before the downfall of the monarchy, Libya and Chad signed agreements aimed at improving mutual communications, the upkeep of Islamic institutions in Chad and the status of Chadian workers in Libya.[2]

Target Israel

With Qaddafi's attention focused on the Mashrek (the Arab East), the revolutionary government's African policy began tentatively with diplomatic missions to African, and largely Muslim, neighbours such as Niger and Mauritania. The primary objective of this early diplomatic offensive was a reduction of Israeli influence in Africa. In Libyan eyes, Israel's presence in Africa was a fifth column behind the Arab front lines, sapping its strength at the back door. Related objectives included opposition to Western interests and influence, the elimination of foreign military bases, opposition to apartheid and white minority regimes, support for African liberation movements, the propagation of Islam and enhancing African and Libyan control over the continent's natural resources.[3]

In the late 1950s, Israel had initiated an intense diplomatic effort in sub-Saharan Africa which aimed to counterbalance the hostility of its Arab neighbours as well as Arab influence in the Third World. Israel's African policy focused on diplomatic relations, trade and aid. In the decade after 1957, Israel established diplomatic representation in 29 African countries. By 1965 Israel had the world's fourth largest diplomatic corps; and by 1970 it had more diplomatic missions in Africa than all the Arab states combined. Israel's diplomatic efforts were complemented by a modest but steadily increasing volume of trade. While trade with Africa represented a fraction of Israel's total world trade, it increased by some 42 per cent in 1966-69. Moreover, expanding Israeli-African trade relations established important economic foundations between infant economies. At the same time, it was important to recognize that the Republic of South Africa remained Israel's most important trading partner in Africa, followed by the Central African Republic, Ethiopia, Uganda and Gabon. Israeli aid, while modest in financial terms, focused on small, practical projects which were quickly beneficial to the recipient country.

The 1967 Arab-Israeli war was a measure of the effectiveness of Israeli diplomacy. During the war, the majority of African states remained silent. Only seven openly took sides, with six supporting the Arab position and Malawi supporting Israel. In effect, Israeli diplomacy had neutralized the continent in terms of the Arab-Israeli conflict.[4]

Qaddafi's strategy was to establish diplomatic relations with African states, offer one or more forms of aid and then urge the recipients to break relations with Israel. At the same time, Libya moved to reduce all Western power and influence on the continent by eliminating Western military bases and undermining moderate African governments opposed to Libyan policies. Support was provided to African liberation movements as well as radical, anti-Western governments; and the white minority regimes in southern Africa were repeatedly denounced. Libya provided significant military assistance to the liberation movements in Angola, Guinea-Bissau and Mozambique, for example; and in 1973 it closed Libyan air space to South African over-flights. In many places, albeit not all, Libyan foreign policy assumed an Islamic hue, as preference was shown to governments and groups which expressed their opposition to the status quo in religious terms.[5]

The Libyan government eventually developed a variety of institutions to support its sub-Saharan objectives. In 1970 the Association for the Propagation of Islam was founded to train Muslim missionaries sympathetic to Qaddafi's reformist approach to Islam. As mentioned earlier, a Jihad Fund was also established in 1970 to strengthen the Libyan Armed Forces and to support the Arab nation in its struggle against Zionist forces and imperialist perils. At the Fourth Conference of Foreign Ministers of Islamic Countries, held in Benghazi in March 1973, the Jihad Fund assumed both an Islamic and an African character. A central objective of the fund was described as African liberation through assistance to Islamic liberation movements and aid to Islamic welfare associations. Direct action groups, such as the Bureau to Export Revolution, were also formed to train non-Arab Africans in guerrilla tactics. Finally, towards the end of the decade, Libya organized the Islamic Legion, largely consisting of recruits from African states, to further its Saharan and Sahelian objectives.[6]

Libyan foreign policy in sub-Saharan Africa had an Islamic element, but it was important to keep it in perspective. Islam was only one factor, together with Arab nationalism, positive neutrality, Arab unity and a pragmatic assessment of Libya's political and strategic interests, which both motivated and constrained the conduct of Libya's external relations. Qaddafi's policy was never Islamic to the extent of automatically taking the Muslim side in any dispute, and he did not equate Islamic revival and anti-communism. Libya supported the Marxist regime in Ethiopia against the predominantly Muslim Eritrean independence movement, as well as the Soviet intervention in Muslim Afghanistan. While Libya actively supported Islam, the most distinctive and controversial feature of Libya's approach to Africa was the extent to which religious assistance was linked to the development of economic relations, the provision of secular economic support and the pursuit of often aggressive political goals.[7]

Growing oil revenues, especially after the price increases of 1971-74, enhanced the ability of Arab states in general and Libya in particular to influence other Third World states. The developing states, especially those in sub-Saharan Africa, were anxious for economic aid and thus receptive to Libyan overtures. In this context, the RCC used Libya's economic resources as an effective political tool for the first time. Even after the discovery of oil, the monarchy had pursued a defensive policy using finance to reduce or avoid political agitation from surrounding countries. In contrast, the RCC quickly initiated an aggressive policy which disbursed oil revenues, largely on a bilateral basis, to support friends, attack enemies and further its foreign-policy objectives.[8]

Of all Arab donors, Libya was the most actively involved politically and economically in sub-Saharan Africa, especially in the belt of states along the rim of the Sahara with dominant or large Muslim communities.[9] Unfortunately, it was seldom easy to analyse the exact nature, level or impact of Arab aid in general or Libyan aid in particular. Serious discrepancies existed between aid commitments and aid disbursements because many Arab states, particularly Libya, did not translate commitments into disbursements. Nevertheless, it appears that Libya contributed at least $500 million through bilateral and multilateral channels in 1973-79. Zaire and Uganda were the largest individual recipients of aid, receiving almost one-half of total Libyan bilateral aid to sub-Saharan Africa in 1973-80. In terms of recorded sums, Libya ranked second to Saudi Arabia as an Arab donor of African aid. Overall, Africa was a far more important region, relatively speaking, to Libya than to any other Arab donor.[10]

A prominent feature of Libya's growing economic intercourse with Africa was its participation in the ownership and management of companies engaged in African trade and development. With the first such company established as early as 1972, Libya eventually developed no less than 50 joint-venture companies in a wide variety of economic sectors. Such companies were established in Benin, Burundi, the Central African Republic, Chad, Gabon, Gambia, Mali, Niger, Sierra Leone, Togo, Uganda and Upper Volta, usually as part of wide-ranging economic, financial and commercial agreements. Although the capital of each company seldom exceeded a few million dollars, Libyan ownership tended to be at least 51 per cent, so that control rested with the Libyan government.

The second type of aid which Libya practised widely was the allocation of loans in the form of protocol agreements which often promoted Islamic culture or the Arabic language. Such economic-cum-cultural agreements were concluded with the governments of Gambia, Niger, Mali, Burundi, the Central African Republic, Gabon, Liberia, Togo and Uganda. The amount disbursed annually by Libya for purely Islamic purposes does not appear to have been large; but it was often highly visible, politically sensitive, economic assistance.[11]

Despite Libya's comparative lack of emphasis on sub-Saharan Africa in 1969-73, its approach to the region was rewarded by a series of early diplomatic victories. Following a late 1971 meeting between Qaddafi and Ugandan President Idi Amin Dada, which had been preceded by several months of aid negotiations, Uganda expelled several hundred Israeli advisers and later broke off diplomatic relations. In September 1972, during Amin's first confrontation with Tanzania, Libya successfully intervened with an airlift of troops, justifying its action as support for the Ugandan struggle against colonialism and Zionism. Nine months later, at a ceremony marking the closure of the US air base outside Tripoli, Qaddafi praised Amin for transforming Uganda from a backward satellite of Zionism into one of the vanguard African countries combating Zionist colonialism and apartheid.[12]

Libya scored another early diplomatic victory in Chad. After two years of acrimonious relations, Libya had resumed diplomatic ties with Chad in April 1972. In return for Libyan friendship, a withdrawal of official support for Frolinat and a promise of aid from Libya and other Arab states, Chad broke relations with Israel in November 1972. The reconciliation between Libya and Chad was crowned by a treaty of friendship signed in December 1972.[13]

After these two successes, Libya's diplomatic offensive against Israeli influence in Africa gained momentum, especially in the predominantly Muslim states on the southern rim of the Sahara. By mid-1973, the governments of Mali, Niger, the Congo and Burundi had also severed diplomatic relations with Israel. Libya even raised the issue at meetings of the OAU, a body which had previously been largely neutral on the Arab-Israeli conflict. Libya urged OAU members to break off relations with Israel and to shift the OAU headquarters from Ethiopia to a country more suitable for achieving the freedom and unity of Africa. Libya's emphasis on the Israeli issue at the OAU summit conference in May 1973 polarized the membership, and some states felt it was counterproductive.[14]

While African support for the Arab position on Palestine grew in 1972-73, the litmus test for the Libyan approach came during and after the October 1973 Arab-Israeli war. Skilfully exploiting African concerns raised by the oil embargo and oil price increases, Libya and other Arab states pressured African states to abandon their neutrality on the Palestinian issue and rid the continent of Zionism. By the end of 1973, over 20 more African states had broken off relations with Israel, and many opened relations with Libya for the first time. Only four member states of the OAU refused to sever diplomatic links with Israel. Hence, by the beginning of 1974, Libya's foremost goal in Africa, the reduction of Israeli influence, had been largely achieved, with Libya often supplanting the Israeli presence. The aftermath of the October 1973 war marked the nadir of Israeli authority in Africa and the apogee of Libyan prestige.[15]

The failure to consolidate

After 1973 Qaddafi maintained the anti-Israeli emphasis of Libyan foreign policy in the third circle, but focused more on the related goals of attacking colonialism and neo-colonialism, as well as increasing African control of the continent's natural resources. Libya provided both rhetorical and practical support for African liberation movements, including arms supplies and military training. Its favourite targets were the white minority governments in Rhodesia and South Africa which Qaddafi grouped with Israel as racist regimes.

His emphasis on this association helped set the stage for the controversial UN General Assembly vote in November 1975 which equated Zionism with racism. Twenty-eight African states voted for the resolution, with 12 abstaining and only five opposing. Meanwhile, the Libyan government continued to use the OAU as a forum to advocate stronger policies against all forms of imperialism and colonialism. Already on the OAU Liberation Committee, in February 1978 Libya had been made a member of a new military committee whose members included the front-line states of southern Africa. One purpose of the committee was to secure sophisticated weaponry for African liberation movements.[16]

Libya's approach to the Western Sahara conflict was complex; but a significant element, in addition to the promotion of popular democracy and the development of a wider Saharan Islamic state, was its opposition to imperialism and colonialism. As early as February 1972, Qaddafi signalled a willingness to provide military support to liberate the Western Sahara; and in June 1972 he announced he would back a people's war of liberation if Spain did not leave by the end of the year. When the Polisario campaign began in May 1973, Libya was the only Arab state ready to provide significant material support, although its ability to do so was hampered when neighbouring states refused to co-operate.

At the same time, Libya's policy on the Western Sahara proved erratic, largely because Qaddafi disagreed with the policies of both Algeria and Polisario. As noted earlier, his emphasis on Arab unity made him especially reluctant to support Polisario's goal of creating its own national state. Libya did not recognize the Saharan Arab Democratic Republic until 1980, four years after its proclamation. Even then, Qaddafi hoped it would eventually merge with Mauritania, proposing such a union to Mauritania's prime minister in 1981.[17]

A second major Libyan objective at this time — enhanced African control over the continent's natural resources — achieved only limited economic and political success. Unable to offer technical assistance, Libya's ability to influence African mineral producers was largely confined to being an alternative source of capital. In Zaire, for example, Libya joined the World Bank and the European Investment Bank as a co-financier of a multi-million–dollar loan to finance cobalt and copper production. In Gabon and Niger, Libyan attempts to buy into the uranium reserves upon which France relied to reduce its dependence on imported petroleum were largely rebuffed, in part due to the strong opposition of the French government.[18]

Libya's focus on Africa's mineral wealth was not entirely disinterested. It involved territorial ambitions in mineral-rich northern Chad and Niger, as well as determined efforts to buy into reserves of strategic minerals in Guinea, the Central African Republic, Mauritania, Rwanda, Upper Volta and Zaire, as well as Gabon and Niger. As its oil reserves diminished and tentative exploration failed to uncover major non-hydrocarbon mineral deposits beyond the iron ore reserves at Wadi Ash Shati, Libya sought to consolidate its position as an energy supplier by gaining access to other natural resources. The location of mineral reserves in the border areas accounted in part for the significance Libya attached to the resolution of its border disputes. In addition, Libya's borders were an especially sensitive issue for Qaddafi because they were largely the product of arbitrary decisions by European colonial powers. Concern for its natural resources also aggravated its disputes with Algeria, Tunisia and Malta, especially the international litigation with Tunisia and Malta over maritime boundaries. In 1976-81 Libya also attempted to strengthen its regional economic position by meeting regularly with Niger and Algeria, and occasionally with Chad, Mali and Mauritania, to promote economic and political co-operation and integration.[19]

By 1979 Libyan influence in sub-Saharan Africa was on the decline. This was particularly evident in Uganda and the Central African Republic. In Uganda Libya had provided considerable financial, moral and military backing for Idi Amin since 1972. At the end of 1978, when Uganda was invaded by a mixed force of Ugandan exiles and Tanzanian armed forces, Qaddafi again responded by sending Libyan troops and supplies to Kampala to repel the invaders. These Libyan forces suffered a crushing defeat, and Libya reportedly paid a sizeable ransom to secure the release of the survivors. In the Central African Republic self-proclaimed emperor Jean Bedel Bokassa was deposed in September 1979 while in Libya negotiating for Libyan aid. Three days later, the official Libyan news agency denounced French involvement in the coup as an attempt to thwart the spread of Islam. Nevertheless, it was abundantly clear that what the French government had really thwarted was Libya's efforts to bolster one of Africa's most bizarre and unpleasant regimes. Uncritical support for notorious regimes like those of Amin and Bokassa reflected badly on Libya but were consistent with Qaddafi's overall approach to Africa. Personalities and internal policies were generally irrelevant as long as governments professed support for Islam and opposed imperialism, colonialism and Zionism.[20]

Setbacks

By 1980 Libyan diplomacy in Africa and elsewhere was coming under extreme pressure, in part because of the growing French and American opposition to its strategy and tactics. In particular, Libya's continuing involvement in Chad alarmed Western and African policy-makers because they feared success there would encourage intervention elsewhere. In the course of the year, nine nations, including Senegal, Gambia, Ghana and Gabon, either expelled Libyan diplomats, closed Libyan embassies or broke diplomatic relations with Libya. In addition, strong tensions or a serious deterioration in relations occurred with at least six other states, including Uganda and Upper Volta.

African governments were especially concerned about the intricate nexus of politics, religion and foreign aid which characterized Libyan foreign policy. Often secular in tenor and outlook, many African states resented Libya's use of Islam as an instrument of foreign policy. Other states with large Muslim populations or a geographic split between Muslims in the north and Christian or animist faiths in the south, such as Sudan, Niger, Mali, Nigeria and Cameroon, complained that the Libyan emphasis on religion exacerbated sensitive national cleavages. Continuing recruitment for Libya's Islamic Legion was also a source of widespread concern, particularly in the states along the southern fringe of the Sahara. In Senegal and Gambia, for example, diplomatic relations with Libya were severed because the latter was allegedly providing military training and support for anti-regime forces. Throughout Africa governments also complained, with apparent justification, that the discrepancy between Libyan aid commitments and disbursements continued to widen.[21]

Events in Chad in 1980–81 highlighted Libya's diplomatic isolation. Intent on drawing Chad into its sphere of interest, Libya had been deeply involved in Chad's internal affairs for most of the previous decade. In fact, it was largely due to Libya's diplomatic and military intervention that the civil war became irrevocably internationalized as early as 1978. At that time, Libya hosted a series of international conferences attended by representatives of adjacent states; but an agreement reached in Benghazi in April 1978 was soon breached.

One year later, the Nigerian government launched a fresh diplomatic initiative, eventually supported by the OAU, which aimed at bringing peace and unity to Chad; but it met with a similar lack of success. In 1980, Libya and Chad signed a treaty of friendship providing for Libyan support of Chadian independence and territorial integrity, an agreement which provided the legal justification for increasing Libyan involvement in Chad in the second half of the year. It was also the forerunner of the Libyan communiqué issued on 6 January 1981, stating that Libya and Chad would work together to achieve complete unity between the two states.[22]

Intervention in Chad gave Qaddafi his first real military success, but it came at a substantial political cost, especially in sub-Saharan Africa. Five days after the announcement of the proposed merger, the chairman of the OAU called for a withdrawal of Libyan troops from Chad; and an emergency OAU meeting later in the month collectively denounced Libya for the first time, condemning the suggested union.[23] At a subsequent OAU meeting in the summer of 1981, a more tactful approach was pursued, in that a resolution was passed thanking Libya for establishing peace in Chad and suggesting that the Libyan troops in the country be replaced by a pan-African peace-keeping force. An African peace-keeping force was later organized and sent to Chad, where it failed to meet the objectives set for it, and the Chadian government collapsed in June 1982.[24]

The reaction of individual African states to the proposed merger varied considerably. In some cases, the level of indignation seemed to be in direct proportion to the distance of the state from Libya and the size of its indigenous Muslim population. By the end of January 1981 Mali, Mauritania, Niger and Nigeria joined the list of African nations breaking diplomatic relations with Libya, while other states either expelled Libyan diplomats or closed Libyan embassies. Liberia, Sudan and Somalia also broke diplomatic relations later in the year. Ironically, the only African government publicly to defend Libyan policy in Chad was Ethiopia, whose head of state, Mengistu Haile Mariam, was not a Muslim.[25] Sub-Saharan Africa was beginning to show the unity which Qaddafi had long advocated, the common bond being opposition to Libyan policy.

The opposition to Libya voiced in 1981-82 included the concerns raised in 1980 with some larger strategic considerations added. Many African states feared Libya would use control of Chad to increase its influence in the Sahel region and West Africa, as well as to harass Sudan. Around the time of the union announcement, the governments of Niger, Nigeria, Ghana and Mauritania joined Senegal and Gambia in announcing they had discovered evidence of Libyan interference in their internal affairs; and Gabon and Cameroon implied as much. African leaders also expressed concern about Qaddafi's nebulous plans to create an Islamic Republic of the Sahel or Sahara, and about how the Islamic Legion, composed in part of recruits from Niger, Mali and Mauritania, might fit into those plans. Like the United States, some West African states saw Qaddafi's goal to create an Islamic Republic as little more than a public pledge to destabilize Libya's neighbours. Finally, the Nigerian government again raised the old concern about Libyan efforts to subvert a large Muslim minority. In early January 1981 Nigeria crushed a large Islamic sect after its members attacked local officials in what the Nigerian authorities termed a Libyan-backed insurrection.[26]

To cut its military and political losses as well as buttress Qaddafi's candidacy for the chairmanship of the OAU, Libya abruptly withdrew its forces from Chad in November 1981.[27] While the withdrawal temporarily reduced Libya's leverage over Chad, it improved its general political position elsewhere in Africa. On a bilateral level, diplomatic relations with Ghana were restored in January 1982, after Libya supported the second successful coup of Jerry Rawlings and provided oil on favourable terms to his new government. Relations with Tanzania also improved after it backed Libya in the latter's dispute with OAU members over seating Polisario. Elsewhere, relations with Zaire were severed when it renewed diplomatic links with Israel.

On the multilateral level, the key issue for much of 1982–83 was the Libyan effort to convene the 19th summit meeting of the OAU in Tripoli with Qaddafi as chairman. Opposition came from moderate African leaders, acting from personal conviction or under pressure from the US and European governments, who had no desire to attend a high-level meeting which could appear to vindicate Libyan policy in sub-Saharan Africa.[28] A contributing issue was the war in the Western Sahara and the bitterly divisive question of whether or not to seat a representative of Polisario. After two attempts to convene the summit in Tripoli failed, an OAU panel recommended moving it to OAU headquarters in Addis Ababa, where it eventually opened in June 1983 under the chairmanship of the Ethiopian head of state. Qaddafi attended the summit briefly but soon departed after suffering the double indignity of being denied the chairmanship and seeing his protégé, Polisario, effectively barred from the meeting. Qaddafi was the first African leader in OAU history to be denied its chairmanship; hence, the incident aptly illustrated how limited and counterproductive his influence in Africa had become.

More of the same
After 1983 the Libyan government maintained its emphasis on the third circle, but the content and approach of its African policy remained essentially unchanged. Israel continued to be the central concern, especially in the light of its improved position in Africa. The US government, as part of the Reagan administration's efforts to undermine Qaddafi's regime, actively supported Israeli efforts to restore diplomatic links with African states. Israel's rapprochement with the African continent was also boosted by the decline in Arab oil earnings and an apparent Israeli policy of slowly distancing itself from South Africa. In August 1986 Cameroon became the fourth African country, following Zaire, Liberia and the Ivory Coast, to resume diplomatic relations with Israel; and there was speculation that several other African states might follow its lead. Three other countries, Swaziland, Malawi and Lesotho, had never broken ties; and Israel also operated interest sections in Kenya, Togo, Ghana and Gabon.

Libya responded to the growing Israeli presence by cutting diplomatic ties with Liberia as well as Zaire. In addition, it refused to participate in a July 1984 refugee conference because both South African and Israeli delegations were scheduled to attend. In November 1985 Libya announced it was blacklisting Liberian-registered vessels, which made it the first Arab state to implement a 1984 Arab League decision to boycott Liberian ships because of Liberia's ties with Israel. On a more positive note, Libya restored or normalized diplomatic relations with a number of African states, including Niger, Gambia, Somalia and Mauritania.

In support of its efforts to improve relations with sub-Saharan Africa, the Libyan government relied heavily on the familiar tools of economic aid and trade. In a series of often lightning visits to African states, Qaddafi doled out Libyan largesse to at least a dozen different countries in 1983-87. Libyan aid took a multitude of forms, including economic and technical agreements with Nigeria, the establishment of joint companies with Benin and Upper Volta, a one-million-dollar cheque to Mali and concessionary oil sales to Burkina Faso (Upper Volta until 1984) and Ghana. While considerable publicity often accompanied Libyan aid commitments, it remained extremely difficult to compare commitments to disbursements. Although the available evidence was incomplete, it was highly likely that Libya's declining oil revenues had a restraining effect on its diplomacy, especially in Africa, where aid was always more important than the ideology outlined in *The Green Book*. One concrete example of the negative effect Libya's plummeting oil revenues had on its foreign policy was the bitterness expressed by the governments of Mali and Mauritania when their nationals were among the foreign workers expelled by Libya in August-September 1985 as part of an economic austerity programme.

In Chad sporadic outbreaks of fighting continued in 1983-87, prompting renewed intervention by Libyan and French forces. The second major Libyan intervention differed from the first in one fundamental aspect. In 1980 Libyan troops had moved into the Chadian capital at the request of Chad's only legitimate government; but in 1983 Libya threw its weight behind a rebel faction and against a government which enjoyed official recognition by the vast majority of OAU members. As Libya reinforced its military presence and imposed civilian administration in northern Chad, Qaddafi aggressively defended Libya's right to intervene in African affairs, terming Chad an extension of Libya.[29]

In November 1984 Libya and France announced the completion of a mutual phased withdrawal of their armed forces in Chad; however, within a week, France was forced to admit that a sizeable Libyan force remained in Chad. Thereafter, the stalemate in Chad continued, with many African states adopting an ambivalent attitude. Understandably nervous about Libya's regional objectives, many African states remained reluctant to give open support to a former colonial power against an African nation, and thus either quietly supported French policy or remained silent.[30]

The 1983 Libyan intervention in Chad was followed by the series of diplomatic realignments already discussed, realignments which intensified African concern over the direction of Libyan foreign policy. In August 1984 Libya and Morocco signed a treaty of Arab-African Union, in part to counter the 1983 treaty of fraternity and concord signed by Algeria, Tunisia and Mauritania. As well as gaining tangible support for its cherished objective of Arab unity, Libya ruled out the possibility of Moroccan participation in a future peace-keeping force in Chad and caused Morocco's closest ally, the United States, considerable consternation. Following the overthrow of the Numairi regime in Sudan in 1985, Libya and Sudan signed a military co-operation agreement in which Libya agreed to stop supporting the Sudanese rebels in the south. In return, Libya strengthened the likelihood that the Sudanese government would not oppose its policies in northern Chad. Together, the 1984 and 1985 treaties carried serious implications for regional alignments and policies and thus were alarming to African policy-makers. Morocco's subsequent abrogation of the 1984 pact did little to allay the concern of regional leaders. In late February 1987, the OAU issued an appeal to Libya and Chad, together with all interested parties, to seek a peaceful resolution to the Chad-Libya conflict. Later, African leaders meeting in Cairo condemned foreign intervention in Chad.[31]

Nevertheless, the fighting continued between Libyan forces and their rebel allies on the one hand and Chadian government troops on the other. By March 1987, it was apparent that Qaddafi's intervention in northern Chad, not seriously challenged since the early 1970s, was suddenly in serious jeopardy. A Chadian victory over Libyan forces at Fada in January 1987 was followed by a devastating defeat of Libyan troops at Ouadi Doum in mid-March. The Chadian victory at Ouadi Doum marked a major turning-point in the war because it made Libya's position at Faya Largeau, its last major stronghold in northern Chad, untenable. In recognition of this fact, the Libyan forces at Faya Largeau soon began retreating north to the Aouzou strip. Libya's withdrawal from northern Chad was a humiliating military defeat as well as a major setback for Qaddafi's vague plans to create an Islamic federation from Mauritania to Sudan. Although Libya's future in the Aouzou strip was uncertain, the Libyan government appeared determined to continue its role in Chadian politics. In a speech marking the anniversary of the evacuation of British bases in Libya, Qaddafi pledged that the confrontation in Chad would continue as long as French troops were present there. Later, he rejected a Chadian proposal to bring the issue of the Aouzou strip before the International Court of Justice. Qaddafi argued that the disputed territory had been an indivisible part of Libya since the French and Italian occupations and that he would consent to arbitration only if he was sure Libya's rights would be confirmed.[32]

Elsewhere, the Libyan government continued to pursue a variety of non-diplomatic means to regain its former influence in Africa. The Central African Republic, Ghana, Burkina Faso and Uganda, among others, received gifts of Libyan arms and other military equipment in 1983-87. At the same time, the allegations continued, invariably denied by the Libyan government, of unsolicited Libyan involvement in the internal affairs of states from Niger and Mauritania in the north, through Togo and Zaire, to South Africa. Libya also continued its recruitment for the Islamic Legion, focusing its efforts on Djibouti, Ethiopia, Sudan, Nigeria, Mali, Ghana and Burkina Faso, but not restricting itself to Muslims or to Africa. By the spring of 1987, the Islamic Legion included several thousand African recruits, including 2,500 Sudanese. Meanwhile, speculation continued as to whether the objectives of the Islamic Legion had been broadened to include the establishment of an international revolutionary force.[33]

Observations

A mélange of regional, extra-regional and domestic interests and concerns combined to frustrate Qaddafi's ambitions in sub-Saharan Africa. At the root of the problem was the failure to develop a sound ideological base for Libya's African policy. In the early years of the revolution, the revolutionary government focused on Arab concerns, with Africa viewed largely as a secondary arena for the promotion of the Arab position on Palestine. Later, when Libya's growing political isolation in the Mashrek and the Maghreb contributed to a renewed interest in the third circle, Qaddafi never developed a comprehensive ideological approach tailored to the region. African governments greeted Qaddafi's ideology, based on alien forces and objectives, with the same widespread disbelief and lack of interest accorded it in North Africa and the Middle East. However, while the Arab world viewed Qaddafi's ideology as largely obsolete, sub-Saharan Africa saw it as simply irrelevant.

Libyan diplomacy in sub-Saharan Africa was also hampered by its dubious, negative character. The key objective was the destruction of Western, especially Israeli, influence, as opposed to fostering positive long-term socio-economic and political relationships. The negative inspiration for Libyan diplomacy was obvious in the early 1970s, and it continued after Israel's influence had been undermined. Libya's periodic emphasis on Africa over the last decade was largely dictated by the failure of its objectives elsewhere. In a policy with limited ideological substance, the ongoing discrepancy between aid commitments and aid disbursements was fatal because it reinforced the feeling that Libyan solicitude was both insincere and self-serving. In this context, the ambiguity of Libyan policies combined with Qaddafi's overt commitment to revolutionary change to heighten African concerns as to the real motivation and direction of Libyan foreign policy.

7

The Primacy of Oil

The sovereignty of a state over its natural resources always requires that such resources are placed under its control.

Muammar al-Qaddafi

Major oil deposits were not discovered in Libya until 1959, when American prospectors confirmed their location at Zelten in Cyrenaica. The following decade witnessed dramatic increases in oil production and oil revenues but not in the posted price of oil. While the Libyan monarchy considered the posted price undervalued and unjust, it accepted a volume-oriented as opposed to a price-oriented oil policy. This was especially true after the June 1967 war closed the Suez Canal. Oil companies rapidly expanded their production in Libya to achieve the transport savings derived from not having to ship Gulf oil to Europe via the Cape of Good Hope. When the monarchy was overthrown in September 1969, Libya's daily oil production was comparable to that of Saudi Arabia.

The revolutionary government moved quickly to increase the posted price of oil. In the process, an increasingly close connection between oil policy and foreign policy developed. Key aspects of revolutionary foreign policy strongly influenced the speed and degree to which the RCC modified the monarchy's oil policy. Conversely, swelling oil revenues helped determine the direction and emphasis of Libyan foreign policy. No attempt will be made here to evaluate or even discuss all aspects of Libyan oil policy after 1969. The analysis will focus only on those elements of oil policy, such as control, pricing, production and revenues, which had a significant impact on Libyan foreign policy.

First moves

In contrast to early statements in other policy areas, the initial approach of the RCC towards oil was almost conciliatory. Even as the revolutionary government prepared for dramatic changes in oil policy, it reassured foreign governments and oil producers alike that major changes were not being contemplated. On 17 September 1969, for example, the Libyan prime minister, Mahmud Suleiman al-Maghrabi, expressed a desire to co–operate with the oil companies, emphasizing there would be no spectacular changes in Libyan oil policy. Later statements by other members of government stressed there was no intention of nationalizing the oil industry and that revisions to posted prices, clearly desired by the government, would be achieved only through negotiations with the oil companies in agreements satisfactory to both parties.[1]

While the revolutionary government preached conciliation, its obvious intent was to increase its control of Libya's oil sector. At the time it came to power, a debate was raging throughout the oil-producing world as to whether to seek broader control through a strategy of greater participation with the oil companies, or outright nationalization. In Libya the revolutionary government initially opted for the first strategy, but it soon moved to the second. In so doing, it increased its co-operation with the Algerian government which, along with Iran, was an early Opec advocate of enhanced control. By the end of 1969, Libya had established continuing contacts with Algeria for the purpose of co-ordinating their views regarding oil policies in the two countries.[2]

Apart from occasional public statements, the Libyan government took no concrete action to raise oil prices until the end of 1969. On 22 December 1969, a committee of officials from the Ministry of Petroleum was established to negotiate with the oil companies an adjustment in the posted price of Libyan crude oil. At this point, the Libyan government's approach was not dissimilar to earlier, unanswered requests by the Libyan monarchy for adjustments to the posted price. Negotiations began in earnest the following month. On 29 January 1970, the Minister of Petroleum and Minerals addressed oil company representatives; and on 29 January 1970, Qaddafi addressed the heads of oil companies. At the meeting, Qaddafi remarked that the Libyan people had lived for thousands of years without petroleum revenues and were willing to do so again, if necessary. His attitude disturbed the oil companies.[3]

In the spring of 1970, the pricing committee continued to negotiate with the oil companies, but without result. After two unsuccessful sets of meetings with individual oil companies, the government strengthened its approach. On 4 April 1970, the former prime minister Maghrabi was appointed chairman of the pricing committee. Behind the committee, decisions were increasingly guided by Abdel-Salam Jallud, the RCC member who had negotiated the early withdrawal of US and British forces from Libyan base facilities. Jallud's appointment indicated that the RCC put the highest possible priority on its negotiations with the oil companies.[4]

In this round of negotiations, the Libyan government concentrated its pressure on the independent oil producers, particularly Occidental, because Libyan supplies constituted all or a large part of their resources of crude oil outside North America. In addition, their contracts were generally covered by escalation clauses and thus they had the least to fear from consenting to posted price and tax increases in a rising market with supply restrictions.

In May 1970 the Libyan government cut Occidental's production in successive stages by nearly 400,000 barrels per day (bpd), and additional cutbacks by early September had brought the total reduction to 425,000 bpd. In the interim, Esso, Amoseas, Mobil and Oasis were also forced to reduce oil production. In this four-month period, cutbacks to Libyan oil production totalled some 800,000 bpd. Esso was also ordered not to inaugurate the export of liquefied natural gas from Mersa Brega until the dispute over posted prices was settled.

To increase the prevailing atmosphere of uncertainty, the Libyan government then took a series of supportive actions. It imposed new port dues of one cent a barrel on oil tankers, nationalized the domestic marketing of petroleum products and banned overseas payments by oil companies to employees and contractors. By August 1970 rumours were rampant that a total nationalization of the Libyan oil industry was imminent.[5]

Libyan actions in the summer of 1970 had a notable effect. The cuts in Libyan oil production, combined with a temporary break in the Tapline which carried oil from the Middle East to the Mediterranean, caused short-term scarcities in petroleum products. Concern for future oil supplies stimulated stockpiling and thus demand for petroleum products in the consumer countries. The consequent increases in both oil prices and freight rates generated conditions for an increase in the Libyan posted price which the oil companies could neither deny nor ignore. A secondary result was a drastic fall in exploration and development investment in Libya by the oil companies. Understandably concerned at the tone and direction of Libyan oil policy, the oil companies were reluctant to commit more capital to a relatively unfavourable political environment. By May 1970 the number of oil rigs in Libya had dropped by half compared with the previous summer; and the total continued to drop into the autumn of 1970.[6]

The September agreements

Occidental was the first oil company to reach agreement with Libya. It made an offer in early September 1970 which was accepted by the Libyan government and termed the 1 September agreement to coincide with the first anniversary of the revolution. Similar agreements were made with the other oil companies operating in Libya over the next few weeks. Highlights of the agreements included an increase in the posted price of 30 cents a barrel, with an additional two-cents-a-barrel increase on 1 January of each of the five succeeding years. This marked the first significant increase in the posted price since the formation of the Organization of Petroleum Exporting Countries (Opec) in 1960. Moreover, the new posted price was subject to a new gravity escalation of two cents a barrel for each API degree above 40 degrees, and minus one and one-half cents a barrel for each API degree below 40 degrees. This proviso, which eventually altered the oil industry's entire gravity differential structure, was noteworthy as it favoured Libya's lighter crudes. In terms of oil revenues, its effect was to augment the agreed increase in the posted price of oil.[7] The oil companies also agreed to make back payments for underpricing Libyan oil with effect from 1965 or the start of production, whichever came first. In the area of taxes, the agreements ended the old 50–50 profit-sharing pattern based on posted price. The rate of income tax was increased as high as 58 per cent with a new average of around 54 per cent. In addition, the Libyan government imposed harbour dues on all oil tankers; and the entire salaries of foreign workers were now to be paid in local currency.[8]

The worldwide impact of the 1 September agreements was enormous. Opec had been created in 1960 to block the downward movement in oil prices, but the oil companies had continued to block upward movement. The Libyan government changed this situation virtually overnight; and in the process, it ended the myth that the oil companies alone could decide the posted price of crude oil. Recognizing the vulnerability of the independent oil producers, Qaddafi and his cohorts were shrewd enough and forceful enough to capitalize on them. In the process, Libyan actions drove up the market price of oil to a level which enabled the oil companies to make a nice profit in 1970 even after paying the higher posted price. In the case of Libya, the agreement had the benefit of increasing its oil revenues even as the government was reducing crude oil production.[9]

Libya's conduct of negotiations with the oil companies was adroit; however, a myriad of factors contributed to its success in 1970. Its tough tactics were fortified by substantial financial resources, recognized oil reserves and a small population. The regime drew a psychological advantage from its recent nationalization of Libya's banks, and this advantage was bolstered by Qaddafi's pronouncements that Libya could do without the oil companies, and even without oil. The negotiations took place at a time when European demand for oil was rising rapidly, especially Mediterranean oil, because of the closure of the Suez Canal and other temporary supply interruptions. Oil prices and tanker freight rates, due to the need to go round the Cape of Good Hope, were climbing steeply. Since Europe feared a bleak winter, Libya's forced cuts in oil production had an exaggerated effect. The excellent quality of Libyan crude oil, coupled with the RCC's recognized interest in greater conservation measures, also gave Libya extra bargaining advantage. Lastly, the oil companies were divided among themselves, with the majors, in particular, being unwilling to go to great lengths to protect the independents.[10]

While additional arguments could be developed to explain Libya's success, it was partly, if not largely, fortuitous. Unfortunately, Qaddafi misread the affair. The lesson he drew from the 1970 oil negotiations was that a defiant posture, buttressed by anti-colonialist-imperialist rhetoric, had called the bluff of the cartel of oil companies and consumer nations, shaking out considerable additional revenues. Consequently, the Libyan government subsequently applied a similar approach to other aspects of domestic and foreign policy which were not susceptible to such aggressive behaviour. This was especially true after 1973-74, when oil revenues, due to increased oil prices, took a dramatic leap. The results of such sharp policy initiatives were sometimes catastrophic for Libya and its neighbours.[11]

As the negotiations leading to the 1 September 1970 agreements progressed, most Opec states chose to stand aloof. Opec had supported earlier Libyan conservation measures, and its members viewed with satisfaction Libyan production cuts, as they stimulated oil price increases elsewhere. However, only Iraq and Algeria actively supported the Libyan actions. With the conclusion of the 1 September agreements, Libya emerged temporarily as a leader of the oil-producing states as the latter moved to negotiate similar settlements. Libyan influence was clearly visible at Opec's twenty-first conference held in Caracas, Venezuela, on 9-12 December 1970. A resolution adopted by the conference mirrored the Libyan settlement in that it called for negotiations with the oil companies aimed at raising the posted price, increasing tax rates and adopting a new system for the adjustment of the gravity differential. In support of these objectives, a committee was formed at the conference to negotiate on behalf of the six countries in the Gulf.[12]

Tehran–Tripoli agreements

The oil companies, led by the majors and with the support of their home governments, were not slow to respond to events in the Middle East. On 16 January 1971, they proposed to the 10 Opec states an all-embracing negotiation aimed at a comprehensive, durable settlement. Their proposal was stillborn, since the Caracas resolution provided for concerted action only among the Gulf states, while the other Opec members were free to act independently. Libya refused to accept the proposals or to negotiate collectively with the oil companies. Based on its earlier experience, Libya rightly felt the best results would come from continuing to attack the oil companies individually at their weakest points.

On 15 January 1971, the oil companies also agreed to a pact known as the Libyan Producers' Agreement. It was a joint commitment to act in concert vis-à-vis the Libyan government, to prevent the latter from forcing further concessions from individual companies. Specifically, the oil companies declared their intention not to make an agreement, or an offer of an agreement, with the Libyan government concerning government revenues from crude oil without the assent of the other parties. If the government cut the oil production of one of the parties, the others agreed to make good the loss of oil from their Libyan production, or other production if Libyan oil was not available, at cost. The amount of crude oil so supplied would be 100 per cent of cutbacks in 1971, 80 per cent in 1972 and 60 per cent in 1973. Details of the agreement, although its existence was known to the Libyan government, were kept secret for a time; and its text was not made public until 1974, when H.R. Hunt filed a claim for damages against Mobil for allegedly violating it.[13]

The Opec resolution adopted in Caracas in December 1970 led to the Tehran agreement, signed on 15 February 1971, between the oil companies and the oil-producing states in the Gulf. The agreement at Tehran, which stemmed directly from the September 1970 Libyan agreements, incorporated many of the gains won in Tripoli. The oil companies agreed to an immediate increase in the posted price of 35 cents a barrel, followed by annual increases over the next five years. The treatment of gravity was modified to reflect the system outlined in the Caracas resolution. In turn, the Gulf member states agreed not to ask individually for better terms (known as leapfrogging), and not to restrict production to achieve better financial terms.[14]

The Libyan government was furious with the terms of the deal struck at Tehran. While Libya rejected the principle of collective bargaining, the Tehran agreement spoke of a general increase in the posted price of 35 cents a barrel as though that price level should apply to all Opec members, including Libya. The Libyan government also protested at the level of price increases agreed upon, and the value of the short-haul freight premium specified for Libya. On the first point, Libya pointed out that it was already taking from the oil companies royalty oil in kind and selling it for substantially more than the new posted price, which suggested the latter was too low. On the second, it argued that an agreement in Tehran on a Libyan short-haul premium was an unwarranted intervention in Libyan affairs to achieve the kind of all-embracing solution desired by the oil companies but rejected by Libya. In addition, Libya rightly viewed the Tehran provisos which prohibited leapfrogging and production restrictions as designed to frustrate Libyan efforts to seek better terms from the oil companies.[15]

With the conclusion of the Tehran agreement, the limited leadership role which Libya had enjoyed in Opec in the autumn of 1970 faded. Even before the agreement, Libya complained about Opec's lack of aggressiveness, while Opec members in the Gulf viewed Qaddafi's regime as too hard-line and extremist. At an extraordinary Opec conference on 3 February 1971, the organization had limited its support for Libya to the objectives outlined in the Caracas resolution, plus a reasonable premium reflecting the short-haul freight advantage of Libyan crude. After the Tehran agreement, a few Opec states, principally those with Mediterranean outlets for their crude oil, agreed to support separate Libyan negotiations with the oil companies operating in Libya. At about the same time, the Algerian government took over 51 per cent of the oil companies operating in Algeria and nationalized the petroleum pipelines. Because of Libya's close relations with Algeria, the move heightened concern as to what Libya's next step might be. [16]

The Libyan government opened new negotiations with the oil companies in February 1971; and after great difficulty, revised terms were finally agreed upon in April. The so-called Tripoli agreement was backdated to 20 March 1971; and while the terms were uniform, Libya negotiated and signed a separate agreement with each oil company. Although the structure of the Tripoli agreement was similar to that agreed in Tehran, the Libyan government was able to extract better terms from the oil companies. Again resorting to tactics of threat and intimidation, Libya achieved a new posted price of $3.447 a barrel, which was well above the Tehran increase. The new price included a premium to Libya to reflect, in a period of high tanker freight rates, the temporary advantage which the closure of the Suez Canal and the rupture of Tapline had brought to Libya's short-haul crude. The new price was subject to the same gravity escalation agreed upon in September 1970, and there was a proviso for annual price increases over five years. [17]

In line with the resolution adopted at Caracas, the tax rate was established at a minimum 55 per cent, with Occidental paying 60 per cent because of an earlier commitment to spend five per cent of pre-tax profit on the development of the Kufra oasis agricultural project. To compensate for previous underpricing, the oil companies agreed to make a supplemental payment on every barrel of oil exported, for the duration of their concessions. They also agreed that, in each year of the agreement, the oil companies would together have at least one exploration rig in operation on concessions held jointly or individually. The Libyan government insisted on this point. It was concerned about the rapid fall in exploration and development, as well as the natural reluctance of the oil companies to commit money to a country, regardless of its oil prospects, which did not give them confidence in the future security of their investments. While the financial commitment was comparatively small — eight rigs at an average cost each of approximately $3.5 million a year — the oil companies reportedly gave way reluctantly on this point. Although exact figures were not available, the price increases and retroactive payments in the Tripoli agreement brought the Libyan government a net increase in revenues estimated at around $1 billion in the first year of the agreement alone.

It was later argued, largely on the basis that the oil companies achieved a five-year agreement, that the oil producers achieved a victory over Libya at the Tripoli negotiations. At the time, there was little evidence to suggest they felt that way. Moreover, the general feeling in the Gulf states was that

Libya received more than it deserved at Tripoli. As for the Libyan Producers' Agreement, it helped the oil companies to resist Libya's approach but later proved to be fatally flawed. In short, if the oil producers enjoyed any advantage in the March 1971 agreement, it was both limited and fleeting.

The Tehran–Tripoli agreements proved to be unstable, and subsequent events led to participation, price and embargo crises in 1973–74. When the United States devalued the dollar in August 1971, and again in February 1973, it did so with little apparent thought to the impact on the oil industry. The oil-producing states, because their oil exports were denominated in US dollars, responded immediately by demanding and obtaining modifications to the Tehran–Tripoli accords. In an effort to protect oil revenues from the falling value of the dollar, the First Geneva Agreement, dated 20 January 1972, raised posted oil prices by a fixed percentage and also provided for quarterly adjustments as the value of the dollar moved up or down. The agreement was between the Gulf states and the oil companies who were party to the Tehran agreement, and was supplemental to and incorporated into it. The Libyan government remained aloof from the general negotiations, again attempting to achieve a better result on its own. Its actions caused the oil companies to broaden the Libyan Producers' Agreement to cover enforced adjustments for currency fluctuations. In any event, final agreements were reached by Libya and each oil company in May 1972 which contained the same features as the First Geneva Agreement and were effective from 20 January 1972.

On 1 June 1973, the parties to the First Geneva Agreement signed a Second Geneva Agreement, to reflect the February 1973 devaluation of the dollar. On this occasion, Libya signed separate but identical agreements with the oil companies on the same day. The net result was that all Opec countries, including Libya, had incorporated by mid-1973 both inflation and dollar escalation factors into their posted prices until the end of 1975.[18]

Increased participation

The currency and foreign-exchange agreements negotiated by Libya and the other Opec states in 1972–73 were soon superseded by new and more radical alterations in the world oil industry. In June 1971 Opec had established a ministerial committee, consisting of the oil ministers of Iran, Kuwait, Saudi Arabia and Libya, to investigate ways and means to increase government participation in their oil concessions. The committee eventually developed recommendations for increased participation; but by that time, Libya had declared its intention to pursue participation negotiations with its concessionaires on an individual basis. In September 1971, the Libyan government announced that it would shortly demand that concession agreements be changed to participation agreements. While 20 per cent might be acceptable to the other Opec states, Libya emphasized that it would demand at least 51 per cent.[19]

On 7 December 1971, the RCC announced it was nationalizing the British Petroleum (BP) share of the BP–N.B. Hunt Sarir field. BP was replaced by the Arabian Gulf Exploration Company, and the production of the other oil companies operating in Libya was frozen to prevent them from supplying BP. The oil companies responded on 16 December 1971, by amending the Libyan Producers' Agreement to include total or partial nationalization of the properties of any party by the Libyan government. Qaddafi described the action as a protest against the British government's failure to intervene to prevent the Shah of Iran from occupying the Greater and Lesser Tumb islands off the coast of the United Arab Emirates. Developing the twin themes of Arab nationalism and Arab unity, Qaddafi delivered a series of blistering attacks on Britain, arguing that Iran's occupation was an assault on Arab territorial integrity. In this sense, the nationalization of BP was in a different category from later actions; nevertheless, it set the stage for Libya's growing emphasis on participation in 1972-73.[20]

Apart from the nationalization of BP, Libya's first agreement covering participation in an existing concession was with the Italian producer ENI and its subsidiary Agip. After two years of negotiations, Libya accepted a September 1972 company proposal for 50 per cent state participation. Libya then focused its attention on N.B. Hunt, arguing that 50 per cent state participation was not negotiable and was only a preliminary step towards greater state participation. On 11 June 1973, after Hunt refused Libya's participation terms and also refused to market for Libya what had once been BP's share of Sarir crude oil, Libya nationalized N.B. Hunt.[21] Qaddafi termed the action a slap in the face for the United States because of its support for Israel. In a broader context, he described the nationalization of N.B. Hunt as a decisive step in the struggle of the Arab masses to restore their own wealth and to end the drainage of Arab oil by foreign monopolists. In the process, he indicated the extent to which the government's position on nationalization had changed since its conciliatory statements in the early days of September 1969.

> The right to nationalize is one of the rights of the government which owns the oil. There is no law in the whole world which prevents the country that owns the oil from nationalizing oil resources and from handling oil operations or halting the pumping of oil, taking full control of all oil operations. At the same time, any people already moving on the road of the revolution cannot, in any circumstance, halt in the middle of the road.[22]

In August 1973 Jallud intervened in the participation negotiations, making it clear that the Libyan government was now demanding 51 per cent of net book value of all the oil companies. Agreements on those terms were signed the same month with Occidental and Oasis, the largest independent and major group producer respectively. On 1 September 1973, the fourth anniversary of the revolution, Tripoli Radio announced a general nationalization covering 51 per cent of the assets and business of all the producing majors and their partners operating in Libya. The major oil producers, under the terms of the Libyan Producers' Agreement, tried to stand behind N.B. Hunt; but they were unable to provide significant assistance. They attempted to boycott Libyan oil; but with petroleum in short supply, there were simply too many willing buyers.[23]

The terms of the nationalization included similar provisions for each producer. The Libyan government took 51 per cent of the assets and business of the companies concerned, with the exception of Esso's gas liquefaction plant. Compensation was to be decided by three-man committees consisting of representatives from the Appeal Court, the Libyan National Oil Company and the Ministry of the Treasury. The oil companies protested at the actions of the Libyan government, but individual settlements were reached over the next four years.

The year 1973 marked the highpoint of the state's emphasis on participation, although selected refinements to the general nationalization decree occurred thereafter. By 1975–76, the state's share of total Libyan oil production, excluding royalty oil, had reached 64 per cent. At that point, the government suggested it was not considering further increases in participation levels because it needed the oil companies for marketing, new investment and exploration.[24]

War and embargo
In the early 1970s, three separate developments increasingly interacted until they culminated in a major oil crisis. First, there was the growing confidence and power of the oil-producing states of the Middle East vis-à-vis the oil companies which had discovered, developed and long controlled Middle Eastern oil. Second, there was the growing dependence of the United States on Middle Eastern oil.

Third, there was the creation in Palestine of the state of Israel, a development strongly supported by the United States but bitterly opposed by the Arab countries. A fourth development, secondary to the others but which intensified their impact, was the growing tension and confusion in international monetary relationships compounded by escalating rates of inflation in the industrial economies.

The October 1973 war was the culmination of a largely independent course of events, but it brought these separate developments to a head. As the war widened and intensified, the Arab oil-producing countries imposed oil restrictions. They also abandoned all pretence of negotiation over prices and began to impose new price levels by unilateral decree. As might be expected, the Libyan government was at the forefront of this new approach.[25]

As previously discussed, Qaddafi's initial reaction to the Egyptian–Syrian attack on Israel was a mixture of rage and support. Frustrated by his exclusion from the planning for the attack, Qaddafi offered financial and military support to the Arab forces, while criticizing the direction and objectives of their attack.

On 18 October 1973, Saudi Arabia initiated a broad programme of restrictive measures which included both general production cutbacks and an export embargo to specified countries, including the United States. In support of this move, Libya halted oil exports to the United States on 19 October 1973, and cut off oil supplies to the Netherlands on 29 October. In both cases, Qaddafi linked the restrictions to these states' support for Israel. Libya also reduced its overall oil production by five per cent, in accordance with an Opec decision taken in Kuwait on 16 October; and on 20 October it announced the price of oil would be immediately increased from $4.60 to $8.90 per barrel. The resolution announcing the price increase justified the action on the basis of inflation, increased demand for oil and fluctuations in currency exchange rates and freight charges.[26]

Two days later, the United Nations Security Council adopted Resolution 338, which called on all parties to the fighting to cease fire and terminate all military activity in the positions they then occupied. Predictably, Libya, joined by Iraq and Kuwait, denounced the ceasefire as unwarranted foreign intervention in an Arab problem. Egypt's subsequent acceptance of the ceasefire over vigorous Libyan opposition added to Qaddafi's isolation in the Arab world.

The Arab retreat from the oil boycott, strenuously opposed by Libya, was effected in several stages. On 9 December 1973, the Arab oil ministers accepted a Saudi proposal to link the lifting of the embargo to the adoption of a timetable for Israeli withdrawal from occupied Arab territories. Two weeks later, the ministers reduced the schedule of production cutbacks and cancelled a five per cent reduction scheduled for January 1974. In the next stage, President Sadat began to press for an early end to the boycott based on the conclusion, under American auspices, of the Egyptian-Israeli disengagement agreement on 17 January 1974. Because the terms of the agreement fell far short of the conditions outlined on 9 December, Sadat encountered temporary resistance from several Arab governments, especially Syria, Algeria and Saudi Arabia. He was angrily denounced by Qaddafi, who boycotted joint meetings of Arab heads of state in protest.

On 18 March 1974, the Arab oil ministers agreed, with Libya and Syria dissenting, to remove provisionally the embargo against the United States.

After the conclusion of the Syrian-Israeli disengagement agreement on 29 May 1974, the oil ministers tentatively agreed to lift all restrictions except those on the Netherlands, which were finally included on 11 July 1974. Despite Libyan objections, the boycott crisis had ended; however, the oil ministers warned in June and July statements that the boycott could be re-imposed if a new war broke out.[27]

The October 1973 war solidified the basic changes in the oil industry initiated by Libya in 1970. Throughout the Middle East, the old system of oil concessions had been replaced by host government participation. The oil companies no longer owned, or could act as if they owned, the producing properties in the major oil-exporting states. They had become mere buyers of oil. In the future, production levels, and to a lesser extent price levels, would be set by the host governments. The Libyan government had spearheaded these crucial changes in the oil industry, and it enjoyed their fruits for the remainder of the decade.

Oil revenues and foreign policy

While Opec effectively ended the oil embargo on 18 March 1974, the higher oil prices remained. An early proponent of price increases, Libya remained a persistent advocate of higher prices. Qaddafi hinted at the ideological base for Libyan oil price policy in a September 1976 interview.

> It is surprising that the industrial states regret the increase of oil prices at the time when it [sic] should regret the Third World standards of living, whose blood is sucked and chocked [sic] amidst the first of the industrial world which wants to purchase at the lowest prices, while selling at the highest.[28]

In the second half of the decade, the Libyan government, inside and outside Opec councils, continued to push for higher prices. In mid-1977, for example, it temporarily opposed a unified Opec pricing policy on the grounds that the proposed price increase was insufficient. In the absence of co-ordinated Opec action, it also seized on the occasional market crisis to achieve real increases in unit prices. The 1979 Iranian crisis, for example, created general fears of a severe oil shortage which led to panic buying by over-anxious purchasers. In this context, Libya joined other Opec members to triple the price of crude.

At times, Libya's support for higher prices was counterproductive, since it led to low and economically damaging levels of production by the oil companies. It also led to widespread disagreement with the other Opec states, especially when Libya advocated price increases on political as opposed to economic grounds. In late 1977 Libya joined Algeria and Iraq in pressing for a significant price increase as a political show of force on behalf of radical elements in the Arab world. A price freeze was clearly in the economic interests of Saudi Arabia and the Gulf states (as well as Libya and Iraq, for that matter); therefore, the cartel eventually agreed, after heated debate, to postpone consideration of a price increase until June 1978.[29]

Qaddafi's approach to oil production was never as consistent as his policy towards oil price. Production was reduced in 1970-71, largely as a means to force price increases. Oil production continued to drop in 1971-75, but then moved upwards in the second half of the decade. In addition to the growing demand for oil revenues, there was evidence to suggest that Libya increased its oil production after 1975 as one means to help regain the influence it had lost in Opec after 1971. If so, the effort was unsuccessful, since Libya lacked the oil reserves necessary to increase production enough to offset its radical political positions. As the government concluded a 20-year plan for 1981-2000, it was widely assumed that oil production would increase to some 3.5 million bpd in the 1980s. In fact, production was reduced in 1980 as the government evidenced renewed concern at its dwindling reserves. In 1981 Libyan oil production dropped to around 1.1 million bpd, a level not seen since 1964-65; and it remained there.[30]

The discovery of oil in Libya created the conditions which allowed Qaddafi to come to power, as well as providing the necessary means to finance an ambitious, aggressive foreign policy. Oil revenues broke the Libyan government's dependence on income from foreign bases and gave Libya's foreign policy a credibility it had previously lacked. As described elsewhere, Qaddafi employed Libya's new-found wealth in support of Islam and the Arab nation, as well as more parochial interests. As he amassed an arsenal of modern military equipment, he moved to undermine Western political positions from Africa to Latin America. The implementation of this forward policy was of incalculable cost. Opposition to Israel, the United States, imperialism and neo-colonialism involved a continuous flow of funds abroad. Libyan intervention in Uganda in April 1979 and in Chad in late 1981, in particular, proved to be expensive undertakings. Given the limited appeal of the doctrines encompassed in Qaddafi's Third Universal Theory, it was often Libya's oil wealth which gave its foreign policies whatever short-term prominence or success they achieved in the early years of the revolution.[31]

In addition, the Libyan oil industry increased the depth and breadth of the nation's contacts with the outside world. By the end of the 1970s, Libya had developed extensive commercial links with many states in Europe, Africa and Asia which had taken little or no notice of Libya before 1959. Similarly, the discovery of oil served to reverse regional labour patterns, which had important consequences for Libyan foreign policy. Before 1960, there was a substantial emigration of Libyans to Egypt and Tunisia in search of work. After the discovery of oil, this trend was reversed, with expatriate Libyans returning home and an influx of large numbers of other Arabs and Africans, especially Egyptians, Tunisians and Palestinians. By 1981 some 500,000 expatriates were estimated to be living in Libya, including 170,000 Egyptians.[32]

Falling oil revenues

After five years of reasonably stable prices, Opec had grasped the opportunity afforded by the Iranian revolution to make a three-fold increase in the price of crude. It was an example of monopolistic pricing at its most blatant. In the process, Opec members committed themselves to defend a price position which was ultimately indefensible. As oil supply outpaced demand, Libya found it increasingly difficult to find buyers for oil priced, in 1981, at $41 a barrel. Consequently, the last quarter of the year and the first quarter of 1982 witnessed a severe drop in the level of oil exports. Oil production fell from a rate of 1.7 million bpd to 500,000 bpd, and oil revenues for the mid–1981 to mid–1982 period were less than half the $20 billion of the previous 12 months.

Libya's constrained circumstances were of vastly different magnitude from any suffered in the previous 20 years. A fall in revenues in 1975 had been serious, but they dropped by only 20 per cent and then for only a few months. In 1981-82 oil income was down by 50 per cent for almost a year. The decline in oil revenues badly hit spending on domestic consumption and development, defence and foreign affairs.[33]

As might be expected, the Libyan government quickly responded to the new market conditions. In August 1981 Jallud summoned senior executives of the foreign oil companies operating in Libya to a meeting in Tripoli to discuss the drop in their crude oil purchases. Practically all of the companies operating in Libya had reduced the amount of oil taken from Libya in the form of equity crude, oil received for working an oilfield or buyback oil (Libya's share of the oil which the companies market for the country), because vastly cheaper oil was available elsewhere. Actually, this was the second such meeting. Jallud had first summoned the oil executives in February 1981 to express Libya's desire to improve relations with the Reagan administration. Since then, relations with Washington had deteriorated; and Libyan diplomats had been expelled from the United States. A few weeks earlier, Libya had offered the oil companies a price cut of $1.40 a barrel to entice them to increase their oil purchases; but it was rejected as inadequate. At the August 1981 meeting, Jallud urged the oil companies to buy more Libyan oil but refused to grant them the price reductions they demanded as preconditions for increased purchases. Adopting a familiar tactic, Jallud met separately with each oil company's representative; but to the surprise of participants, he adopted a soft approach during the negotiations which contained neither threats nor ultimatums.[34]

With the assistance of its cash and gold reserves, Libya was able to manage its financial problems; however, there were signs that it was short of cash. In October 1981 Libya tested the Euromarket with a $200 million, seven-year Euroloan, apparently designed to establish a credit rating. The size of the loan was reportedly increased to $250 million the following month; and in February 1982 Libya approached the Midland Bank in London for a commercial loan. Reports of defaults on payments to contractors and importers persisted; and in January 1982 the government announced that development spending in 1982 would be five per cent less than in 1981.[35]

Unable to market its expensive oil, the Libyan government grudgingly accepted a lower price. At an August 1981 Opec meeting which failed to produce a unified price, Libya's oil minister signalled the change in policy when he said his country was willing to reduce its price as part of an Opec compromise. A few weeks later, Libya agreed to let Occidental increase its purchase of oil exempt from certain taxes and royalties. While Occidental's contract with Libya was complicated, most experts agreed that the pact marked an unofficial price reduction by Libya. Libya's official price remained at $39.90 a barrel; but Qaddafi had agreed to bend, if not break, his oil-price policy in an effort to keep output from falling even further.

At the end of October 1981, Libya joined Opec in agreeing to peg oil prices on a common benchmark of $34 a barrel, an agreement which ended two years of bickering and chaotic discounting. By April 1982 the official price of Libyan oil was $35.40 a barrel.[36]

Lower oil revenues continued after 1982, as world recession and an embargo on Libyan oil by the United States combined with a world oil glut to restrain Libyan oil exports. As early as 1983 Libya's foreign debt, always difficult to estimate, was reported to be as high as $10–$12 billion, with $2–$3 billion owed to foreign companies exporting to Libya, and $6–$7 billion owed to international construction firms. Total reserves dropped sharply in 1980–84, and real gross domestic product declined annually in 1980–85.

Economic discussions at successive annual meetings of the General People's Congress became a litany of delegate complaints about slowdowns and shortages, coupled with official admonitions for readjustments and reductions. In March 1985, for example, the General People's Congress was asked to approve an administrative budget which was 17 per cent below the allocation for 1984. With oil revenues continuing to run at half the 1980–81 levels, the Libyan government was forced to postpone or scrap several hundred development projects in 1985 alone. Facing lean times, the government increasingly attempted to meet its financial obligations through barter deals and counterpart oil sales. Many such negotiations involved an element of blackmail, since the Libyan government would agree to settle arrears only if the government negotiating on behalf of its companies promised to buy more Libyan oil. As the situation deteriorated, Libya found it increasingly difficult to organize the barter deals and netback arrangements it had come to depend on by 1986.[37]

The economic constraints imposed by lower oil revenues had a negative, albeit difficult-to-quantify, impact on the conduct of Libyan foreign policy. The Libyan intervention in Chad in 1980–81 proved expensive, and there was evidence to suggest that economics as well as politics influenced Qaddafi's sudden withdrawal at the end of 1981. Although Libya subsequently returned to Chad, unscheduled expenditures to support its political and military efforts there, especially in 1986–87, undoubtedly limited its ability to intervene elsewhere in sub-Saharan Africa. As discussed earlier, Libyan largesse did not end; but the ongoing discrepancy between Libyan aid commitments and aid disbursements, especially in Africa, appeared to widen.[38]

As early as February 1983 the General People's Congress had signalled the government's intention to reduce the foreign workforce and increase self-reliance as part of austerity measures. In August 1985 massive deportations of foreign workers, mostly Egyptians and Tunisians, were initiated. While most of the deportees were from countries with poor diplomatic relations with Libya, nationals from countries such as Mali and Mauritania, where workers' remittances were relatively important to national economies, were also included. The abrupt manner in which the Revolutionary Committees conducted the deportations, coupled with delays in concluding reparation payments, led to a sharp deterioration in Libyan relations with several of its neighbours.[39]

In the Mashrek, disagreement over oil-production and oil-price policies combined with the radical elements of Qaddafi's foreign policy to increase Libyan alienation from Saudi Arabia and the Gulf states. The drop in oil revenues also heightened Qaddafi's interest in enhancing Libyan control over the natural resources on its borders. Known petroleum reserves in the Mediterranean, as well as potential mineral deposits in the Sahel and Sahara, contributed to the emphasis Libyan foreign policy placed on these areas in the 1980s.[40] Elsewhere, debt negotiations with suppliers and contractors continued to undermine Libyan relations with Asian and European governments. Finally, Libya's growing economic difficulties, accompanied as they were by visible signs of domestic discontent, clearly encouraged the Reagan administration to step up its efforts after 1981 to isolate the Qaddafi regime.

As the price of oil collapsed, the Opec states engaged in a series of negotiations in 1986–87 aimed at regulating oil production and oil price. In the face of increased Saudi production, Libya joined Iran and Algeria, all three long-standing proponents of higher oil prices, to argue that production quotas were the solution to lower oil prices and reduced oil revenues. In the meantime, Libya endeavoured to dispose of its surplus oil on a netback basis, a procedure which called for the price of oil to be based on the market value of the products made from the crude instead of an official price per barrel.

In April 1986 Opec finally reached a frail accord to reduce output to around 16.5 million bpd. Libya accepted the measure as a first step, while continuing to demand cuts to 14 million bpd. Throughout the summer of 1986, the Libyan government consistently argued that Opec oil production had to be reduced further to increase the price of oil. Its membership of the three-member Opec pricing committee, established in October 1986, was a recognition of Libya's long-term support for higher prices, as well as a sign that support was growing within Opec for the Libyan position. The subsequent sacking of the Saudi oil minister, Ahmed Zaki Yamani, confirmed the triumph of the Libyan viewpoint. At the end of December 1986 Opec agreed, as from 1 February 1987, to limit output to 15.8 million bpd through the first half of 1987 and to fix selling rates around a central reference point of $18 a barrel.[41]

In February 1987 Libya moved to increase its influence inside and outside Opec councils by organizing an African Petroleum Producers' Association. The official objectives of this new organization were to co-ordinate the oil policies of the member states and extend awareness of Opec targets. Saudi Arabia, afraid the new association would weaken its own influence, officially expressed concern that the association amounted to the formation of a new bloc within Opec which would threaten its unity at a particularly sensitive time. A Libyan veto of Egyptian membership of the new organization heightened concern that Qaddafi would indeed seek to use it to increase Libyan influence in Opec's councils.[42]

Oil policy and foreign policy

The revolutionary government reversed the oil policies of its predecessor, a decision which led to a jump in Libya's oil revenues. In terms of daily output, oil production in 1974 was less than half the 1969 figure. While production increased to around two million bpd in the second half of the 1970s, it was again reduced to approximately one million bpd after 1981. The price per unit, on the other hand, went from $2 a barrel in 1969 to as high as $41 a barrel in 1981. In the interim the Libyan government nationalized the oil companies, seizing control of Libyan oil production. The net effect of the oil policies initiated by the Qaddafi regime was greatly to extend the life of Libya's oil reserves, while swelling oil revenues to over $22 billion in 1980, after which they dropped off rapidly.

As Qaddafi's oil policy unfolded, the influence of key tenets of Libyan foreign policy, such as Arab nationalism and positive neutrality, was irrefutable. Regardless of the impact on production, price and revenues, it was simply unacceptable to the revolutionary government to have control of the nation's primary resource in foreign hands. From this perspective, the oil companies were correct to view Qaddafi's suggestion that the Libyan people were willing to exist without oil revenues as more than an idle threat. As elsewhere, Qaddafi appeared willing to go to any extreme to have his way.

While Libya's foreign policy affected its oil policy, the converse was not as true. Oil policy had little impact on the fundamentals of Libyan foreign policy, although early success in the former probably encouraged the regime to be more aggressive in its pursuit of the latter. In addition, the success of Libya's early oil policies, coupled with the rapid escalation in oil revenues, imbued Libyan policy initiatives with a credibility that a provincial, sparsely-populated state would otherwise have found difficult to achieve.

At the same time, oil wealth provided the means for Qaddafi to pursue an extravagant, misguided foreign policy far beyond the point where it might have been abandoned under more realistic economic circumstances. The interdependence of foreign policy and oil policy was increasingly obvious in the mid-1980s, when declining oil revenues severely restricted the regime's ability to achieve its external objectives. As Libya's income plummeted, Qaddafi had the same difficulty in adjusting to Libya's new economic limits as he had experienced earlier in adapting to its political limits.

8

The Foreign Policy Process

> *The instrument of government is the prime political problem which faces human communities.*
>
> **Muammar al-Qaddafi**

Libya is a unitary state governed by a unique organization of congresses and committees. The present system of government evolved slowly after the downfall of the monarchy, and the evolutionary process probably remains incomplete. Fundamental to an analysis of Libyan foreign policy is an understanding of the policy-making process, in particular the impact the congress-committee system has on the formulation and execution of the nation's foreign policy. This chapter focuses on the internal environment of foreign policy, assessing the structure of government, the operation of the political system and the main interest groups.[1]

Libyan policy environment

Colonel Qaddafi and the members of the Revolutionary Command Council (RCC), indeed most members of the Free Unionist Officers' Movement, shared similar backgrounds, motivations and world views. They came largely from lower-middle-class families and minor tribes, and they embarked on a military career because it offered opportunities for education and upward socio-economic mobility. In this sense, the revolutionary movement was rightly characterized as a revolution of the oases and the interior against the more established society of larger, coastal families and dominant tribes.[2]

Moreover, the consistent and closely integrated values and attitudes of the members of the RCC governed the way in which the Libyan government engaged in the decision-making process. Matters that might conventionally be viewed as foreign or external relations became equally or more pertinent as domestic or internal affairs, and vice versa, either because the RCC defined them that way, or because of the progress of events, or both.[3]

The September 1969 coup d'état was totally military in conception, planning and execution; and the RCC initially maintained the military character of the revolution. RCC members remained on active duty, promoting themselves, sometimes more than once, and frequently appeared in uniform to emphasize military affiliation and discipline. In the early days, the RCC monopolized both policy direction and legislative functions, promulgating new laws through RCC decrees which became operative as soon as they were published in the official gazette. RCC dominance was codified on 11 December 1969, when the 1951 constitution was replaced by a constitutional proclamation which designated the RCC as the highest authority in the Libyan Arab Republic. Exercising both executive and legislative functions, the RCC was empowered to take whatever measures it deemed necessary to protect the regime or the revolution. In particular, the RCC could declare war, conclude and ratify treaties, appoint diplomatic envoys and receive diplomatic missions, and direct the armed forces.[4]

Later, the RCC appointed civilians to a Council of Ministers to help run the government; nevertheless, the former reserved supreme authority in all policy areas for itself. Sitting at the top of the pyramid, the RCC issued proclamations and directives, overseeing governmental actions and the development of new institutions to ensure their consistency with the objectives of the revolution. In particular, the RCC refused to allow its considerable civilian support to be channelled into an autonomous political organization. This insistence on total domination highlighted an early contradiction of the revolution. Members of the Free Unionist Officers' Movement, especially the participants on the RCC, repeatedly emphasized they were close to the people and mirrored their thoughts and wishes. At the same time, the RCC showed considerable distrust of the Libyan people and was initially unwilling to allow them to share significantly in the direction of the revolution.[5]

The RCC remained at the apex of the new Libyan political system until approximately 1975. Qaddafi, as the principal architect of the Free Unionist Officers' Movement, was chairman of the RCC and clearly the dominant figure in the movement. Nevertheless, he did not dominate the Libyan system in the early days of the revolution to the same extent that other Arab revolutionary leaders such as Nasser had. In the beginning, the RCC functioned as a collegial executive body with Qaddafi in the role of first among equals. This situation changed as the 1970s progressed, with Qaddafi increasingly becoming the chief activist, ideological innovator and policy initiator on the RCC. Eventually, the attempt at collective leadership broke down completely; and with the 1975 split in the RCC, Qaddafi emerged as undisputed head of the Libyan political system.[6]

The structure of government
Colonel Qaddafi, generally referred to as Leader of the Revolution or simply the Guide, is the head of state. The General Secretary of the General People's

Congress is the chief executive, and the General Secretariat of the Genera. People's Congress is the chief executive's staff and advisory body. The General People's Committee (sometimes known as the General Popular Committee) currently comprises a general secretary and 10 secretaries and serves as a cabinet, replacing the former Council of Ministers, which was abolished in 1977. On the General People's Committee, the Secretary of the Foreign Liaison Bureau is responsible for the conduct of Libyan foreign policy.[7]

The General People's Congress was created in 1976 and serves as the national-level representative body. Delegate composition to the General People's Congress has varied over the years, but has generally included the chairmen of the Basic People's Congresses and the Branch or Municipal People's Committees, as well as representatives from the university student unions and the national federation of unions and professional associations. The General People's Congress is scheduled to meet at least once a year and is intended to be the major arena in which the plans, programmes and policies of the central government, as well as those originating at lower levels of government, are discussed and ratified. Once they are ratified, the responsibility for their implementation rests with the congresses, committees, unions and associations.

Local government in Libya is focused on the zone and the municipality. The zone is the lowest operative level, and its citizens elect a People's Committee (or Popular Committee) to administer the affairs of the zone. There is no congress or legislative body at this level. The municipality is the next echelon of government; and in the larger urban areas, a few municipalities are divided into branch municipalities. Each municipality or branch municipality elects a Basic People's Congress. The Basic People's Congress selects its own chairman, as well as a five-member People's Committee which has day-to-day administrative responsibility. The Basic People's Congresses debate the agenda of the General People's Congress in advance of its annual meetings, as well as administering local concerns such as road networks, water systems and health clinics. In those instances where a municipality is divided into branch municipalities, a municipal People's Leadership Committee is established to co-ordinate the activities of the branch People's Committees. Finally, the national-level General People's Committee was decentralized in 1978 to include a similar organization at the municipal level. Municipal General People's Committees are elected by the Basic People's Congress and are responsible for co-ordinating activities between the latter organization and the national-level General People's Committee.

In addition to the network of zone and municipal congresses and committees, Libyan workers are also organized into union or professional associations. Each union or professional association elects a People's

Committee to administer its affairs and to participate in the national federation of unions. In turn, the national federation of unions and professional associations sends representatives to the General People's Congress in a non-voting capacity to address issues of special relevance to the unions. While the unions and professional associations bring the necessary expertise to selected issues, their concerns as ordinary citizens continue to be represented by the People's Committees and the Basic People's Congresses in their home towns or municipalities.

Libya's universities are largely student-managed through a system of student unions. Under this system, each college or faculty at the university elects a committee with its own chairman to administer the affairs of the college or faculty. Representatives of the committees constitute a university student union which, together with the president of the university, administer the affairs of the university. Like the unions and professional associations, the members of the university student unions attend the General People's Congress in a non-voting capacity.

Evolution of the political system
In terms of political organization, the RCC followed the Egyptian example in that it moved to create a new governmental structure designed to infuse the populace with the ideology of the revolution while generating mass support for the regime. In the process, the RCC learned how difficult it was to create a centralized, authoritarian political system which also generated the levels of popular mobilization and participation required to achieve the government's objectives.[8] The political history of Libya after 1 September 1969, including the evolution of the foreign-policy process, was largely a chronology of the RCC's search for a political organization which would effectively address complex, conflicting challenges of political development.

In 1969, Libya remained a traditional, tribal society with local leadership largely in the hands of tribal sheikhs, urban notables, the religious establishment or appointed representatives. While the monarchy had exercised political authority through these traditional leaders, the latter owed very little to the central government because their legitimacy, in the eyes of the Libyan people, was founded on family status, wealth and symbols of religious piety. Similarly, the boundaries of local administrative units under the monarchy remained the *de facto* boundaries of Libya's major tribes. This traditional system, due to the general ignorance of the masses, their passivity and conformity, and their pervasive sense of fatalism, was largely immune to challenge from below.[9]

The RCC sought to broaden support for the revolution by reducing tribal power and identification, increasing political mobilization and substituting new local leadership supportive of revolutionary goals. It divided Libya into new administrative zones, based on geographical divisions and population density, which crossed the old tribal boundaries and grouped disparate tribes in the same area. This administrative reorganization reduced regional identity and accompanying social and political power, as well as relocating traditional administrative power centres. Its effectiveness increased as it was buttressed by supportive actions such as the replacement of traditional leaders with young technocrats whose selection was based on education and ability as displayed in oral and written exams. In the process, every effort was made to link the traditional leadership to the colonial powers and the negative aspects of the monarchy. In late 1971, for example, a special people's court was convened to try members of the former regime accused of treason and corruption.[10]

By the spring of 1971, the RCC recognized that its new system of government was not generating popular support sufficient to transform traditional Libyan society into a modern progressive state. In part, this was due to the failure of the newly appointed administrators, for the most part outsiders, to achieve the support and co-operation of local communities. The poor performance of the young technocrats also mirrored a failure of the RCC which had under-estimated the power base of the traditional leadership and over-estimated the appeal of its own socio-economic and political programme. Another reason for the failure of the young technocrats was the RCC's reluctance to delegate authority and responsibility, especially to civilians. While this was true of all areas of government policy, it was especially true of foreign policy. Consequently, the attempt to build an effective core of revolutionary administrators through appointment was scrapped after less than two years in favour of a completely new structure.[11]

The Arab Socialist Union

On 11 June 1971, Colonel Qaddafi, as chairman of the RCC, announced the formation of the Arab Socialist Union (ASU), an official mass mobilization party. Modelled on Nasser's Arab Socialist Union, the organization of the Libyan ASU was divided into the national, intermediate and local levels. The intermediate and local levels consisted of two main organizations, a conference or general membership, and a committee or leadership. RCC control of the new organization was transparent, since the chairman of the RCC was appointed president and the other members of the RCC were designated as 'the Supreme Leading Authority of the Arab Socialist Union'. Initially the RCC appointed constituent committees at the intermediate level, with an RCC member chairing each of these committees. Committees were later elected at the intermediate and local levels; but with ideological and policy discussions banned, participants lapsed into familiar patterns of family and factional politics. The RCC eventually opened ASU membership to Arabs outside Libya, but there was minimal interest in other Arab states.[12]

The RCC assigned the ASU a host of complex, contradictory goals. It hoped the ASU would become the primary link between the central government and the Libyan people, and thus fill the void created by the abolition of the tribal system. In this sense, the ASU offered the potential for a meaningful increase in political participation, especially at the lower levels of the new system. At the same time, the RCC expected the ASU to be a source of support for the revolutionary leadership and its policies whenever such support was required. The ASU offered a pervasive network of organizations throughout Libyan society capable of monitoring citizens' activities at all levels. Members of the RCC emphasized that consensus was the goal of the Libyan political system, and openly admitted they might have to circumvent normal democratic processes in the early stages of the revolution to promote revolutionary change and check counter-revolutionary activity. The length of this transitional stage was not discussed.[13]

In effect, the Arab Socialist Union was stillborn. It never resolved the fundamental contradiction inherent in trying to be both an organization which reflected government interests and objectives on the one hand, while remaining sensitive to public demands and aspirations on the other. Members of the RCC, concerned with maintaining control of the revolution, stifled local initiatives and suffocated local leadership. In the few instances where local ASU leadership attempted to articulate local needs or grievances, committee members were reprimanded or the local committee was simply dissolved and replaced with one more amenable to RCC directives. The ASU organizational structure also proved to be complex and unwieldy and was undercut by existing government organizations and by the young technocrats appointed after October 1969, since both groups rightly viewed it as a competitor. Finally, the ASU, like its predecessors, failed to take full account of the nature and extent of the traditionalism of the Libyan people as well as the central role of traditional leaders in developing public perceptions and attitudes.

Popular revolution
On 15 April 1973, Colonel Qaddafi proclaimed a popular revolution intended to heighten revolutionary change. The Libyan people were told to seize power through People's Committees which were to be elected throughout Libya in villages, schools, airports and popular organizations. As with many RCC proclamations, Qaddafi's call for elections was not accompanied by detailed guidelines or procedures, and this led to considerable uncertainty in the early stages of the popular revolution. Occasionally, a People's Committee was elected and then replaced in an RCC-sanctioned election after the former was denounced by workers as being unrepresentative. In a few cases, this happened three or four times before a suitably radical group of discontented, lower-level employees was

elected to the People's Committee. Direct elections were also held in public corporations and selected government bureaucracies; but to prevent anarchy the RCC banned their formation in government ministries. The initiation of the popular revolution ended the early experiment with young technocrats, since most rural People's Committees quickly dismissed the RCC appointees and replaced them with local individuals far less modern in outlook but still more receptive to change than the traditional rural élites.[14]

A complex web of ideological and tactical considerations was behind the decision to initiate a popular revolution. First, the RCC hoped to increase public participation and involvement, thus fostering the supportive attitudes and roles believed necessary for the success of its internal and external goals. Second, the formation of the People's Committee system reflected the paranoia of the revolutionary government, since each committee became an adjunct to the security services, denouncing individuals opposed or even ambivalent to the objectives of the revolution. In conjunction with the election of the People's Committees, a wave of arrests occurred which focused on members of Marxist, Baathist, Muslim Brotherhood or other international political circles which had not identified themselves satisfactorily with the new regime's policies. While the majority of these arrests were instigated by the secret police, there were cases in which individuals were denounced by the local People's Committees. Finally, the RCC hoped the popular revolution would mobilize public opinion in both Libya and Egypt for the union with Egypt scheduled for September 1973. Prior announcement of the forthcoming merger was met in Libya with apathy, scorn and even resentment.[15]

The creation of the People's Committee system was a revolutionary step in Libya's political evolution which produced mixed but largely positive results. The new political system, for the first time in Libyan history, required popular participation in the selection of local leadership and popular involvement in the local policy-making process. People's Committees assumed responsibility for administrative functions at both the local and the provincial levels. Hence, the RCC increased the political involvement and experience of the Libyan people through active participation, while focusing their attention on the issues of most importance to the local community.[16] In the process, the revolutionary government consolidated its control of the revolution by further weakening the influence of the traditional leadership and exposing or arresting a number of actual or potential critics of the regime. On the negative side of the ledger, People's Committees disrupted the management and functioning of a variety of institutions, in particular public-sector companies and agricultural development projects, which had a detrimental influence on the economic development objectives of the regime.

General People's Congress

While the People's Committee system was a general success, especially in the area of political participation, it did not satisfy the RCC in terms of political mobilization. In part, the problem was a continuing conflict between the ASU and the People's Committees as to which was to be the central institution for popular mobilization. This conflict, as well as other considerations not so clearly understood, led to a fourth major stage of reform intended to increase mobilization by reducing conflict and competition between the ASU and the People's Committees. Late in 1975, Qaddafi introduced a number of institutional changes, including the election of Basic People's Congresses at the intermediate level and the creation of a new, national-level representative body called the General People's Congress. The Basic People's Congresses subsequently became the primary area for the debate of foreign and domestic policy issues prior to meetings of the General People's Congress. Qaddafi became Secretary General of the General People's Congress, with the remaining members of the now defunct RCC forming its General Secretariat. In March 1977, Qaddafi concluded this stage in the evolution of the committee-congress system by declaring the formal establishment of the people's authority and renaming Libya the Socialist People's Libyan Arab Jamahiriya.[17]

To the surprise of most observers, the central government began submitting major plans and policies to the General People's Congress for its review and authorization at its first session in early 1976. Both the general administrative budget for 1976 and the five-year plan (1976-80) were presented, for example, as well as several major foreign-policy items. Thereafter, the practice was continued. At the fifth session of the General People's Congress in January 1980, a wide range of domestic and foreign-policy questions were discussed, including a progress report on the five-year plan, the bilateral pacts concluded by Libya in 1979, financial support for Syria and Jordan, an end to economic co-operation and trade with China and a break in relations with the Fatah leadership of the Palestine Liberation Organization (PLO). At the ninth session held in Pripoli in February 1984, the General People's Congress adopted an unusually wide range of resolutions relating to foreign-policy issues. Issues addressed included the United Nations Charter, US missile bases in southern Italy, events in Lebanon, Arab unity in the Maghreb, relations with African states and the policies of the PLO. The agenda for the session held in February-March 1986 focused on Libya's deteriorating economic position and a government reshuffle, but also included a call for the Central Bank of Libya to seek the assistance of other central banks to end the US freeze on Libyan assets and the formation of suicide squads to strike at Libya's enemies.[18]

When the RCC and the former Council of Ministers were officially abolished with the formal establishment of the people's authority in March

1977, both executive and legislative power was theoretically vested in the General People's Congress. In practice, the General People's Congress delegated many of its major responsibilities to the General Secretariat and the General People's Committee. In December 1978, for example, the General People's Congress authorized the General People's Committee to appoint ambassadors and the then Secretary of Foreign Affairs to receive the credentials of foreign diplomats. Colonel Qaddafi served as General Secretary of the General People's Committee from 1977 until early 1979, when he resigned to concentrate on what he described as revolutionary activities with the masses. He retained his position as *de facto* commander-in-chief of the armed forces and assumed the new title of Leader of the Revolution. At the same time, the former members of the RCC who had been serving as the General Secretariat of the General People's Congress resigned their posts to focus on revolutionary activities. Regardless of position or title, Qaddafi and the former members of the RCC continued to control and direct the Libyan government. Members of the General Secretariat of the General People's Congress were selected by them and served at their convenience. Members of the General Secretariat, in turn, appointed members of the General People's Committee who served three-year terms.[19]

The fourth session of the General People's Congress, held in December 1978, first illustrated some of the practical limits of its power and authority. In the first two days of the meeting, delegates called for wage increases after the recently published second volume of *The Green Book*, Qaddafi's socio-economic and political manifesto, had called for their abolition, and demanded an end to the military draft when the General Secretariat had announced a programme of universal conscription. As a result of these and related actions, the session was postponed on the third day, officially out of respect for the death of the president of Algeria. In reality, the delegates' independence had convinced Qaddafi and the members of the General Secretariat of the need to reassert control of the revolution. After the meeting was adjourned, several People's Committees were told to elect new members before the General People's Congress reconvened, and mobile election teams were dispatched to monitor the new elections.[20]

To avoid such problems, the Libyan intervention in Chad, a policy which provoked increasing domestic opposition in Libya, was a taboo subject at the sixth session of the congress in January 1981. Nevertheless, delegates continued to criticize key policies. At the ninth session of the congress in February 1984, delegates rejected several proposals originating with the Leader of the Revolution, including liberalized divorce laws, a reduction in educational facilities and a military training programme which included females as well as males. In response, Qaddafi criticized the reactionary nature of the deliberative body and again reorganized it to ensure such opposition was not repeated. Later in the year, the General People's Congress issued a law requiring all Libyan citizens to undergo military training.[21]

Despite the fact that the activities of the General People's Congress have been closely supervised and it has not grown significantly in authority or responsibility, it has served as a clearing house and sounding board for the views of the Libyan people as transmitted by their local representatives. This was especially true in the realm of domestic policy but also applied to a number of foreign-policy issues. At the same time, it provided an effective organization for the national leadership to communicate their ideas and objectives to the people. Hence, while Colonel Qaddafi and the former members of the RCC remained the principal decision-makers, especially in the realm of foreign policy, the refined political system introduced a level of representation and participation hitherto unknown in Libya.

Revolutionary Committees

At the same time that Qaddafi announced his resignation from the position of General Secretary to the General People's Congress, he called for the establishment of Revolutionary Committees, a new level of organization drawn from the most revolutionary elements of the Basic People's Congresses. Established as revolutionary watchdogs, the objectives of the Revolutionary Committees were described by Qaddafi as to exercise revolutionary supervision, to protect and defend the Great First of September Revolution, to activate and guide the People's Committees and the leadership of the Basic People's Congresses, and to urge the masses to seize authority. Qaddafi insisted, somewhat naively, that the Revolutionary Committees would not exercise power, but indicated that their members were true revolutionaries who believed in the revolution and the cause of the masses. Qaddafi also maintained that the Revolutionary Committees were an integral part of his revolutionary theory, an assertion belied by the fact that they were not mentioned in *The Green Book* or his other early revolutionary musings.[22]

Over the next two years, official attention focused on the composition and role of the Revolutionary Committees. Drawn from the Basic People's Congresses, Revolutionary Committee members were described as a progressive vanguard for the protection of the revolution, a security belt to affirm the authority of the people. An article in a May 1980 issue of *The Green March*, the official publication of the Revolutionary Committees, emphasized that Revolutionary Committee members were expected to make a total commitment. It said that the Revolutionary Committees were to become suicide squads who did not fear death and were willing to make any sacrifice for the sake of Arab unity and the elimination of reactionary idols.[23] Revolutionary Committees were established throughout Libyan society, including within the police and armed forces, parallel to the congress and committee system. Where the latter had largely administrative responsibilities and reported to the General People's Congress, the former were responsible for maintaining revolutionary ardour throughout the political system and reported direct to the Leader of the Revolution. As Qaddafi emphasized, the People's Committees exercised authority, while the Revolutionary Committees exercised revolutionary control.[24]

The formation of Revolutionary Committees complicated international as well as domestic affairs. The Libyan government urged Arab expatriates working in Libya, especially Egyptians and Palestinians, to form Revolutionary Committees as a first step towards forming People's Committees. Such activities were condemned by both foreign governments and the Palestine Liberation Organization, and they were one of the reasons why diplomatic relations between Libya and the PLO deteriorated in late 1979. The PLO charged that Libya's proposed organization of Palestinians into Revolutionary Committees or People's Committees violated the Arab League's declaration that the PLO was the sole legitimate representative of the Palestinian people.[25]

On 1 September 1979, Qaddafi called on Libyans living abroad to organize popular marches to seize Libyan embassies, because the latter represented government bodies whereas traditional forms of government had been abolished in Libya and replaced by the authority of the people. His announcement marked the culmination of a long-standing dispute between the Libyan foreign ministry, largely staffed by professional diplomats, and the Foreign Liaison Bureau, a revolutionary organization initially responsible for Libyan relations with non-governmental bodies, liberation movements and guerrilla groups. In the beginning, Qaddafi had encouraged the competition; however, by 1979, he concluded that the foreign ministry and its missions abroad, especially in sub-Saharan Africa, were frustrating the objectives of the Foreign Liaison Bureau. In response to his appeal, Libyan embassies were turned into Libyan People's Bureaus, with Libyan ambassadors replaced by People's Committees which reported to the Foreign Liaison Bureau. Qaddafi's purge of the Libyan foreign ministry and its missions abroad decimated the Libyan diplomatic corps, since most professional diplomats were transferred home or resigned in protest. Thereafter, members of the foreign ministry tended to avoid postings abroad because it was the People's Committees, largely composed of Revolutionary Committee members, which actually ran most embassies.[26]

Apart from the fact that few of the committee members who seized control of Libyan embassies had diplomatic experience, the projection of Libya's domestic revolution into an international arena where traditions and conventions had developed over centuries created considerable problems. A harbinger of things to come were the attacks on the US and French embassies in Tripoli in 1979–80. On 1 September 1982, Qaddafi charged that certain Arab governments had forfeited their right to exist after remaining passive during the siege of Beirut, and argued it was the duty of the Revolutionary Committees to destroy those governments. Less than three years later, in a speech to the General People's Congress, Qaddafi claimed the right to kill political dissidents inside and outside Libya.[27] In the interim, Libya's People's Bureaus in Europe, Africa and the Middle East were increasingly identified with state-sponsored terrorism ranging from unsolicited involvement in the internal affairs of African and Middle Eastern states to participation in the assassination of Libyan dissidents throughout western Europe.

In the summer of 1985, the Revolutionary Committees were reorganized in an effort to increase their effectiveness and enhance their orthodoxy. An article in the 26 July 1985 issue of the revolutionary periodical *Al-Jamahiriya*, for example, criticized them for inadequate performance, immaturity, emotionalism and parochialism, and encouraged their thorough reorganization.[28] Thereafter, the Revolutionary Committees, which by then numbered some 50,000 members, appeared to gain influence and control at the expense of the military and the state bureaucracy, as well as the People's Congress. Disaffection in the armed forces, in particular, was muted, albeit not eliminated, by the system of close surveillance imposed by the Revolutionary Committees.

The power of the Revolutionary Committees continued to grow in 1986–87. The April 1986 bombing raid by the United States rallied revolutionary elements in Libya behind the Leader of the Revolution, and he seized the opportunity to strengthen the power and authority of the Revolutionary Committees. While there was little evidence to support the suggestion that the Revolutionary Committees would eventually supplant the congress-committee system of government, their influence over the latter, as well as over the armed forces, obviously increased. In the process, members of the Revolutionary Committees became more active and outspoken in their efforts to silence the voices of dissent.

Political parties

The monarchy had effectively banned the organization and operation of political parties, and the RCC continued this policy. The combined impact of the December 1969 Decision on the Protection of the Revolution, the Penal Code and Law No. 71 of 1972 was to render political party activity of any kind criminal and to constitute a strict legal injunction against unauthorized political activity. Like many Islamic philosophers, Qaddafi rejected the Western political party system, not because it was incompatible with the basic tenets of Islam, but because he was unfavourably impressed with party organization and competition. In *The Green Book*, he described the political party as the modern dictatorial instrument of governing, and the party system as an overt form of dictatorship.[29]

Qaddafi's condemnation of the political party system was multi-faceted. He argued that political parties, because they consisted of people with similar beliefs, represented and promoted only the special interests of select segments of society. Such segments formed parties to attain their ends and impose their doctrines and interests on society as a whole. Moreover, competition in the multi-party political system frequently escalated to the point where a dominant party or parties gained control of the system and then ignored the rights and interests of minority party members. Finally, Qaddafi argued that political parties, in their desire to consolidate political power, often distorted or destroyed the accomplishments of their predecessors, even when those accomplishments were for the general good. Qaddafi's solution to these dilemmas was the committee-congress system of government.[30]

The military

As noted, the September 1969 coup was completely military in conception and execution. It was accomplished without the participation or even knowledge of civilian groups; and initially, the RCC maintained the military direction of the revolution. Under attack from diverse elements of the former élite structure, the RCC worked to create a reliable coercive arm capable of sustaining the revolution. Within a year, the military establishment tripled in size, largely due to the merger of regional and specialized security forces; and it continued to increase in quantity and quality throughout the decade. Expenditures for military equipment also increased dramatically, and Libya's armed forces entered the 1980s with the highest ratio of military equipment to manpower in the developing world.[31]

In the first decade of the revolution, the Libyan armed forces rewarded Qaddafi's paternalism with a general absence of major upheavals or open dissent, although there were occasional coup attempts. However, opposition within the armed forces grew as Qaddafi moved to abolish the formal military hierarchy and replace it with a vaguely defined people's militia, or so-called armed people. To promote this objective, senior army officers were reduced in rank; and the government moved ahead with plans to remove the army headquarters from Tripoli to a remote desert region. Qaddafi's insistence on universal military service was also very unpopular within the ranks of the regular armed forces.[32]

In 1980-83, there were as many attempted coups as in the previous 10 years, with at least eight attempts reported in the international media; and there was no respite for Qaddafi after 1983. In the 12 months preceding May 1986, for example, a further six coup attempts were reported. In the spring of 1987, nine men, including several soldiers, were executed in public, the first such spectacle in three years. Later in the year, members of the Libyan armed forces serving in Chad hijacked a plane and flew to Egypt, where they requested political asylum. The most significant challenge to Qaddafi's rule undoubtedly remained the Libyan armed forces, especially the army, because it was the only group in the country with the requisite power and organization.[33]

The possibility of a palace coup was also raised, especially in the aftermath of the April 1986 air raids on Tripoli and Benghazi. The difficulty with such a scenario was that no one in Qaddafi's inner circle appeared to have cultivated a power base independent of Qaddafi himself. Indeed, Qaddafi made himself so central to the prevailing system that it was very unlikely that any of the present members of the regime could sustain the system without him. This was especially true after the US bombing attack rallied Libyan revolutionary elements behind their Leader of the Revolution. In short, a palace coup was unlikely if for no other reason than that it would probably bring down the palace along with Qaddafi.[34]

Petit bourgeoisie

Domestic civilian opposition to Qaddafi's rule increased at the end of the first decade of the revolution. After 1977, the government followed a progressively radical socio-economic policy which included housing redistribution and demonetization and led to a state takeover of import, export and distribution functions. The consequent redistribution of wealth and power directly affected the economic well-being of different sectors of the population, activating latent political opposition. Members of the nascent middle class were most affected, since they had prospered during the early years of the revolution when the government's emphasis on the service and housing sectors created lucrative opportunities in trade, real estate and small consumer manufacture.[35]

Internal opposition was not limited to a single socio-economic group but incorporated diverse elements of Libyan society including the nation's religious leadership. The reformist elements of Qaddafi's approach to Islam were a deliberate attempt to reduce the role of religious scholars and jurists and to bring Islam under the control of the revolution. When Libya's religious leaders increasingly opposed this policy, Qaddafi purged them in mid-1978, emphasizing that mosques were meant to be places of worship and not arenas to discuss socio-economic and political issues. Qaddafi's harsh reaction had a significance beyond the immediate issue, since it symbolized the extent to which he sought to make Islam a domestic and international instrument in support of the revolution.[36]

While significant levels of internal opposition to the Qaddafi regime developed, the opposition was badly fragmented and had to deal with considerable support for the regime, especially among the younger, less

well-to-do elements of society. Nevertheless, internal discontent continued to grow, fuelled by unpopular foreign and domestic policies.[37] More recently, the austerity policies resulting from the collapse of oil prices in the first half of 1986 combined with Qaddafi's refusal to reduce military expenditures to result in increasing shortages of basic necessities and growing unemployment.

Organized opposition

Organized opposition abroad to the revolutionary government increased in visibility, if not in effectiveness, in the early 1980s, as domestic opposition mounted and the government resorted to increasingly stringent coercive measures to silence opposition inside and outside Libya. In 1980 Qaddafi first articulated his so-called doctrine of physical liquidation, according to which after all other efforts at disarming counter-revolutionary elements had failed, physical liquidation could be used as a last resort. Thereafter, Qaddafi's use of violence to suppress organized opposition abroad increasingly strained Libya's diplomatic relations with Western governments.[38]

Nevertheless, the character and prospects of the external opposition, in part because of its clandestine nature, remained uncertain. Opposition groups tended to be organized more in theory than in practice, with groupings coming and going, uniting and dividing, as time passed. Hence, the very existence of some such groups, to say nothing of their organization, membership, funding and ideology, was open to question. For this reason, while it was possible to discuss credible dissident groups such as the National Front for the Salvation of Libya, the Libyan National Democratic Group or the Libyan Liberation Organization, it was more fruitful to discuss the organized opposition to Qaddafi's regime outside Libya in terms of the generations which composed it.[39]

As two decades of revolutionary government approached, at least five generations of opposition groups were identifiable. The first group to be disenchanted with the new government was the élite of the old regime. While this group included a few active monarchists, the bulk of its membership consisted of the traditional élite, which was aggressively attacked by the RCC in the early days of the revolution.

The next group, often characterized as conservative nationalists, consisted of individuals who initially supported the strong Arab nationalist position taken by the government on issues such as the foreign air bases and the Palestinian question, but could not abide by its increasingly radical socio-economic policies. The next two groups, the country's technocrats and its religious leadership, have already been discussed. In the early years, young technocrats were fêted as a substitute for the traditional élite; but their power waned with the increasing power of the ideologues who championed revolution before economic development. As this occurred, the brain drain

of technocrats from Libya accelerated. An early ally of the regime, Libya's religious establishment parted company with Qaddafi when his rigid interpretation of the Third International Theory challenged their position and power.[40]

The stream of defections swelled in the 1980s, with individual complaints varying from policy implementation as opposed to policy content, to charges of corruption, inefficiency and increased repression. Many of the newcomers to the ranks of the organized opposition were not welcomed with enthusiasm, either because of a feeling they had reaped the benefits of the regime before deserting it, or out of fear they might be government agents sent to infiltrate their ranks.

Therefore, a manifest diversity of organization, motives and objectives continued to characterize the opposition to the Qaddafi regime. If they were united at all, it was in their opposition to Qaddafi. If they shared a single characteristic, it was their mistrust of each other. While the ideology of one or more of them might help shape the outlook of a successor regime, it was unlikely that any of them in their current form would significantly contribute to the overthrow of the revolutionary government.

New foreign-policy process

Muammar al-Qaddafi fashioned a new form of government for Libya. The system of congresses and committees, largely without precedent, remains unique. Qaddafi also created new structures to manage the foreign-policy process. Today, Libyan foreign policy is formulated and executed through an intricate network of governmental bodies paralleled by private directives from the Guide and his inner circle. While the Foreign Liaison Bureau is at the centre of foreign-policy implementation, its efforts are often circumvented by other official bodies such as the Secretariat of Justice, the Islamic Call Society and divisions of General Intelligence and Military Intelligence. The Secretariat for External Security, created in 1984, has often appeared to play an especially important role, since one of its tasks is to co-ordinate the activities of other intelligence and security organizations.[41]

In the beginning, the RCC tightly controlled all aspects of the formulation and execution of Libyan foreign policy. The Libyan people accepted this approach, both because they were in general agreement with the redirection of Libyan foreign policy, and because no previous Libyan government had offered them a more significant role in the nation's foreign-policy process. Almost two decades later, ultimate control over the nation's foreign policy remains in the hands of Colonel Qaddafi and his immediate circle; however, the congress-committee system has offered new opportunities for Libyans to discuss and influence the government's foreign policy. For example, Basic People's Congresses throughout the country debate foreign and domestic policy items on the agenda of the General

People's Congress in advance of the meetings of the latter where the debate continues. Similarly, the Revolutionary Committee network offers a degree of foreign as well as domestic policy involvement to tens of thousands of young Libyans. It is true that one objective of such organizations and debates is to reach a consensus in support of central government policies. Nevertheless, it must be recognized that the new system of government offers more opportunities for more people to participate in the foreign-policy process than was available before the September revolution.

9
Conclusions

Under the direction of Muammar al-Qaddafi, the Libyan government has pursued a vigorous, aggressive foreign policy which has been remarkable for the broad scope of its interests and objectives. No state in the Arab world since Egypt under Nasser has attempted such a multifarious regional and global policy. Moreover, it was a rational foreign policy pursued with tactical flexibility and driven by a strong ideological perception of the world outside Libya.

The revolutionary leadership of Libya, and to a certain extent the Libyan people, rejected what they saw as the fundamental inequality of the international system and moved to revise it to the benefit of the non-industrialized states. In effect, Libyan foreign policy pursued a new world order in which the Middle East in general and Libya in particular would have a more central role. In this context, Libya's refusal to recognize the state of Israel was symbolic of a wider rejection of the existing international system and the world powers which had created and sustained it. While this Libyan perspective was not unique in the Third World, few states shared Qaddafi's concomitant desire to make himself a major player in the new world order.

Both regional and global powers reacted to the threat of Libyan foreign policy, and their collective responses highlighted the importance both of regional systems to individual states, and of the Arab world to the global system. In the Mashrek, the Maghreb and sub-Saharan Africa, Libyan foreign policy was condoned or condemned, ignored or attacked, largely in terms of its impact on individual states and their place within regional systems. At the global level, the United States and its allies in western Europe recognized Libya's destabilizing impact on regional systems as well as on the international system. While individual interests shaped specific responses, the Western allies were generally united in their specific opposition to Libyan attempts to reshape the existing political system inside or outside the Arab world. The Soviet Union, while sharing Libya's general desire to reorder the international system, provided less than total support, since it lacked confidence in the ability and stability of the Libyan leader.

Oil revenues gave the revolutionary government the means to pursue a new foreign policy, but it did not dictate the content of that policy. The major changes in the direction and emphasis of Libyan foreign policy initiated by the revolutionary government were determined by the ideology it embraced. The new ideological framework for Libyan foreign policy, largely borrowed from the Egyptian experience, centred on the tenets of Arab nationalism, *jihad*, Arab unity and positive neutrality. The revolution's ideology, especially the emphasis on Arab nationalism, was accorded general support by the Libyan populace because there was a high degree of consonance between that ideology and fundamental values of Libyan political culture. Nonetheless, not all the tenets of Libyan foreign policy were equally applicable to all events in all places at all times. In this regard, one of the benefits of the thematic approach employed here has been to highlight areas of commonality and dissimilarity. The remainder of this chapter will focus on the most significant patterns which have emerged from the analysis, discussing early continuity, policy innovation, constant principles, tactical flexibility and political isolation.

Early continuity
A number of observers, including the author, have previously examined the early continuity which existed between the foreign policies of the Libyan monarchy and the revolutionary government. While the relevance of the monarchical legacy diminished with each year Qaddafi continued in power, it remained important to recognize that Libyan foreign policy after 1969 was not *sui generis*. Especially in the early years of the revolution, it shared a degree of continuity in content and emphasis with that of the monarchy.

In particular, the full extent to which the revolutionary government simply adopted or expanded policies originating with the monarchy was seldom recognized. For example, considerable domestic support for the Palestinian people was obvious in Libya after 1947; and the Idris regime supported and encouraged this to a limited degree. In the area of oil policy, the monarchy advocated higher posted prices and greater government participation after 1959. While it later consented to increase oil production, it remained vocal in its concern that oil prices were too low. Finally, as oil revenues came to replace revenues from military bases, the monarchy moved to reduce the Western presence and influence in the kingdom in an effort to add substance to its policy of non-alignment. While Qaddafi's impact on the foreign policy he inherited cannot be underestimated, it is incorrect to assume there was little or no continuity between the two regimes.

Both governments also showed an understanding and appreciation for the extent to which the Libyan nation had developed within a special milieu. The revolutionary government sought to legitimize external objectives by placing them within the context of the Libyan heritage and by appealing to traditional values, especially Islam. Its rationale for legitimacy was not dissimilar to that of the monarchy, although both the essence and the emphasis of their policies varied considerably. The revolutionary government stressed brotherhood, but it shifted the emphasis from narrow tribal structures to the larger Arab community. It recalled the heroic struggle against Italian colonialism, but added condemnation of the more recent corruption of the palace and its co-operation with neo-colonialism and imperialism. Religion was also invoked repeatedly, but it was promoted in the context of justice and right rule as opposed to the parochial lodges and brotherhoods of the Sanusi movement. Qaddafi was personally an austere and devout Muslim, and he often expressed his desire to increase the role of Islam as a cultural and religious factor in international affairs.

Policy innovation

Despite the early continuity between the monarchical and revolutionary regimes, the most striking aspect of Qaddafi's foreign policy vis-à-vis that of its predecessor remained the change it introduced. Qaddafi embarked on a broad range of new activities and objectives which had been rejected or actively opposed by the Idris regime. Moreover, he created new institutions and organizations, such as the Islamic Call Society and the Foreign Liaison Bureau, to accomplish his new policies.

In part because the monarchy was so vulnerable to external actors, Qaddafi was determined to pursue a more independent course. He removed Libya from a close association with the Western alliance system and placed it in a close, albeit tempestuous, relationship with the rival Arab system. As political ties with the Western democracies deteriorated, Qaddafi moved to replace them with growing ties to the east European communist states. In the process, he blurred the traditional concept of positive neutrality, openly and repeatedly advocating membership of the Warsaw Pact. Nevertheless, Qaddafi completely failed to develop the sustained credibility necessary to become a truly independent actor on the world stage. Cynical Libyans remained wont to inquire what kind of freedom came from selling oil to the Western democracies in order to buy arms from the communist states.

Whereas the monarchy was wary of Egypt and viewed Arab nationalism as a competing ideology, Qaddafi sought to succeed Nasser as its principal spokesman. Embracing Arab nationalism, he assigned the movement a central place in Libyan foreign policy. He also revived Islam as a key element of Arab nationalism. While this development paralleled the growth of Islamic fundamentalism, Qaddafi was not, as some suggested, a precursor of that movement, since his variant of Islam bore only a limited relationship to the mainstream religion. Instead, his emphasis on Islam was based on the belief that the Arab revolution must be an Islamic one because the Arab and Islamic identities were intertwined. While Qaddafi insisted on an Islamic base for his approach to Arab nationalism, Libyan foreign policy was never controlled by Islamic precepts. Like Nasser, Qaddafi used Islam as an instrument of the revolution to advance its objectives.

On the Palestinian issue, Qaddafi not only moved Libya from sympathy to active support, but also placed the issue in the forefront of Libyan policy. He viewed Palestine as an integral part of the Arab nation and argued that the latter could not be free until Palestine was free. In terms of Arab unity, Qaddafi endorsed the discarded idea that the Arabs had to unite before they could hope to free Palestine. He obstinately stuck to this position as growing numbers of Palestinians concluded that the freedom of Palestine would precede and thus advance Arab unity. Qaddafi also eagerly endorsed the concept of a war of total liberation, advocating direct armed action against Israel even as most Palestinians explored other alternatives. Of course, Qaddafi's military support for the Palestinian and other liberation movements was also self-serving as it brought much coveted attention and prestige to a state of otherwise limited, fleeting importance.

In Africa, the objectives of the revolutionary regime reflected the depth and breadth of its expanded interests. Whereas the monarchy had focused primarily on the propagation of Islam, Qaddafi pursued a wide-ranging policy which included a reduction in the Israeli presence, opposition to Western interests and influence, and increased local control over the continent's resources. In addition to creating new organizations and institutions tailored to support its objectives in the region, Libya also played a more active role in existing organizations such as the Organization of African Unity.

Constant principles

After 1969, Libyan foreign policy was conducted on the basis of fairly constant principles. On issues such as Arab nationalism and Arab unity, Qaddafi established a position at the outset of the revolution; and he refused to modify it despite changing political realities in the Middle East and Africa. Indeed, the bizarre quality of Libyan foreign policy often derived from its utter certainty and constancy.

Concerning Arab nationalism, Qaddafi patterned the content and emphasis of his approach on the Nasser of the early years of the Egyptian revolution. Hence, while it was simplistic to label Qaddafi's total revolution anachronistic, his policy on Arab nationalism certainly belonged to an earlier time. Even after the 1982 Beirut war aptly demonstrated the limits of pan-Arabism, Qaddafi continued to articulate a stand on Arab nationalism largely drawn from speeches delivered by Nasser 30 years earlier.

In particular, Qaddafi adopted the common Arab nationalist viewpoint on the Palestinian issue, seizing on *jihad* as the only appropriate solution to the problem. Over the years, neither his assessment of the issue nor his solution changed appreciably. Faced with shifts in strategy and tactics, Qaddafi remained the confirmed rejectionist, refusing to negotiate with Israel. When his insistence on armed struggle put him at odds with the mainstream Fatah leadership of the Palestinian movement, he shifted his support to more radical Palestinian factions. A founding member of the Steadfastness and Confrontation Front, Libya was also a frequent host to conferences of the more radical member groups of the PLO.

As Qaddafi shifted Libyan support towards the more extreme Palestinian organizations, he also increased his support for other revolutionary movements. Unable or unwilling to differentiate between support for liberation movements and state-sponsored terrorism, he supported both long after other states found alternative approaches more practical and effective. In the process, he moved closer politically to the governments of Syria and Iran, the other two radical regimes in the region. In addition to giving bilateral support which was difficult to identify and quantify, he hosted a series of multilateral conferences for the world's dissident organizations, parties, groups and movements, including two elaborate meetings in 1983 and 1986 and a smaller one in 1987. Qaddafi's emphasis on *jihad* was destabilizing regionally and globally, since Libya often intervened aggressively in the domestic affairs of other states in pursuit of its objectives.

Tactical flexibility

To appreciate fully the nature and extent of the policy changes initiated by Qaddafi, it was important to distinguish clearly policy from tactics. The failure to do so was one of the major reasons why the origins and consistency of Libyan foreign policy were so widely misunderstood. Under Qaddafi, the focus of Libyan foreign policy often moved from one issue or geographical area to another. While such tactical shifts were sometimes influenced by domestic policy, more often they were dependent on where external opportunities — or obstacles — were the greatest. The cyclical nature of Libyan foreign policy, most notable in terms of the quest for Arab unity, tended to mask Qaddafi's inflexibility on that issue and others. It also caused analysts to underestimate Libya's continuing involvement in geographical areas like sub-Saharan Africa.

Initially, Libyan interest in Arab union focused on the Mashrek. In 1969–73, Qaddafi engaged in intense, prolonged negotiations with Egypt, Sudan and Syria. At the same time, he decried regionalism as represented by periodical consultations in the Maghreb aimed at increased political or economic co-operation. Unable to achieve comprehensive unity in the

Mashrek, Qaddafi later turned his attention to the Maghreb with the January 1974 proposal for total union with Tunisia. However, this tactical shift was not as abrupt as some observers suggested. While adamantly opposed to regionalism, Qaddafi had already tried to bring the Maghreb into union discussions in the early 1970s. Algeria had been invited to join the Federation of Arab Republics in 1971, and Qaddafi first proposed an immediate union with Tunisia in late 1972.

In 1975–80, Qaddafi continued to advocate Arab unity but more as a long-term goal than an immediately achievable objective. With Libya's diplomatic relations with most Mashrek states strained, practical efforts were limited and focused on the Sahara and Sahel as well as North Africa. A mutual defence pact was concluded with Algeria in 1975; and in early 1978 Qaddafi again proposed union with Tunisia. In the interim, a series of meetings were held with Saharan and Sahelian neighbours aimed at greater regional co-operation. In 1980 comprehensive union with Syria was announced, a move which appeared to presage a tactical shift to the Mashrek but soon proved aberrant. In 1981–84, Qaddafi's efforts at Arab unity continued to focus on the Sahara. A brief union with Chad was proclaimed in January 1981; and in August 1984 Libya and Morocco announced an alliance which endured for some two years. At the same time, Qaddafi continued to promote wider co-operation with Tunisia and Algeria; but significant policy differences thwarted advancement. Additional progress towards Arab unity subsequently eluded Qaddafi despite his announcement in 1984 that the 1971 Federation of Arab Republics was being resurrected and union proposals with Sudan in 1985 and 1986.

Libyan involvement in sub-Saharan Africa, especially in key areas such as Chad and the Western Sahara, was also marked by tactical shifts in policy and emphasis. Libyan foreign policy tended to focus on Africa when its diplomatic efforts stalled in the Mashrek and Maghreb. Examples are the periods from late-1972 to 1974, from 1976 to 1981 and from 1983 to 1987. Of course, such cycles between geographical areas were only approximate, since Libyan foreign policy was also opportunistic and tried to react to apparent political openings in countries such as Uganda and the Central African Republic. Moreover, a recognition of peak periods of Libyan involvement in the region should not obscure the depth and breadth of Libya's continuing involvement in Africa after 1969. While its initial overtures were hesitant, early success led to a substantial, sustained involvement in the economic and political affairs of the region.

The tactical flexibility of Libyan foreign policy contributed to its contradictory nature. While the Libyan government preached Arab unity, it severely restricted Arab immigration and often harassed Arab expatriates working in Libya. In Eritrea and again during the Gulf war, it took the non-Arab side in international disputes. While it condemned neo-colonialism and imperialism, its policies in north and central Africa were widely viewed by its neighbours as designed to establish Libyan hegemony if not Libyan control. While it advocated self-determination, it sought to subvert a variety of governments in Africa and the Middle East simply because they rejected the socio-economic and political theories outlined in *The Green Book*. Abroad, commitment to the Islamic cause was compromised in Afghanistan, where affinity with the Soviet Union led to support for anti-Islamic forces. Finally, while the government condemned the Western way of life, the Qaddafi regime bought Western technology and invested the profits from the sale of petroleum in Western economies.

Political isolation

Innovative but doctrinaire, Qaddafi's foreign policy was also singularly unsuccessful. Leaders in the Arab world generally ignored its emphasis on Arab nationalism while condemning the distortion and misuse of Islam. In pursuit of Arab, African and Islamic unity, Libyan policies were most often a source of discord and disunity. While Qaddafi made the Palestinian issue a focal point of Libyan foreign policy, his government never played a significant role in the wider search for a viable solution to the problem. Similarly, he never equalled his mentor, Nasser, in his ability to play off one major power bloc against the other. As for the Third Universal Theory, it was widely dismissed throughout the Third World as simplistic, idiosyncratic and irrelevant.

Qaddafi sought a wider role for Libya in regional and global affairs, but the policies he pursued progressively isolated his regime. Libya's relations with its North African neighbours were mercurial; and after the dissolution of the Arab-African Union with Morocco, it enjoyed normal diplomatic ties only with Algeria. In the Arab east, Qaddafi's radical policies, in particular his insistence on a violent solution to the Palestinian problem, alienated Libya from much of the region's leadership. In Africa, Qaddafi was the first political leader to be denied the chairmanship of the Organization of African Unity, and the Chadian rout of Libyan forces in the spring of 1987 was a humiliating political and military defeat. Elsewhere, Qaddafi's association with state-sponsored terrorism distanced Libya from the Western democracies as well as its erstwhile allies in the communist bloc.

Intent on reshaping the world, Libyan foreign policy today is in retreat around the globe. A variety of factors combined to produce the current state of bankruptcy. Externally as well as internally, the Qaddafi regime took a simplistic approach to problems of overwhelming complexity. For a time, oil wealth tended to mask the undesirable, inappropriate and hostile aspects of Libyan foreign policy; however, Qaddafi found it increasingly difficult to establish a satisfactory relationship now between aspirations and accomplishments. As the regime's frustration mounted, Qaddafi faced repeated opportunities to reorient Libyan foreign policy to address the changing political realities in the international environment. Instead, he chose to endorse the same policies and repeat the same errors which had caused his growing political isolation. Hence, it was the inflexibility of Qaddafi more than any other factor which was responsible for the singular lack of success of Libyan foreign policy.

Notes

Chapter 1

1. Ronald Bruce St John, 'The Determinants of Libyan Foreign Policy', *The Maghreb Review*, 8, 3-4 (May–August 1983): 96-97.

2. Majid Khadduri, *Modern Libya: A Study in Political Development* (Baltimore: Johns Hopkins Press, 1963), 111-140.

3. Fouad Ajami, 'Stress in the Arab Triangle', *Foreign Policy*, 29 (Winter 1977-78): 91. Qaddafi's remark invites comparison with the observation attributed to the German writer Bertolt Brecht, that if the rulers cannot get along with the people they will just have to elect a new people.

4. Gus H. Goudarzi, *Geology and Mineral Resources of Libya — A Reconnaissance*, Geological Survey Professional Paper 660 (Washington: United States Government Printing Office, 1970), 2-18.

5. Benjamin Higgins, *Economic Development: Problems, Principles and Policies*, revised edition (New York: W.W. Norton, 1968), 26.

6. Nathan Alexander [Ronald Bruce St John], 'The Foreign Policy of Libya: Inflexibility Amid Change', *Orbis*, 24, 4 (Winter 1981): 821-824.

7. Elizabeth R. Hayford, 'The Politics of the Kingdom of Libya in Historical Perspective' (unpublished PhD dissertation, Tufts University, 1971): 401-402 and 469-470.

8. Mohammed Zahi el-Mogherbi, 'Arab Nationalism and Political Instability in Monarchical Libya: A Study in Political Ideology' (unpublished MA thesis, Kansas State University, 1973): 2-3, 15-41 and 92-96.

9. John Norman, *Labor and Politics in Libya and Arab Africa* (New York: Bookman Associates, 1965), 174.

10. In October 1969 Qaddafi emphasized that the 1967 war was one of the factors that precipitated the revolution. Mirella Bianco, *Gadafi: Voice from the Desert* (London: Longman, 1975), 68.

11. Ruth First, *Libya: The Elusive Revolution* (Harmondsworth: Penguin, 1974), 18, 84-85 and 198-199.

12. Nicola A. Ziadeh, *Sanusiyah: A Study of a Revivalist Movement in Islam* (Leiden: E.J. Brill, 1968 [1958]), 27; E.E. Evans-Pritchard, *The Sanusi of Cyrenaica* (Oxford: Oxford University Press, 1973), 228-229; Salaheddin S. Hasan, 'The Genesis of the Political Leadership of Libya, 1952-1969: Historical Origins and Development of Its Component Elements' (unpublished PhD dissertation, George Washington University, 1970): 63; Benjamin Rivlin, 'Unity and Nationalism in Libya', *The Middle East Journal*, III, 1 (January 1949): 31.

13. Khadduri, *Modern Libya*, 111-140 and 330-333; F. LaMond Tullis, *Politics and Social Change in Third World Countries* (New York: John Wiley, 1973), 187-188; Mustafa S. el-Ghariani, 'Libya's Foreign Policy: The Role of the Country's Environmental and Leadership Factors, 1960-1973' (unpublished MA thesis, Western Michigan University, 1979): 13.

14. Rivlin, 'Unity and Nationalism in Libya', 34-42; Hayford, 'The Politics of the

Kingdom of Libya in Historical Perspective', 17; William H. Lewis and Robert Gordon, 'Libya after Two Years of Independence', *The Middle East Journal*, VIII, 1 (Winter 1954): 49-51; Frank Ralph Golino, 'Patterns of Libyan National Identity', *The Middle East Journal*, 24, 2 (Summer 1970): 338-352.

15. I. William Zartman, *Government and Politics in North Africa* (New York: Praeger, 1963), 85; Khadduri, *Modern Libya*, V, 9-10, and 334-337.

16. Ali Muhammad Shembesh, 'The Analysis of Libya's Foreign Policy, 1962–1973: A Study of the Impact of Environmental and Leadership Factors' (unpublished PhD dissertation, Emory University, 1975): 188-189; Salaheddin Hasan Sury, 'The Political Development of Libya 1952–1969: Institutions, Policies and Ideology', in *Libya since Independence: Economic and Political Development*, ed. J.A. Allan (London: Croom Helm, 1982), 128-132.

17. 'The Libyan Revolution in the Words of Its Leaders: Proclamations, Statements, Addresses, Declarations and Interviews from September 1 to Announcement of the Counter-Plot (December 10)', *The Middle East Journal*, 24, 2 (Spring 1970): 203.

18. Meredith O. Ansell and Ibrahim Massaud al-Arif, eds., *The Libyan Revolution: A Sourcebook of Legal and Historical Documents*, Vol. I: *1 September 1969 – 30 August 1970* (Stoughton, Wisconsin: The Oleander Press, 1972), 63-69.

19. Henri Habib, *Politics and Government of Revolutionary Libya* (Ottawa: Le Cercle du Livre de France, 1975), 96.

20. Jacques Roumani, 'From Republic to Jamahiriya: Libya's Search for Political Community', *The Middle East Journal*, 37, 2 (Spring 1983): 163-168; First, *Libya*, 218.

Chapter 2

1. William L. Cleveland, 'Sources of Arab Nationalism: An Overview', *Middle East Review*, XI, 3 (Spring 1979): 25-33.

2. William L. Cleveland, *Islam Against the West: Shakib Arslan and the Campaign for Islamic Nationalism* (London: Al Saqi Books, 1985), XVI; Nikki R. Keddie, *An Islamic Response to Imperialism: Political and Religious Writings of Sayyid Jamal al-Din al-Afghani*, 2nd ed. (Berkeley: University of California Press, 1983), 36-53.

3. Cleveland, *Islam Against the West*, 40 and 45; George Antonius, *The Arab Awakening: The Story of the Arab National Movement* (New York: Capricorn Books, 1965), 276-412.

4. Albert Hourani, *Arabic Thought in the Liberal Age, 1798–1939* (Cambridge: Cambridge University Press, 1983), 278-279; Majid Khadduri, *Political Trends in the Arab World: The Role of Ideas and Ideals in Politics* (Baltimore: Johns Hopkins Press, 1970), 199.

5. Maxime Rodinson, *The Arabs* (Chicago: University of Chicago Press, 1981), 92-93; Cleveland, 'Sources of Arab Nationalism', 27; Najm A. Bezirgan, 'Islam and Arab Nationalism', *Middle East Review*, IX, 2 (Winter 1978–1979): 38-39.

6. William B. Quandt, Fuad Jabber and Ann Mosley Lesch, *The Politics of Palestinian Nationalism* (Berkeley: University of California Press, 1973), 7-42; Rodinson, *The Arabs*, 96-100; Hourani, *Arabic Thought*, 291-294.

7. Hayford, 'The Politics of the Kingdom of Libya in Historical Perspective', 100 and 110; Lisa Anderson, *The State and Social Transformation in Tunisia and Libya, 1830–1980* (Princeton: Princeton University Press, 1986), 251-252. While Arab

nationalist leaders such as Shakib Arslan actively protested at the Italian subjugation of Libya, there is little evidence to support Hayford's suggestion that the demand for a united and independent Libya became a popular Arab issue second only in intensity to the Palestinian question. Ibid., 100.

8. Cleveland, *Islam Against the West*, XX; Hourani, *Arabic Thought*, 295-297 and 313-316; Bezirgan, 'Islam and Arab Nationalism', 40-41; Anouar Abdel-Malek, ed., *Contemporary Arab Political Thought* (London: Zed Books, 1983), 138-140.

9. Khadduri, *Modern Libya*, 83-84; Hayford, 'The Politics of the Kingdom of Libya in Historical Perspective', 143-144; William R. Polk, *The United States and the Arab World*, 3rd ed. (Cambridge: Harvard University Press, 1976), 205.

10. Hisham B. Sharabi, *Nationalism and Revolution in the Arab World* (Princeton: D. Van Nostrand, 1966), 56-66.

11. R. Hrair Dekmejian, *Egypt Under Nasir: A Study in Political Dynamics* (Albany: State University of New York Press, 1971), 49-51; Nissim Rejwan, *Nasserist Ideology: Its Exponents and Critics* (Jerusalem: Israel Universities Press, 1974), 1-8 and 70-90; Leonard Binder, 'Ideological Foundations of Egyptian-Arab Nationalism', in *Ideology and Discontent*, ed. David E. Apter (New York: The Free Press of Glencoe, 1964), 128-154.

12. George Lenczowski, *The Middle East in World Affairs*, 4th ed. (Ithaca: Cornell University Press, 1980), 536; P.J. Vatikiotis, *Nasser and His Generation* (New York: St. Martin's Press, 1978), 232-233 and 244; Dekmejian, *Egypt Under Nasir*, 40, 43 and 93; Robert A. Divine, *Eisenhower and the Cold War* (New York: Oxford University Press, 1981), 80-83 and 91-92.

13. Lenczowski, *The Middle East in World Affairs*, 537-539; Rodinson, *The Arabs*, 110-115; Carl Leiden, 'Arab Nationalism Today', *Middle East Review*, XI, 2 (Winter 1978–1979): 48.

14. James B. Mayfield, *Rural Politics in Nasser's Egypt: A Quest for Legitimacy* (Austin: University of Texas Press, 1971), 102-116; P.J. Vatikiotis, *The History of Egypt*, 2nd ed. (Baltimore: Johns Hopkins University Press, 1980), 399-402; Jean Leca, 'Algerian Socialism: Nationalism, Industrialization, and State-Building', in *Socialism in the Third World*, eds. Helen Desfosses and Jacques Levesque (New York: Praeger, 1975), 121-160.

15. Fouad Ajami, 'The End of Pan-Arabism', *Foreign Affairs*, 57, 2 (Winter 1978–1979): 357.

16. Dekmejian, *Egypt Under Nasir*, 303; Vatikiotis, *The History of Egypt*, 406; Qandt, Jabber and Lesch, *The Politics of Palestinian Nationalism*, 45-51.

17. Qaddafi's subsequent practice of repeating Nasser's speeches almost verbatim became a standing joke in the Arab world. Sensitive to such criticism, Qaddafi later described the Libyan revolution as a continuation of the Egyptian revolution but not a mirror image. Ansell and al-Arif, *The Libyan Revolution*, 280.

18. Mu'Ammar Qathafi, *Discourses* (Valletta: Adam Publishers, 1975), 129; Ansell and al-Arif, *The Libyan Revolution*, 83; Hervé Bleuchot, 'Les fondements de l'idéologie du Colonel Mouammar el-Kadhafi', *Meghreb*, 46 (March/April 1974): 21-27.

19. The Libyan Arab Republic, Delivered by Col. Mo'ammar el-Gadhafi, *1. The Broadlines of the Third Theory; 2. The Aspects of the Third Theory; 3. The Concept of Jihad; 4. The Divine Concept of Islam* (Tripoli: Ministry of Information and Culture,

1973), 41-42; *The Jamahiriya Mail* (Tripoli), 18 November 1978; United States Department of Commerce, Foreign Broadcast Information Service, *Daily Report: Middle East and North Africa (FBIS-MEA)*, 4 March 1981, I10; 4 March 1982, Q3. For a copy of the 1969 constitutional proclamation, see Rawle Farley, *Planning for Development in Libya: The Exceptional Economy in the Developing World* (New York: Praeger, 1971), 313-320.

20. Fouad Ajami, *The Arab Predicament: Arab Political Thought and Practice Since 1967* (Cambridge: Cambridge University Press, 1981), 200.

21. Mu'ammar al-Qadhdhafi, 'A Visit to Fezzan', in *Man, State, and Society in the Contemporary Maghrib*, ed. I. William Zartmann (New York: Praeger, 1973), 131-132; Ansell and al-Arif, *The Libyan Revolution*, 88; 'The Libyan Revolution in the Words of Its Leaders', 204.

22. Ansell and al-Arif, *The Libyan Revolution*, 217-218; El-Gadhafi, *The Broadlines of the Third Theory*, 28-29; Ronald Bruce St John, 'The Ideology of Mu'ammar al-Qadhdhafi: Theory and Practice', *International Journal of Middle East Studies*, 15, 4 (November 1983): 474.

23. *FBIS-MEA*, 3 March 1986, Q2; Ahmed M. Ashiurakis, *A Concise History of the Libyan Struggle for Freedom* (Tripoli: General Publishing, Distributing and Advertising Co., 1976), 82-87; William H. Lewis, 'Libya: The End of Monarchy', *Current History* (January 1970): 38; Hayford, 'The Politics of the Kingdom of Libya in Historical Perspective', 425 and 483-484.

24. Ansell and al-Arif, *The Libyan Revolution*, 67; *FBIS-MEA*, 6 March 1979, I2.

25. J.A. Allan, *Libya: The Experience of Oil* (London: Croom Helm, 1981), 222; *FBIS-MEA*, 22 January 1981, I2.

26. Ansell and al-Arif, *The Libyan Revolution*, 87. In September 1972, the RCC created a Higher Council for National Guidance to guarantee a unity of thought among citizens with regard to their roles in and responsibilities towards the revolution. Libyan Arab Republic, Ministry of Information and Culture, *The Revolution of 1st September: The Fourth Anniversary* (Benghazi: The General Administration for Information, 1973), 174-181.

27. El-Gadhafi, *The Broadlines of the Third Theory*, 14; The Embassy of the Libyan Arab Republic, 'Interview with Colonel Kaddafi', *Progressive Libya*, 5, 9-10 (May-June 1976): 1-2; St John, 'The Ideology of Mu'ammar al-Qadhdhafi', 475. Hajjar has argued that Qaddafi's political theory was part of a tradition of radical democratic thought initiated by Rousseau and that the source of Qaddafi's ideas was *The Social Contract*. Sami J. Hajjar, 'The Jamahiriya Experiment in Libya: Qadhafi and Rousseau', *The Journal of Modern African Studies*, 18, 2 (June 1980): 181-200.

28. Muammar Al Qathafi, *The Green Book, Part III: The Social Basis of the Third Universal Theory* (Tripoli: Public Establishment for Publishing, Advertising and Distribution, 1979); 'Gathafi's Press Conference in Paris', *Progressive Libya*, 3, 3-4 (November-December 1973): 4. The economic aspects of the Third Universal Theory were based on Qaddafi's approach to socialism.

29. *FBIS-MEA*, 16 May 1973, T1-T9 and 12 August 1980, I1; The Libyan Arab Republic, Ministry of Information and Culture, *The Fundamentals of the Third International Theory* (Tripoli: The General Administration for Information, 1974), 3 and 14-16; Qathafi, *Discourses*, 135-136.

30. At different times, both the Yemen Arab Republic and Burkina Faso have shown some interest in establishing a Jamahiriya along the lines of the Third Universal Theory. *FBIS-MEA*, 5 March 1986, Q20.

31. United States Department of Commerce, Office of Technical Services, *Joint Publications Research Service (JPRS)*, 'Al-Qadhdhafi Ties His Policies to Koran', 70813, No. 1772 (21 February 1978): I30; John F. Devlin, *The Baath Party: A History from Its Origins to 1966* (Stanford: Hoover Institution Press, 1976), 7-15.

32. El-Gadhafi, *The Aspects of the Third Theory*, 38.

33. Raymond N. Habiby, 'Mu'amar Qadhafi's New Islamic Scientific Socialist Society', in *Religion and Politics in the Middle East*, ed. Michael Curtis (Boulder: Westview Press, 1981), 250.

34. El-Gadhafi, *The Divine Concept of Islam*, 86-117; Harold D. Nelson, ed., *Libya: A Country Study*, 3rd ed. (Washington: The American University, 1979), 175; Libyan Arab Republic, Ministry of Information and Culture, *The Third International Theory: The Divine Concept of Islam and the Popular Revolution in Libya* (Tripoli: The General Administration for Information, 1973), 11-15.

35. *FBIS-MEA*, 21 August 1980, I2-I6.

36. Ajami, *The Arab Predicament*, 61; Khadduri, *Political Trends*, 194-198; Leonard Binder, *The Ideological Revolution in the Middle East* (New York: John Wiley, 1964), I68.

37. Ziadeh, *Sanusiyah*, 3, 80-81 and 86-87; Hasan, 'The Genesis of the Political Leadership of Libya, 1952–1969', 57; Roumani, 'From Republic to Jamahiriya', 166-167.

38. Anderson, *The State and Social Transformation*, 262; Marius K. Deeb and Mary Jane Deeb, *Libya since the Revolution: Aspects of Social and Political Development* (New York: Praeger, 1982), 98.

39. Deeb and Deeb, *Libya since the Revolution*, 99-100; Ann Elizabeth Mayer, 'Islamic Resurgence or New Prophethood: The Role of Islam in Qadhdhafi's Ideology', in *Islamic Resurgence in the Arab World*, ed. Ali E. Hillal Dessouki (New York: Praeger, 1982), 196-198.

40. Mayer, 'Islamic Resurgence', 198; Ann Mayer, 'Developments in the Law of Marriage and Divorce in Libya since the 1969 Revolution', *Journal of African Law*, 22, 1 (Spring 1978), 30-49.

41. Qathafi, *Discourses*, 122; Deeb and Deeb, *Libya since the Revolution*, 101-103; *The Jamahiriya Mail* (Tripoli), 18 November 1978; Habiby, 'Mu'amar Qadhafi's New Islamic Scientific Socialist Society', 248-254.

42. El-Gadhafi, *The Aspects of the Third Theory*, 42-43; *JPRS*, 70813, No. 1772 (21 March 1978): 130-131, 135-136 and 140; *FBIS-MEA*, 14 July 1980, I1; Raymond A. Hinnebusch, 'Charisma, Revolution, and State Formation: Qaddafi and Libya', *Third World Quarterly*, 6, 1 (January 1984): 70-71. For an analysis of the legal implications of Qaddafi's remarks, see Mayer, 'Islamic Resurgence', 202-218.

43. Shembesh, 'The Analysis of Libya's Foreign Policy, 1962–1973', 202; Nelson, *Libya*, 167.

44. Deeb and Deeb, *Libya since the Revolution*, 103.

45. Gamal Abdul Nasser, *Egypt's Liberation: The Philosophy of the Revolution* (Washington: Public Affairs Press, 1955), 111-114; Dekmejian, *Egypt Under Nasir*, 132-133; Rejwan, *Nasserist Ideology*, 34-39.

46. Morroe Berger, *Islam in Egypt Today: Social and Political Aspects of Popular Religion* (Cambridge: Cambridge University Press, 1970), 46–47, 60–61 and 128–129; Vatikiotis, *Nasser*, 229.

47. *FBIS-MEA*, 5 March 1986, Q1–Q22; 25 September 1985, Q1–Q8; 25 January 1982, Q4; Deeb and Deeb, *Libya since the Revolution*, 103–104.

Chapter 3

1. 'The Libyan Revolution in the Words of its Leaders', 214–215 and 218–219.

2. Quandt, Jabber and Lesch, *The Politics of Palestinian Nationalism*, 7–42 and 45–51; Ansel and al-Arif, *The Libyan Revolution*, 74–75.

3. El-Gadhafi, *The Concept of Jihad*, 53; The Libyan Arab Republic, Ministry of Information and Culture, *Aspects of First of September Revolution* (Tripoli: The General Administration for Information, 1973), 5–9.

4. Ansell and al-Arif, *The Libyan Revolution*, 115–117.

5. Ibid., 131; Daniel Pipes, 'No One Likes the Colonel', *The American Spectator*, 14, 3 (March 1981): 18–22.

6. *FBIS-MEA*, 22 May 1979, I1–I2; Colin Legum, 'Recruiting to Reform the World', *International Herald Tribune* (Zurich), 26–27 April 1986; *Jeune Afrique*, No. 1315 (19 March 1986): 49.

7. Nelson, *Libya*, 186; First, *Libya*, 218–219.

8. Qathafi, *Discourses*, 32–33, 43–46 and 100–101; Eric Rouleau, 'The Palestinian Quest', *Foreign Affairs*, 53, 2 (January 1975): 264–283.

9. Richard H. Sanger, *Libya's Multi-Step Revolution*, Middle East Problem Paper No. 8 (Washington: The Middle East Institute, 1974), 9; Sam Younger, 'Qaddafi: Faith and Freedom', *Middle East International*, 25 (July 1973): 14; Qathafi, *Discourses*, 32 and 37. Earlier, Qaddafi had favoured conventional warfare. First, *Libya*, 231.

10. *FBIS-MEA*, 7 January 1982, Q8 and 18 November 1982, Q2.

11. Nelson, *Libya*, 186–187; Walter Laqueur, *Terrorism*, Abacus edition (London: Sphere Books, 1978), 236–237; *FBIS-MEA*, 4 March 1981, I11.

12. The Libyan Arab Republic, *Aspects of First of September Revolution*, 4 and 20–21; Laqueur, *Terrorism*, 248–249; Nelson, *Libya*, 179 and 186–187.

13. Quandt, Jabber and Lesch, *The Politics of Palestinian Nationalism*, 157 and 176; Eric Rouleau, *Les Palestiniens* (Paris: Editions la Découverte, 1984), 26–28.

14. Helena Cobban, *The Palestinian Liberation Organization: People, Power and Politics* (Cambridge: Cambridge University Press, 1984), 36–53; Quandt, Jabber and Lesch, *The Politics of Palestinian Nationalism*, 52 and 179. From the start of their association, Fatah's leaders had explicitly rejected the idea of espousing a pan-Arabist or universalist ideology.

15. Cobban, *The Palestinian Liberation Organization*, 53; Rouleau, *Les Palestiniens*, 26–51. The September 1970 crisis in Jordan preoccupied the Libyan government, which first stopped economic aid to Jordan and then broke diplomatic relations.

16. Rouleau, 'The Palestinian Quest', 278.

17. Richard Clutterbuck, *Guerrillas and Terrorists* (London: Faber, 1977), 82–84; David Fromkin, 'The Strategy of Terrorism', *Foreign Affairs*, 53, 4 (July 1975): 695–697.

18. Qathafi, *Discourses*, 140–141; Amos Perlmutter, 'A Race Against Time: The Egyptian-Israeli Negotiations Over the Future of Palestine', *Foreign Affairs*, 57, 5

(Summer 1979): 1000-1001; Deeb and Deeb, *Libya since the Revolution*, 136.

19. Nelson, *Libya*, 187.

20. John Wright, *Libya: A Modern History* (Baltimore: Johns Hopkins University Press, 1982), 214; Nicole Grimaud, *La politique extérieure de l'Algérie* (Paris: Editions Karthala, 1984), 252; Jonathan Bearman, *Qadhafi's Libya* (London: Zed Books, 1986), 165-166.

21. *FBIS-MEA*, 17 February 1984, Q3-Q4; Arnold Hottinger, 'L'expansionnisme libyen: Machrek, Maghreb et Afrique noire', *Politique étrangère*, 46, 1 (March 1981): 144; David Blundy and Andrew Lycett, *Qaddafi and the Libyan Revolution* (London: Weidenfeld and Nicolson, 1987), 157.

22. Lisa Anderson, 'Libya and American Foreign Policy', *The Middle East Journal*, 36, 4 (Autumn 1983), 527-528; *Financial Times* (London), 27 June 1985; *Middle East Economic Digest (MEED)*, 29, 26, (29 June – 5 July 1985): 22. The most complete account of Musa al-Sadr is Fouad Ajami, *The Vanished Imam: Musa al-Sadr and the Shia of Lebanon* (Ithaca: Cornell University Press, 1986); *The Middle East*, No. 149 (March 1987): 19.

23. Deeb and Deeb, *Libya since the Revolution*, 136; Cobban, *The Palestinian Liberation Organization*, 93-94; Bearman, *Qadhafi's Libya*, 174.

24. Deeb and Deeb, *Libya since the Revolution*, 136-137.

25. *FBIS-MEA*, 2 January 1980, I1-I5.

26. Judith Miller, 'The PLO in Exile', *New York Times Magazine*, 18 August 1985: 30 and 63; John Kifner, 'Scattering of Rebels Cuts PLO Power', *International Herald Tribune* (Zurich), 21 November 1984; Rouleau, *Les Palestiniens*, 169-193.

27. Farid el-Khazen, 'The Middle East in Strategic Retreat', *Foreign Policy*, 64 (Autumn 1986): 154.

28. *New York Times*, 3 September 1982; *FBIS-MEA*, 25 September 1985, Q7.

29. *MEED*, 26, 38 (17-23 September 1982): 45; Bearman, *Qadhafi's Libya*, 180-181.

30. *MEED*, 27, 3 (21-27 January 1983): 2; *Wall Street Journal* (Europe), 12 January 1983, and 19 January 1983. For the text of President Reagan's address to the nation on the future of the West Bank and the Palestinians, see *New York Times*, 2 September 1982.

31. P. Edward Haley, *Qaddafi and the United States since 1969* (New York: Praeger, 1984), 306-308 and 317; *New York Times*, 21 April 1983, and 1 May 1983. Earlier, the Libyan government had extended a balance-of-payments loan to the Nicaraguan government.

32. *FBIS-MEA*, 23 March 1983, Q1-Q3, and 5 March 1984, Q5. Libya's continuing involvement in Lebanon occasionally strained Libyan-Syrian relations; but it did not, as Qaddafi hoped, enhance Libya's international position or cause other Arab states to recognize it as a front-line state in the struggle against Israel.

33. *FBIS-MEA*, 21 November 1983, Q1-Q2. Qaddafi's support for the Lebanese Shiites was not always repaid. In July 1984, a Shiite faction calling itself the Imam Sadr Brigades blew up part of the building housing the Libyan People's Bureau in Beirut. The group had been conducting a campaign against Libyan diplomats to protest at the 1978 disappearance of Imam Musa al-Sadr.

34. *FBIS-MEA*, 24 February 1984, Q1-Q2, and 7 March 1984, Q1-Q2; *MEED*, 28, 8 (24 February – 1 March 1984): 17.

35. *New York Times*, 2 September 1984; *International Herald Tribune* (Zurich), 3 September 1984, and 5 September 1984. Economist Intelligence Unit, *Quarterly Economic Review of Libya, Tunisia, Malta*, 4 (London: Economist Publications, 1984): 23.

36. *Wall Street Journal* (Europe), 25 November 1986; *MEED*, 30, 50 (13-19 December 1986): 22; *International Herald Tribune* (Zurich), 23 December 1986; *MEED*, 31, 10 (7-13 March 1987): 15; *Jeune Afrique*, No. 1365 (4 March 1987): 27.

37. Laqueur, *Terrorism*, 100; Claire Sterling, *The Terror Network* (New York: Holt, Rinehart and Winston, 1981), 258-271.

38. *The Times* (London), 4 March 1985 and 11 March 1985; *El País Internacional* (Madrid), 11 March 1985.

39. *La Suisse* (Geneva), 1 January 1986; *Wall Street Journal* (Europe), 2 January 1986, and 6 January 1986; *Financial Times* (London), 2 January 1986; *International Herald Tribune* (Zurich), 2 January 1986, and 6 January 1986.

40. *International Herald Tribune* (Zurich), 10 January 1986; 17 January 1986; 29 January 1986; and 5 March 1986; *Wall Street Journal* (Europe), 4 February 1986; *Jeune Afrique*, No. 1322 (7 May 1986): 48.

41. *Le Monde* (Paris), 11 April 1986; *International Herald Tribune* (Zurich), 5 March 1986; 7 April 1986; 11-12 April 1986; 18 April 1986; and 26-27 April 1986; *Jeune Afrique*, No. 1340 (10 September 1986): 28. In a later interview, Qaddafi admitted Libya was training freedom fighters, and repeated the threat made on 1 September and again at the Non-Aligned Movement conference in Zimbabwe, to raise an international army to fight the United States and its aggression. *International Herald Tribune* (Zurich), 17 October 1986.

42. *International Herald Tribune* (Zurich), 22 April 1987, and 2-3 May 1987; *The Times* (London), 2 May 1987.

Chapter 4

1. James A. Bill and Carl Leiden, *The Middle East: Politics and Power* (Boston: Allyn and Bacon, 1974), 259.

2. Al-Qadhdhafi, 'A Visit to Fezzan', 132-134.

3. First, *Libya*, 124.

4. Ansell and al-Arif, *The Libyan Revolution*, 74-75; Shembesh, 'The Analysis of Libya's Foreign Policy, 1962–1973', 51, 196-198 and 216-217; Juliette Bessis, *La Libye contemporaine* (Paris: L'Harmattan, 1986), 130.

5. Al-Qadhdhafi, 'A Visit to Fezzan', 134; 'The Libyan Revolution in the Words of its Leaders', 216.

6. Ansell and al-Arif, *The Libyan Revolution*, 66 and 74.

7. Daniel Pipes, *In the Path of God: Islam and Political Power* (New York: Basic Books, 1983), 154-155.

8. Ansell and al-Arif, *The Libyan Revolution*, 66.

9. First, *Libya*, 214-215.

10. Nelson, *Libya*, 176-177.

11. Anwar el-Sadat, *In Search of Identity* (London: William Collins, 1978), 216-217; Deeb and Deeb, *Libya since the Revolution*, 131.

12. Arnold Hottinger, 'Colonel Ghadhafi's Pan-Arab Ambitions', *Swiss Review of World Affairs*, XXI, 3 (June 1971): 24; First, *Libya*, 232-233.

13. First, *Libya*, 219-220; Nelson, *Libya*, 176-177.

14. Hottinger, 'Colonel Ghadhafi's Pan-Arab Ambitions', 23; Polk, *The United States*, 244; Peter Mansfield, *The Arabs* (London: Allen Lane, 1976), 506-508 and 444-445.

15. Michael C. Hudson, *Arab Politics: The Search for Legitimacy* (New Haven: Yale University Press, 1977), 334-335; Mansour Khalid, *Nimeiri and the Revolution of Dismay* (London: KPI, 1985), 318-322; William D. Brewer, 'The Libyan-Sudanese "Crisis" of 1981: Danger for Darfur and Dilemma for the United States', *The Middle East Journal*, 36, 2 (Spring 1982): 207-210.

16. Nelson, *Libya*, 177; First, *Libya*, 232-233.

17. Nelson, *Libya*, 184; Deeb and Deeb, *Libya since the Revolution*, 131; John K. Cooley, *Libyan Sandstorm: The Complete Account of Qaddafi's Revolution* (New York: Holt, Rinehart and Winston, 1982), 105.

18. Sadat, *In Search of Liberty*, 233.

19. Nelson, *Libya*, 179-181; First, *Libya*, 233-234; Deeb and Deeb, *Libya since the Revolution*, 131. Qaddafi was also actively promoting union between North and South Yemen in 1972.

20. Cooley, *Libyan Sandstorm*, 105-106; Qathafi, *Discourses*, 13-14; First, *Libya*, 235-236.

21. Bessis, *La Libye*, 111-113; Mansfield, *The Arabs*, 463-465; *Progressive Libya*, 2, 12 (August 1973): 1.

22. *Progressive Libya*, 3, 1 & 2 (September-October 1973): 1-2; Cooley, *Libyan Sandstorm*, 109.

23. Qathafi, *Discourses*, 30; *Progressive Libya*, 3, 1 & 2 (September-October 1973): 1 and 7; Fouad Ajami, 'Between Cairo and Damascus: The Arab World and the New Stalemate', *Foreign Affairs*, 54, 3 (April 1976): 449-450.

24. Qathafi, *Discourses*, 62-63 and 82-85; Ajami, 'Between Cairo and Damascus', 445 and 451; Deeb and Deeb, *Libya since the Revolution*, 134.

25. For example, see Hottinger, 'L'expansionnisme libyen', 144-145.

26. Brian Crozier, ed., *Libya's Foreign Adventures*, Conflict Studies No. 41 (London: The Institute for the Study of Conflict, 1973), 4-5; Nelson, *Libya*, 189-190; Grimaud, *La politique extérieure de l'Algérie*, 217-218.

27. The Libyan Arab Republic, Ministry of Information and Culture, *The Revolution of 1st September: The Fourth Anniversary* (Benghazi: n.p., 1973), 234; Bessis, *La Libye*, 131; Grimaud, *La politique extérieure de l'Algérie*, 213-244; Hottinger, 'Colonel Ghadhafi's Pan-Arab Ambitions', 22.

28. Nelson, *Libya*, 189-190; Hottinger, 'Colonel Ghadhafi's Pan-Arab Ambitions', 22.

29. Libyan Arab Republic, *The Revolution of 1st September*, 235; *Progressive Libya*, 2, 5 (January 1973): 1, 2 and 4; First, *Libya*, 229-230; Bernard Cohen, *Habib Bourguiba* (Paris: Flammarion, 1986), 131-132.

30. First, *Libya*, 245-246; Deeb and Deeb, *Libya since the Revolution*, 133.

31. John Damis, 'Prospects for Unity/Disunity in North Africa', *American-Arab Affairs*, 6 (Autumn 1983): 38; Qathafi, *Discourses*, 88-89; Cooley, *Libyan Sandstorm*, 125-126; Cohen, *Habib Bourguiba*, 134-141. A measure of Qaddafi's frustration over the lack of progress towards union was an April 1974 exchange of views with the Maltese government on the subject. Malta accepted Libyan aid but resisted efforts to

Arabize and Islamicize the island. Qathafi, *Discourses*, 60–61; Bessis, *La Libye*, 137–138.

32. Ajami, 'Between Cairo and Damascus', 447–448; Mohamed Hassanein Heikal, 'Egyptian Foreign Policy', *Foreign Affairs*, 56, 4 (July 1978): 725.

33. Ajami, 'The End of Pan-Arabism', 365–368.

34. Perlmutter, 'A Race Against Time', 989; Adeed I. Dawisha, 'Syria in Lebanon — Assad's Vietnam?', *Foreign Policy*, 33 (Winter 1978-79): 135; William B. Quandt, *Decade of Decisions* (Berkeley: University of California Press, 1977), 271–281). The most complete study of the Camp David accords is William B. Quandt, *Camp David: Peacemaking and Politics* (Washington, DC: The Brookings Institution, 1986).

35. Khalid, *Nimeiri*, 319; Hudson, *Arab Politics*, 324–325; Mohamed Heikal, *Autumn of Fury: The Assassination of Sadat* (London: Corgi, 1984), 102–103.

36. Grimaud, *La politique extérieure de l'Algérie*, 327–328; Wright, *Libya*, 208; Nourredine Abdi, 'Common Regional Policy for Algeria and Libya: From Maghribi Unity to Saharan Integration', in *Social and Economic Development of Libya*, eds. E.G.H. Joffé and K.S. McLachlan (Wisbech: Menas Press, 1982), 223–227.

37. Cooley, *Libyan Sandstorm*, 127–128; *MEED*, 25, 10 (6–12 March 1981): 43; Cohen, *Habib Bourguiba*, 140–141.

38. *FBIS-MEA*, 2 September 1980, I1-I4 and 10 September 1980, I5-I7.

39. John Kifner, 'Libya and Syria Proclaim a Merger and Call On Other Arabs to Join', *New York Times*, 11 September 1980; Susannah Tarbush, 'Syrian Economy: A Web of Politics and Red Tape', *MEED*, 24, 42 (17–23 October 1980): 6–8; *MEED*, 24, 42 (17–23 October 1980): 16–17. The Libya-Chad union is discussed in Chapter 6.

40. The new treaty of friendship and co-operation between Libya, Ethiopia and South Yemen was, in effect, an alliance against Western policy in the Indian Ocean and the Gulf. Syria, Algeria and the PLO were invited to participate in the negotiations but declined. Somalia immediately broke diplomatic relations with Libya over the treaty, terming it an unholy alliance. *New York Times*, 29 August 1981; Oye Ogunbadejo, 'Qaddafi's North African Design', *International Security*, VIII, 1 (Summer 1983): 168.

41. *MEED*, 25, 35 (28 August – 3 September 1981): 2; *FBIS-MEA*, 2 September 1981, Q4-Q5 and 10 September 1985, Q2.

42. *MEED*, 27, 10 (11–17 March 1983): 2; *International Herald Tribune* (Zurich), 5 April 1984.

43. Economist Intelligence Unit, *Quarterly Economic Review of Libya, Tunisia, Malta*, 2 (1984): 19 and 129; and 4 (1984): 22; *MEED*, 29, 36 (7–13 September 1985): 20.

44. Ann Mosely Lesch, 'Confrontation in the Southern Sudan', *The Middle East Journal*, 40, 3 (Summer 1986): 410–412; Cooley, *Libyan Sandstorm*, 209; William Gutteridge, ed., *Libya: Still a Threat to Western Interests?*, Conflict Studies No. 160 (London: The Institute for the Study of Conflict, 1984), 17; *FBIS-MEA* (29 March 1984): Q1-Q6; Brewer, 'The Libyan-Sudanese "Crisis" of 1981', 205–216.

45. *MEED*, 29, 21 (24–30 May 1985): 22; *MEED*, 29, 28 (13-19 July 1985): 22 and 27; *International Herald Tribune* (Zurich), 12 April 1985; 20 May 1985; and 15 July 1985; Lesch, 'Confrontation in the Southern Sudan', 422.

46. *Le Monde Diplomatique* (Paris), 12 October 1985; *MEED*, 30, 1 (4–10 January 1986): 25; *Africa Economic Digest (AED)*, 7, 16 (19-25 April 1986): 7–8; *Jeune Afrique*,

No. 1322 (7 May 1986): 33; *International Herald Tribune* (Zurich), 8 December 1986, and 20-21 December 1986.

47. L. Carl Brown, 'Tunisia: The Record since Independence', *American-Arab Affairs*, 6 (Autumn 1983): 80; Damis, 'Prospects for Unity/Disunity', 38; L.B. Ware, 'The Role of the Tunisian Military in the Post-Bourguiba Era', *The Middle East Journal*, 39, 1 (Winter 1985): 45-46.

48. *MEED*, 26, 9 (26 February – 4 March 1982): 3; Gutteridge, *Libya*, 9-10. The judgement put the offshore Bouri oil field in Libya's sector. While its total reserves are unknown, it should represent a substantial source of revenue in the late 1980s and 1990s when Libya's existing oilfields will begin to run down. The decision encouraged Libya to pursue a similar dispute with Algeria.

49. *New York Times*, 1 March 1982; *FBIS-MEA* (3 December 1982): Q1.

50. *MEED*, 27, 14 (8-14 April 1983): 35; *FBIS-MEA* (5 December 1983): Q1-Q2.

51. *FBIS-MEA* (14 May 1984): Q3-Q4.

52. *FBIS-MEA* (17 February 1984): Q2.

53. *MEED*, 29, 19 (10-16 May 1985): 47; *MEED*, 29, 25 (22-28 June 1985): 27; Bessis, *La Libye*, 154.

54. Damis, 'Prospects for Unity/Disunity', 42-44; John P. Entelis, 'Algeria in World Politics: Foreign Policy Orientation and the New International Economic Order', *American-Arab Affairs*, 6 (Autumn 1983): 70-78; *New York Times*, 29 January 1982.

55. Economist Intelligence Unit, *Quarterly Economic Review of Libya, Tunisia, Malta*, 4 (1984): 15-16; *El País Internacional* (Madrid), 7 May 1984.

56. John Damis, 'Morocco, Libya and the Treaty of Union', *American-Arab Affairs*, 13 (Summer 1985): 45-46.

57. Ibid., 46; Damis, 'Prospects for Unity/Disunity', 44.

58. Richard B. Parker, 'Appointment in Oujda', *Foreign Affairs*, 63, 5 (Summer 1985): 1099; William H. Lewis, 'Morocco and the Western Sahara', *Current History*, 84, 502 (May 1985): 216; *Le Monde* (Paris), 25 October 1984; 'Assessment of Moroccan-Libyan Unity Agreement', *JPRS-NEA* 86-018 (11 February 1986): 39-43.

59. Parker, 'Appointment in Oujda', 1100-1108; Lewis, 'Morocco and the Western Sahara', 216; Lisa Anderson, 'Assessing Libya's Qaddafi', *Current History*, 84, 502 (May 1985): 226; *International Herald Tribune* (Zurich), 18 March 1985. Concerning the Western Sahara, Libyan officials later revived a position taken by Qaddafi in the early 1970s when he had argued it was a mistake to create yet more Arab states from disputed territories when the real goal was greater Arab unity.

60. Parker, 'Appointment in Oujda', 1100; Lewis, 'Morocco and the Western Sahara', 216; *International Herald Tribune* (Zurich), 7 September 1984, and 18 March 1985; Robert S. Barrett, 'US Policy in North Africa', *American-Arab Affairs*, 13 (Summer 1985): 42.

61. *La Suisse* (Geneva), 31 August 1986; *Financial Times* (London), 1 September 1986; *Jeune Afrique*, No. 1340 (10 September 1986): 26-29.

62. *MEED*, 30, 5 (1-7 February 1986): 3; *MEED*, 30, 13 (29 March – 4 April 1986): 10; *FBIS-MEA*, 5 March 1986, Q20 and 2 May 1986, Q3-Q7.

63. Jean Raffaelli, 'La stratégie libyenne', *La Suisse* (Geneva), 1 September 1985; 'Bank Governor Discusses Labor Expulsions, Payment Delays', *JPRS-NEA* 86-029 (10 March 1986): 31-35; *MEED*, 30, 11 (15-21 March 1986): 25; *Jeune Afrique*, No.

1340 (10 September 1986): 26-29.

64. François Soudan and Mohamed Selhami, 'Algérie-Libye: Convergences et divergences', *Jeune Afrique*, No. 1354 (17 December 1986): 44-45; *MEED*, 30, 49 (6-12 December 1986): 2 and 23.

65. *FBIS-MEA* (5 March 1986): Q20.

66. *FBIS-MEA* (25 September 1985): Q2.

67. *FBIS-MEA* (5 March 1986): Q3 and Q16.

Chapter 5

1. St John, 'The Ideology of Mu'ammar al-Qadhdhafi', 479.

2. Dekmejian, *Egypt Under Nasir*, 109-118.

3. 'The Libyan Revolution in the Words of Its Leaders', 211-212.

4. Libyan Arab Republic, *The Fundamentals of the Third International Theory*, 5-6.

5. Nelson, *Libya*, 187-188; *FBIS-MEA* (2 September 1981): Q12-Q14 and (14 March 1984): Q5.

6. Qathafi, *Discourses*, 25-29, 47 and 87; Gadhafi, *Broadlines*, 9-14 and 23-26.

7. Claudio G. Segrè, *Fourth Shore: The Italian Colonization of Libya* (Chicago: University of Chicago Press, 1974), 173-177; Khadduri, *Modern Libya*, 111-140.

8. Arieh Yodfat, 'The USSR and Libya', *New Outlook*, 13, 6 (June 1970): 37-40.

9. James M. McConnell and Bradford Dismukes, 'Soviet Diplomacy of Force in the Third World', *Problems of Communism*, XXVIII, 1 (January-February 1979): 24. Although there were no legal grounds for British intervention, the RCC was apparently concerned that Britain might use as a pretext its pledge in the 1953 treaty to defend Libya's territorial integrity from outside attack.

10. Yodfat, 'The USSR and Libya', 38; Blundy and Lycett, *Qaddafi*, 60-61.

11. Ansell and al-Arif, *The Libyan Revolution*, 70; Qathafi, *Discourses*, 25-29, 47 and 87; Libyan Arab Republic, *The Revolution of 1st September*, 250.

12. Yodfat, 'The USSR and Libya', 39-40; Roger F. Pajak, 'Arms and Oil: The Soviet-Libyan Arms Supply Relationship', *Middle East Review*, XIII, 2 (Winter 1980-81): 51.

13. Richard H. Sanger, 'Libya: Conclusions on an Unfinished Revolution', *The Middle East Journal*, 29, 4 (Autumn 1975): 411-413; Pajak, 'Arms and Oil', 51-53.

14. 'Libya: Russian Rapprochement', *Africa Confidential*, 15 (31 May 1974): 2-3.

15. Deeb and Deeb, *Libya since the Revolution*, 134; Pajak, 'Arms and Oil', 53.

16. John C. Campbell, 'Communist Strategies in the Mediterranean', *Problems of Communism*, XXVIII, 3 (May-June 1979): 3-5, quote on 7; Wright, *Libya*, 216-217. To minimize its public involvement in arms transfers to Libya, the Soviet Union after 1974 channelled many of the sales and deliveries through East Germany. To ensure adequate spare parts, Libya felt obliged to improve its relations with other holders of large Soviet military stocks such as China, Romania, Yugoslavia and North Korea. Dennis Chaplin, 'Libya: Military Spearhead Against Sadat?', *Military Review*, 59, 11 (November 1979): 45.

17. *MEED*, 22, 48 (1-7 December 1978): 38; *FBIS-MEA* (5 October 1978): I4; Lisa Anderson, 'Qadhdhafi and the Kremlin', *Problems of Communism*, XXXIV, 5 (September-October 1985): 34-35; Pajak, 'Arms and Oil', 52-54.

18. Anderson, 'Qadhdhafi and the Kremlin', 35-36.

19. Fallaci, 'Iranians Are Our Brothers', 120; *FBIS-MEA* (12 October 1978): I6.

20. *FBIS-MEA* (22 July 1983): Q2 and (1 June 1983): Q5; Robert Bailey, 'Arab Armed Forces Expansion Brings Manpower Headaches', *MEED*, 25, 40 (2-9 October 1981): 26; Drew Middleton, 'A Soviet Peril: Bases in Libya', *New York Times*, 1 March 1981.

21. *FBIS-MEA* (29 April 1981): Q1 (30 April 1981): Q1-Q3 and (4 May 1981): Q4-Q5; Serge Schmemann, 'Qaddafi's Moscow Trip Ends in Amity', *New York Times*, 30 April 1981.

22. Anderson, 'Qadhdhafi', 38 and 41.

23. Edward Schumacher, 'The United States and Libya', *Foreign Affairs*, 65, 2 (Winter 1986-87): 345; *MEED*, 29, 37 (14-20 September 1985): 24; Dankwart A. Rustow, 'Realignments in the Middle East', *Foreign Affairs*, 63, 3 (1984): 593.

24. *MEED*, 29, 42 (19-25 October 1985): 30; *FBIS-MEA* (30 September 1985): Q3; Helen Kitchen, 'Africa: Year of Ironies', *Foreign Affairs*, 64, 3 (1986): 566-567.

25. *MEED*, 29, 42 (19-25 October 1985): 30 and 30, 14 (5-11 April 1986): 20; *International Herald Tribune* (Zurich), 11-12 January 1986; Lillian Craig Harris, *Libya: Qadhafi's Revolution and the Modern State* (Boulder: Westview Press, 1986), 99. In 1984 the Belgian government, under strong pressure from the United States, agreed not to enter into a nuclear co-operation agreement with Libya providing no other European country took the contract.

26. *MEED*, 29, 51/52 (21 December 1985 – 3 January 1986): 63; Kitchen, 'Africa', 566.

27. Hugo Sada, 'Libye-URSS: je t'aime, moi non plus', *Jeune Afrique*, No. 1339 (3 September 1986): 34-35; Jim Hoagland, 'One Winner of·Libya Raid: Gorbachev's Image', *International Herald Tribune* (Zurich), 23 April 1986.

28. Amir Taheri, 'Qu'est-ce que Kaddafi peut attendre de Moscou?', *Jeune Afrique*, No. 1327 (11 June 1986): 38-39; Schumacher, 'The United States and Libya', 345-346.

29. 'The Libyan Revolution in the Words of Its Leaders', 214-215; Wright, *Libya*, 214-216; First, *Libya*, 242.

30. Claudia Wright, 'Shadow on Sand: Strategy and Deception in Reagan's Policy towards the Arabs', *Journal of Palestine Studies*, 11, 3 (1982): 7 and 9-10; Nelson, *Libya*, 192-193; Ann T. Schulz, 'United States Policy in the Middle East', *Current History*, 74, 433 (January 1978): 2-3.

31. Haley, *Qaddafi*, 4-5 and 20-32; Parker, *North Africa*, 68. On the conspiracy theory, see Cooley, *Libyan Sandstorm*, 80 and 83, or I. William Zartman and A.G. Kluge, 'Heroic Politics: The Foreign Policy of Libya', in *The Foreign Policy of Arab States*, eds. Bahgat Korany and Ali E. Hillal Dessouki (Boulder: Westview Press, 1984), 187.

32. Haley, *Qaddafi*, 5-6; Schumacher, 'The United States and Libya', 334; Wright, 'Shadow on Sand', 26-27; Bernard Reich, 'United States Middle East Policy', *Current History*, 76, 443 (January 1979): 6-8 and 41-42.

33. Haley, *Qaddafi*, 5-6; Wright, *Libya*, 215-216.

34. Ellen Laipson, 'US Policy in Northern Africa', *American-Arab Affairs*, 6 (Autumn 1983): 51-52; Wright, 'Shadow on Sand', 26-27; Wright, *Libya*, 214-216.

35. Ronald Bruce St John, 'Terrorism and Libyan Foreign Policy', *The World Today*, 42, 7 (July 1986): 113; Barrett, 'US Policy in North Africa', 42; *New York Times*, 7 May 1981.

36. Wright, 'Libya and the West', 12-16; Haley, *Qaddafi*, 248-249; *New York Times*, 20 August 1981. The Gulf of Sirte is also known as the Gulf of Sidra.

37. Laipson, 'US Policy', 52-53; *New York Times*, 11 March 1982; *International Herald Tribune* (Zurich), 17-18 December 1983.

38. Wright, 'Libya', 14.

39. *International Herald Tribune* (Zurich), 9 January 1986 and 25-26 January 1986; *MEED*, 29, 19 (10-16 May 1985): 47 and 29, 47 (23-29 November 1985): 31.

40. *International Herald Tribune* (Zurich), 26 March 1986; J.L. Brierly, *The Law of Nations: An Introduction to the International Law of Peace*, 6th ed. (Oxford: Oxford University Press, 1963), 197-198.

41. *International Herald Tribune* (Zurich), 3 April 1986; 16 April 1986; and 24 April 1986; *Jeune Afrique*, No. 1318 (9 April 1986): 20; Seymour M. Hersch, 'Target Qaddafi', *New York Times Magazine*, 22 February 1987, 48 and 71-74.

42. *International Herald Tribune* (Zurich), 28 March 1986; *Wall Street Journal* (Europe), 21 April 1986 and 26-27 April 1986; *Financial Times* (London), 16 April 1986.

43. Ashiurakis, *A Concise History*, 87; *FBIS-MEA* (8 February 1984): Q1; Michael Ritchie, 'Closer Ties Win Libya's Favour', *MEED Special Report: Italy* (June 1985): 16 and 18. In October 1986 the Italian government protested at remarks made by Qaddafi at ceremonies marking the 16th anniversary of the Italian expulsion from Libya. He had referred to Italy as 'enemy number one' because its facilities on Lampedusa had served as a base for US terrorism against Libya. *MEED*, 30, 42 (18-24 October 1986): 23.

44. Nelson, *Libya*, 229-230.

45. Wright, *Libya*, 217; *The Times* (London), 23 April 1984 and 8 March 1985; *Financial Times* (London), 3 October 1986; *Le Monde* (Paris), 26-27 October 1986; *MEED*, 30, 44 (1-7 November 1986): 19.

46. Nelson, *Libya*, 193-194; Andrew Carvely, 'Libya: International Relations and Political Purposes', *International Journal*, XXVIII, 4 (Autumn 1973): 715-716.

47. Wright, *Libya*, 209-210; Cooley, *Libyan Sandstorm*, 188; Paul Balta, 'French Policy in North Africa', *The Middle East Journal*, 40, 2 (Spring 1986): 247-248; *Le Monde* (Paris), 8-9 February 1987.

48. First, *Libya*, 240; Nelson, *Libya*, 194-195.

49. Wright, *Libya*, 213-214; Gutteridge, *Libya*, 10; *International Herald Tribune* (Zurich), 1-2 December 1984.

50. St John, 'Terrorism and Libyan Foreign Policy', 111-115; *Financial Times* (London), 16 April 1986; *International Herald Tribune* (Zurich), 23 April 1986.

51. *Financial Times* (London), 29 April 1986; Parker, 'Appointment in Oujda', 1098; Wright, 'Libya', 38.

52. Tony Walker, 'The Financial Squeeze on Qaddafi', *Financial Times* (London), 22 April 1986; *MEED*, 29, 51/52 (21 December 1985 – 3 January 1986): 65.

53. *Le Monde* (Paris), 27 March 1986; Anderson, 'Assessing Libya's Qaddafi', 226.

54. Jonathan Marcus, 'French Policy and the Middle East Conflicts: Change and Continuity', *The World Today*, 42, 2 (February 1986): 28; *Italian Business Trends* (London), 24 January 1986, 2-4.

55. *Jeune Afrique*, No. 1322 (7 May 1986): 43-44; *Financial Times* (London), 18 April 1986; *Wall Street Journal* (Europe), 29 December 1986. The European Parlia-

ment, by a vote of 154 to 148, condemned US military action against Libya as a flagrant violation of international law. *Wall Street Journal* (Europe), 18 April 1986.

56. *International Herald Tribune* (Zurich), 9 January 1986 and 19-20 April 1986; *Wall Street Journal* (Europe), 24 April 1986.

57. Schumacher, 'The United States and Libya', 344-345; Robin Allen, 'Gulf States Warm to the Soviet Union', *MEED*, 31, 4 (24-30 January 1987): 2-3. On 11 November 1986, Tripoli Radio announced that Libya was halting weapons purchases from the European Community states and would urge other Arab states to follow suit. *MEED*, 30, 46 (15-21 November 1986): 25.

58. Ronald Bruce St John, 'Whatever's Happened to Qaddafi?', *The World Today*, 43, 4 (April 1987): 58-59.

Chapter 6

1. Y. Hasan, 'The Historical Roots of Afro-Arab Relations', in *The Arabs and Africa*, ed. Khair El-Din Haseeb (London: Croom Helm and Centre for Arab Unity Studies, 1985), 37; Evans-Pritchard, *The Sanusi of Cyrenaica*, 15-16.

2. Virginia Thompson and Richard Adloff, *Conflict in Chad* (London: C. Hurst, 1981), 121-122; Benjamin Neuberger, *Involvement, Invasion and Withdrawal: Qadhdhafi's Libya and Chad, 1969–1981*, Occasional Papers No. 83 (Tel Aviv: The Shiloah Center for Middle Eastern and African Studies, 1982), 15-20 and 22-24; Guy Jérémie Ngansop, *Tchad: Vingt ans de crise* (Paris: Editions L'Harmattan, 1986), 53.

3. First, *Libya*, 222; Nelson, *Libya*, 191-192.

4. Tareq Y. Ismael, 'Africa and the Middle East', in *The Middle East in World Politics*, ed. Tareq Y. Ismael (Syracuse: Syracuse University Press, 1974), 175-178; Habib, *Politics and Government*, 356.

5. Libyan Arab Republic, *The Revolution of 1st September*, 262-265; Shembesh, 'The Analysis of Libya's Foreign Policy: 1962–1973', 212-213; Robert Anton Mertz and Pamela MacDonald Mertz, *Arab Aid to Sub-Saharan Africa* (Munich: Chr. Kaiser, 1983), 97-98.

6. Pipes, 'No One Likes the Colonel', 21; Cooley, *Libyan Sandstorm*, 188; Hottinger, 'L'expansionnisme libyen', 145-147. Ostensibly an instrument for the propagation of the faith, the Association for the Propagation of Islam, or Islamic Call Society, was also used for political propaganda and subversion. Harris, *Libya*, 85.

7. Libyan Arab Republic, *The Revolution of 1st September*, 174-181; El-Ghariani, 'Libya's Foreign Policy', 118-121 and 139; Mertz and Mertz, *Arab Aid*, 89-91.

8. El-Ghariani, 'Libya's Foreign Policy', 57; Abdi, 'Common Regional Policy', 220-221.

9. M. Beshir, 'The Role of the Arab Group in the Organization of African Unity', in *The Arabs and Africa*, ed. Khair El-Din Haseeb (London: Croom Helm and Centre for Arab Unity Studies, 1985), 233.

10. Mertz and Mertz, *Arab Aid*, 10, 87 and 94.

11. J. Howe, 'Gaddafi and Africa', *Africa*, 115 (May 1981): 16-17; Mertz and Mertz, *Arab Aid*, 90-96.

12. *Progressive Libya*, 2, 11 (July 1973): 1 and 6; Crozier, *Libya's Foreign Adventures*, 13.

13. A. Carvely, 'Libya: International Relations and Political Purposes', *International Journal*, XXVIII, 4 (Autumn 1973): 713; Wright, *Libya*, 168; Ngansop, *Tchad*,

49. While the Tombalbaye government in Chad received some aid from Libya, total disbursements never approached the amount reportedly promised.

14. Libyan Arab Republic, *The Revolution of 1st September*, 265–266; Grimaud, *La politique extérieure de l'Algérie*, 282.

15. Ismael, 'Africa and the Middle East', 178–180; Wright, *Libya*, 166 and 168–169. Several African states were very disappointed with the economic rewards resulting from their support of Libya, especially resenting the fact that little was done to help them meet the greatly increased cost of oil imports. Many of them voiced their displeasure at the first African oil conference convened in Tripoli, Libya, in February 1974.

16. Qathafi, *Discourses*, 118–119 and 138; *Progressive Libya*, 4, 11–12 (July–August 1975): 3; C. Legum, 'The Middle East Dimension', in *International Politics in Southern Africa*, eds. C.M. Carter and P. O'Meara (Bloomington: Indiana University Press, 1982), 118–121.

17. Tony Hodges, *Western Sahara: The Roots of a Desert War* (Westport: Lawrence Hill, 1983), 326–328; Grimaud, *La politique extérieure de l'Algérie*, 327–328.

18. Mertz and Mertz, *Arab Aid*, 94–95.

19. Abdi, 'Common Regional Policy', 215–231; Charles Gurdon, 'A Preliminary Assessment of the Distribution of Non-Hydrocarbon Minerals in Libya', in *Planning and Development in Modern Libya*, eds. M.M. Buru, S.M. Ghanem and K.S. McLachlan (Wisbech: Menas Press, 1985), 178–186.

20. Wright, *Libya*, 212–213; Fallaci, 'Iranians Are Our Brothers', 121.

21. Hasan, 'The Historical Roots of Afro-Arab Relations', 42; Haley, *Qaddafi*, 224.

22. Thompson and Adloff, *Conflict in Chad*, 79–80; A. Rondos, 'Civil War and Foreign Intervention in Chad', *Current History*, 84, 502 (May 1985): 211; Neuberger, *Involvement, Invasion and Withdrawal*, 69–72; Chris Chidebe, 'Nigeria and the Arab States', *The American Journal of Islamic Social Sciences*, 2, 1 (1985): 121–122.

23. While most African governments viewed Libya's intervention in Chad as a destabilizing influence, a few took the opposite position. In their view, Libya had intervened to restore a degree of order after the Chadians had proved unable to govern themselves, and they had then departed when asked to leave. Parker, *North Africa*, 73.

24. Brewer, 'The Libyan-Sudanese "Crisis" of 1981', 212; René Lemarchand, 'Chad: The Road to Partition', *Current History*, 83, 491 (March 1984): 115.

25. Neuberger, *Involvement, Invasion and Withdrawal*, 53–54.

26. Cooley, *Libyan Sandstorm*, 199–203; Chidebe, 'Nigeria', 122. While Qaddafi's willingness to finance and train dissidents was unquestionable, there was also evidence to suggest that some African governments used him as a scapegoat for domestic discontent.

27. David S. Yost, 'French Policy in Chad and the Libyan Challenge', *Orbis*, 21, 1 (Winter 1983): 978–979.

28. Claudia Wright, 'Libya and the West: Headlong into Confrontation?', *International Affairs*, 58, 1 (Winter 1981-82): 14.

29. Lemarchand, 'Chad', 116; *Le Matin* (Paris), 1 July 1983; *International Herald Tribune* (Zurich), 27 April 1984.

30. François Mitterrand, *Réflexions sur la politique extérieure de la France* (Paris: Lib-

rairie Arthème Fayard, 1986), 124-126; Ngansop, *Tchad*, 134-170; François Soudan, 'La nouvelle guerre du Nord', *Jeune Afrique*, No. 1353 (10 December 1986): 47 and 49.

31. *Financial Times* (London), 10 March 1987; *Jeune Afrique*, No. 1365 (4 March 1987): 24; *The Middle East*, No. 149 (March 1987): 17.

32. *Le Monde* (Paris), 24 March 1987 and 14 April 1987; *International Herald Tribune* (Zurich), 26 March 1987 and 3 April 1987; *MEED*, 31, 18 (2-8 May 1987): 18.

33. *Le Monde* (Paris), 11 April 1986; *MEED*, 30, 33 (16-22 August 1986): 19; *AED*, 8, 10 (7-13 March 1987): 12.

Chapter 7

1. The Libyan Revolution in the Words of Its Leaders', 209-210; Ansell and al-Arif, *The Libyan Revolution*, 94-95; Frank C. Waddams, *The Libyan Oil Industry* (London: Croom Helm, 1980), 229-230.

2. Yusif A. Sayigh, *Arab Oil Policies in the 1970's: Opportunity and Responsibility* (London: Croom Helm, 1983), 44-49; Nelson, *Libya*, 248; First, *Libya*, 210. Libya also turned to Venezuela for advice on oil production and price.

3. S.M. Ghanem, *The Pricing of Libyan Crude Oil* (Valletta: Adam Publishers, 1975), 148; Cooley, *Libyan Sandstorm*, 62-64; Edith Penrose, 'The Development of Crisis', in *The Oil Crisis*, ed. Raymond Vernon (New York: W.W. Norton, 1976), 40; Waddams, *Libyan Oil Industry*, 230.

4. Waddams, *Libyan Oil Industry*, 230; Ghanem, *The Pricing of Libyan Crude Oil*, 150.

5. Paul Barker and Keith McLachlan, 'Development of the Libyan Oil Industry', in *Libya Since Independence: Economic and Political Development*, ed. J.A. Allan (London: Croom Helm, 1982), 39; Waddams, *Libyan Oil Industry*, 231-232 and 269; Shukri Ghanem, 'The Libyan Role within Opec', in *Planning and Development in Modern Libya*, eds. Buru, Ghanem and McLachlan, 169. The eight major oil producers included British Petroleum, Esso or Exxon, Gulf, Mobil, Shell, Socal, Texaco and the para-statal Compagnie Française des Pétroles. Independents working in Libya included Oasis (Continental, Marathon and Amerada Hess), N.B. Hunt, Occidental, Sinclair (Liamco), Grace, Phillips and Pan-American (Amoco). Amoseas was a Texaco-Socal joint venture in Libya.

6. Waddams, *Libyan Oil Industry*, 232; Bearman, *Qadhafi's Libya*, 83-84.

7. The adjustment for gravity, termed the gravity differential allowance, had been part of Opec agreements with the oil companies for a number of years. The adjustment had been introduced by the oil companies which contended that the market for lighter crudes was not as firm as that for heavier crudes.

8. Mohamed R. Buzakuk, 'Libya Took the Lead', *Progressive Libya*, 2, 4 (December 1972): 6; Ghanem, 'Libyan Role within Opec', 169; Waddams, *Libyan Oil Industry*, 233-236.

9. Penrose, 'Development of Crisis', 39; Carvely, 'Libya', 710-711; Waddams, *Libyan Oil Industry*, 233.

10. Mira Wilkins, 'The Oil Companies in Perspective', in *The Oil Crisis*, ed. Raymond Vernon (New York: W.W. Norton, 1976), 166-167; First, *Libya*, 201-205; Dankwart A. Rustow, *Oil and Turmoil: America Faces Opec and the Middle East* (New York: W.W. Norton, 1982), 135; Peter R. Odell, *Oil and World Power*, 8th ed. (Har-

mondsworth: Penguin, 1986), 222.

11. Allan, *Libya*, 186-187 and 309-310.

12. Ghanem, 'Libyan Role within Opec', 169-172; Waddams, *Libyan Oil Industry*, 236-238. A 1971 amendment to the Petroleum Law embodied the Libyan government's approach to conservation or controlled production.

13. Waddams, *Libyan Oil Industry*, 238-240; Bearman, *Qadhafi's Libya*, 86-87.

14. Mohamed R. Buzakuk, 'Opec's Unified Price Strategy — 1971', *Progressive Libya*, 2, 5 (January 1973): 8; Barker and McLachlan, 'Development of the Libyan Oil Industry', 39; Penrose, 'Development of Crisis', 39.

15. Waddams, *Libyan Oil Industry*, 240-241; Ghanem, 'Libyan Role within Opec', 172-173.

16. Waddams, *Libyan Oil Industry*, 241; Ghanem, 'Libyan Role within Opec', 173-174.

17. First, *Libya*, 203-204; Mohamed R. Buzakuk, 'More Price Increases for Short-Haul Crudes', *Progressive Libya*, 2, 6 (February 1973): 8; Ghanem, 'Libyan Role within Opec', 174-175.

18. Wilkins, 'Oil Companies in Perspective', 168; Waddams, *Libyan Oil Industry*, 245-248; Rustow, *Oil and Turmoil*, 137-138.

19. First, *Libya*, 211; Waddams, *Libyan Oil Industry*, 253-254; Bill and Leiden, *The Middle East*, 253-254.

20. Cooley, *Libyan Sandstorm*, 71-72; *Progressive Libya*, 2, 11 (July 1973): 2.

21. First, *Libya*, 209-210; Wilkins, 'Oil Companies in Perspective', 172.

22. Libyan Arab Republic, *The Revolution of 1st September*, 226.

23. *Progressive Libya*, 3, 1 and 2 (September–October 1973): 9-10; Wilkins, 'Oil Companies in Perspective', 172; First, *Libya*, 211.

24. Waddams, *Libyan Oil Industry*, 253-260.

25. Penrose, 'Development of Crisis', 39 and 54; Rustow, *Oil and Turmoil*, 147; *Petroleum Economist*, LIII, 8 (August 1986): 278.

26. Crozier, *Libya's Foreign Adventures*, 2; *Progressive Libya*, 2, 3 and 4 (November–December 1973): 9 and 10; George Lenczowski, 'The Oil-Producing Countries', in *The Oil Crisis*, ed. Raymond Vernon (New York: W.W. Norton, 1976), 67; Quandt, *Decade of Decisions*, 192-193.

27. Lenczowski, 'The Oil-Producing Countries', 64 and 67; Wilkins, 'Oil Companies in Perspective', 174; Mansfield, *The Arabs*, 529.

28. *Progressive Libya*, 1, 1-2 (September–October 1975): 4.

29. Sayigh, *Arab Oil Policies*, 115-120; Barker and McLachlan, 'Development of the Libyan Oil Industry', 39-40; Robert S. Pindyck, 'Opec's Threat to the West', *Foreign Policy*, 30 (Spring 1978): 41. Despite Qaddafi's emphasis on price, the level of inflation in 1974-79 was such that the real price of oil did not keep pace with the nominal price. Allan, *Libya*, 195.

30. Barker and McLachlan, 'Development of the Libyan Oil Industry', 40 and 47; Allan, *Libya*, 116, 217 and 310.

31. J.A. Allan, 'Libya Accommodates to Lower Oil Revenues: Economic and Political Adjustments, *International Journal of Middle East Studies*, 15, 3 (August 1983): 377-385.

32. Shembesh, 'The Analysis of Libya's Foreign Policy, 1962–1973', 112; Nelson, *Libya*, 217; Allan, 'Libya Accommodates to Lower Oil Revenues', 383.

33. *Petroleum Economist*, LIII, 11 (November 1986): 398; Allan, 'Libya Accommodates to Lower Oil Revenues', 377; Barker and McLachlan, 'Development of the Libyan Oil Industry', 49-50.

34. Youssef M. Ibrahim, 'Libya Urges Foreign Oil Firms to Purchase More of Its Crude, but Doesn't Reduce Price', *Wall Street Journal* (New York), 6 August 1981.

35. *MEED*, 25, 44 (30 October – 5 November 1981): 28-29 and 26, 2 (8-15 January 1982): 19; *Wall Street Journal* (New York), 30 November 1981.

36. Youssef M. Ibrahim, 'Opec Moves Closer to Price Compromise That Would Cut Top Oil Quote $4 a Barrel', *Wall Street Journal* (New York), 18 August 1981; Bill Paul, 'Libya Lets Occidental Petroleum Buy More Lower-Cost Oil, Insuring Profit On It', *Wall Street Journal* (New York), 2 October 1981; Youssef M. Ibrahim, 'Opec Sets $34 Oil Price, Bars Discounts, But Some Analysts Doubt Pact Will Hold', *Wall Street Journal* (New York), 30 October 1981.

37. *MEED*, 30, 15 (12-18 April 1986): 39; 29, 51/52 (21 December 1985 – 3 January 1986): 63 and 65; 26, 51 (17-23 December 1982): 102; *FBIS-MEA* 84-032 (15 February 1984): Q2-Q3; Odell, *Oil and World Power*, 109.

38. Allan, 'Libya Accommodates to Lower Oil Revenues', 384; Gutteridge, *Libya*, 6-7.

39. Michael Ritchie, 'Libya: Qaddafi Warns of Further Austerity', *MEED*, 29, 36 (7-13 September 1985): 20-21.

40. As one observer emphasized, 'political analysts would do well to brush up on their economics rather than search for Islamic fundamentalist explanations or historical precedent (e.g. the Sanusi) to explain the Libyan leader's ventures in the Sahara.' Allan, 'Libya Accommodates to Lower Oil Revenues', 384.

41. *MEED*, 30, 7 (15-21 February 1986): 5-6; *FBIS-MEA* (5 March 1986): Q11-Q12; *Wall Street Journal* (Europe), 23 October 1986; Richard Johns, 'Opec Pact Expected to Trigger Sharp Rise in World Oil Prices', *Financial Times* (London), 22 December 1986.

42. *MEED*, 31, 5 (31 January – 6 February 1987): 17; *Petroleum Economist*, LIV, 2 (February 1987): 71.

Chapter 8

1. To encourage comparative analysis of the foreign-policy process in the Middle East, this chapter is patterned after the approach taken by R.D. McLaurin, Mohammed Mughisuddin and Abraham R. Wagner in *Foreign Policy Making in the Middle East* (New York: Praeger, 1977).

2. First, *Libya*, 115. Two RCC members represented prominent tribes.

3. Nelson, *Libya*, 175.

4. Ansell and al-Arif, *The Libyan Revolution*, 108-113.

5. Nathan Alexander [Ronald Bruce St John], 'Libya: The Continuous Revolution', *Middle Eastern Studies*, 17, 2 (April 1981): 213.

6. Raymond A. Hinnebusch, 'Libya: Personalistic Leadership of a Populist Revolution', in *Political Elites in Arab North Africa: Morocco, Algeria, Tunisia, Libya and Egypt*, ed. I. William Zartman (New York: Longman, 1982), 193-194.

7. For the theoretical organization and operation of the committee-congress system, see Qaddafi, *The Green Book, Part I*. For a more realistic appraisal, see Ronald Bruce St John, 'Socialist People's Libyan Arab Jamahiriya', in *World Encyclopedia of*

Political Systems and Parties, ed. George E. Delury (2nd ed.; New York: Facts on File, 1987), 685–693. For consistency, the author is using *The Green Book* as the source for the official nomenclature of all revolutionary organizations.

Two case studies of the committee-congress system in operation have been published. J. Davis, 'Qaddafi's Theory and Practice of Non-Representative Government', *Government and Opposition*, 17, 1 (1982): 61–79, and John P. Mason, 'Qadhdhafi's "Revolution" and Change in a Libyan Oasis Community', *The Middle East Journal*, 36, 3 (Summer 1982): 319–335.

8. Mobilization can be defined as a broad process of social change 'in which major clusters of old social, economic and psychological commitments are eroded or broken and people become available for new patterns of socialization and behavior'. Karl W. Deutsch, 'Social Mobilization and Political Development', *The American Political Science Review*, 55, 3 (September 1961): 493.

9. Hasan, 'The Genesis of the Political Leadership of Libya, 1952–1969', 192; Omar I. El Fathaly, Monte Palmer and Richard Chackerian, *Political Development and Bureaucracy in Libya* (Lexington, Massachusetts: Lexington Books, 1977), 58–59, 63–67 and 75.

10. Fathaly et al., *Political Development and Bureaucracy*, 39–40; Richard F. Nyrop, et al., *Area Handbook for Libya* (Washington: US Government Printing Office, 1973), 168.

11. Alexander, 'Libya', 214.

12. Habib, *Politics and Government*, 204–208; First, *Libya*, 129–130.

13. Alexander, 'Libya', 215–216.

14. George Lenczowski, 'Popular Revolution in Libya', *Current History*, 73 (February 1974): 57 and 59; Libyan Arab Republic, *The Revolution of 1st September*, 239–245; Omar I. Fathaly and Monte Palmer, 'Opposition to Change in Rural Libya', *International Journal of Middle East Studies*, 11, 2 (April 1980): 248.

15. Habib, *Politics and Government*, 220–221; First, *Libya*, 26, 138 and 253–254; Fathaly et al., *Political Development and Bureaucracy*, 58–59, 63, 66–67, 87–88 and 95.

16. Fathaly et al., *Political Development and Bureaucracy*, 96–99.

17. 'The Revolutionary Committees: Aims and Programs', *JPRS*, 70405, No. 1745 (3 January 1978): 17; Alexander, 'Libya', 219–220; Hinnebusch, 'Charisma, Revolution and State Formation: Qaddafi and Libya', 65–69.

18. *FBIS-MEA*, 17 February 1984, Q8–Q9, and 5 March 1986, Q1–Q22. With the creation of the General People's Congress, the ASU structure was allowed to lapse. *Progressive Libya*, 5, 5–6 (January–February 1976): 3.

19. *FBIS-MEA*, 20 December 1978, I3–I6.

20. Abdelaziz Dahmani, 'Le messager en difficulté', *Jeune Afrique*, No. 943 (31 January 1979): 28–29; *MEED*, 23, 2 (12 January 1979): 39.

21. *FBIS-MEA*, 16 February 1984, Q1, and 15 March 1984, Q3.

22. *FBIS-MEA*, 19 April 1979, I2; 12 February 1979, I1–I2; and 15 September 1980, I1; Timothy Niblock, 'Libya: The Emergence of a Revolutionary Vanguard', *New Statesman*, 96 (22 September 1978): 357. While student-based Revolutionary Committees were established in universities as early as 1976, they were not systematically organized. Bearman, *Qadhafi's Libya*, 187.

23. *FBIS-MEA*, 22 May 1980, I4; 'The Revolutionary Committees: Aims and Programs', *JPRS*, 70405, No. 1745 (3 January 1978): 16–19.

24. *FBIS-MEA*, 19 April 1979, I2.

25. *FBIS-MEA*, 10 December 1979, I3-I4; 3 March 1980, I3-I4; 7 August 1980, I1; *MEED*, 24, 3 (18 January 1980): 33.

26. Wright, 'Libya', 27-28; Schumacher, 'The United States and Libya', 338.

27. Alan Cowell, 'OAU Said To Try To Revive Meeting', *New York Times*, 16 September 1982; *El País Internacional* (Madrid), 11 March 1985.

28. 'Reorganization of Revolutionary Committees Urged', *JPRS-NEA* 85-119 (16 September 1986): 63-64.

29. Qaddafi, *The Green Book, Part I*, 23-24; 'Libyan RCC Issues Law Amending Penal Code', *JPRS*, 65623 (18 August 1975): 49; Ansell and al-Arif, *The Libyan Revolution*, 113-114.

30. Qaddafi, *The Green Book, Part I*, 23-25.

31. *FBIS-MEA*, 15 December 1982, Q1-Q2; *Jeune Afrique*, No. 1322 (7 May 1986): 43.

32. Schumacher, 'The United States and Libya', 338-339.

33. Lisa Anderson, 'Qadhdhafi and His Opposition', *The Middle East Journal*, 40, 2 (Spring 1986): 233-234; Christopher Dickey, 'Libya Without Qadhdhafi: Chaos Is Feared', *International Herald Tribune* (Zurich), 19-20 April 1986; *Financial Times* (London), 4 March 1987.

34. Anderson, 'Qadhdhafi and His Opposition', 234; Nora Boustany, 'Poorer But Still, It Seems, Loyal', *Financial Times* (London), 6 September 1986.

35. Allan, *Libya*, 179-316; Qaddafi, *The Green Book, Part II*.

36. Daniel Pipes, *In the Path of God*, 220-223; 'Al-Qadhdhafi Ties His Policies to the Koran', *JPRS*, 70813, No. 1772 (21 March 1978): 129-147.

37. Tony Walker, 'Gaddafi's Libya: Why Testing Times Lie Ahead', *Financial Times* (London), 15 September 1985.

38. 'Libyan National Movement's Muhammad Ahmad al-Sukkar Interviewed', *JPRS-NEA* 85-124 (25 September 1985): 37-41.

39. William Gutteridge, *Libya*, 22-24; *MEED*, 29, 6 (8-14 February 1985): 22; *FBIS-MEA*, 12 May 1980, I3-I4, and 15 May 1980, I4-I5; Bearman, *Qadhafi's Libya*, 243-250.

40. Anderson, 'Qadhdhafi and His Opposition', 229-233.

41. Harris, *Libya*, 85-86.

Select Bibliography

In recent years, sources of information about Libyan foreign policy have become increasingly abundant. Listed below are a few books and articles which provide the general reader with an introduction to the subject. Readers interested in the specialized bibliography of particular questions should consult the footnotes at appropriate passages.

Abdi, Nourredine. 'Common Regional Policy for Algeria and Libya: From Maghribi Unity to Saharan Integration', in *Social and Economic Development of Libya*, E.G.H. Joffé and K.S. McLachlan (eds.), Wisbech, 1982.

Alexander, Nathan [Ronald Bruce St John]. 'The Foreign Policy of Libya: Inflexibility Amid Change'. *Orbis*, 24, 4 (1981), 819–846.

Alexander, Nathan [Ronald Bruce St John]. 'Libya: The Continuous Revolution'. *Middle Eastern Studies*, 17, 2 (1981), 210–227.

Allan, J.A. *Libya. The Experience of Oil*. London, 1981.

Allan, J.A. (ed.). *Libya since Independence*. London. 1982.

Anderson, Lisa. 'Qadhdhafi and the Kremlin'. *Problems of Communism*, XXXIV, 5 (1985), 29–44.

Anderson, Lisa. 'Libya and American Foreign Policy'. *The Middle East Journal*, 36, 4 (1982), 516–534.

Anderson, Lisa. *The State and Social Transformation in Tunisia and Libya, 1830–1980*. Princeton, 1986.

Ansell, Meredith O., and Ibrahim Massaud al-Arif (eds.). *The Libyan Revolution: A Sourcebook of Legal and Historical Documents*, Vol. I: *1 September 1969 – 30 August 1970*. Stoughton, 1972.

Bearman, Jonathan. *Qadhafi's Libya*. London, 1986.

Bessis, Juliette. *La Libye contemporaine*. Paris, 1986.

Bianco, Mirella. *Gadafi: Voice from the Desert*. London, 1975.

Blundy, David and Andrew Lycett. *Qaddafi and the Libyan Revolution*. London, 1987.

Brewer, William D. 'The Libyan-Sudanese "Crisis" of 1981: Danger for Darfur and Dilemma for the United States'. *The Middle East Journal*, 36, 2 (1982), 205–206.

Cooley, John K. *Libyan Sandstorm: The Complete Account of Qaddafi's Revolution*. New York, 1982.

Damis, John. 'Morocco, Libya and the Treaty of Union'. *American-Arab Affairs*, 13 (1985), 44–55.

Deeb, Marius K., and Mary Jane Deeb. *Libya since the Revolution: Aspects of Social and Political Development.* New York, 1982.

First, Ruth. *Libya: The Elusive Revolution.* Harmondsworth, 1974.

El-Ghariani, Mustafa S. 'Libya's Foreign Policy: The Role of the Country's Environmental and Leadership Factors, 1960–1973'. Western Michigan University, 1979.

Gutteridge, William (ed.). *Libya: Still a Threat to Western Interests?* Conflict Studies No. 160. London, 1984.

Habib, Henri. *Politics and Government of Revolutionary Libya.* Ottawa, 1975.

Haley, P. Edward. *Qaddafi and the United States since 1969.* New York, 1984.

Harris, Lillian Craig. *Libya: Qadhafi's Revolution and the Modern State.* Boulder, 1986.

El-Khawas, Mohamed. *Qaddafi: His Ideology in Theory and Practice.* Brattleboro, 1986.

Lanne, Bernard. *Tchad–Libye: La querelle des frontières.* Paris, 1982.

Mattes, Hanspeter. 'Libya's Economic Relations as an Instrument of Foreign Policy', in *The Economic Development of Libya*, Bichara Khader and Bashir el-Wifati (eds.), London, 1987.

Nelson, Harold D. (ed.). *Libya: A Country Study.* 3rd ed. Washington, 1979.

Neuberger, Benjamin. *Involvement, Invasion and Withdrawal: Qadhdhafi's Libya and Chad, 1969–1981.* Occasional Papers No. 83. Tel Aviv, 1982.

Otayek, René. *La politique africaine de la Libye (1969–1985).* Paris, 1987.

el Qathafi, Mu'Ammar. *Discourses.* Valletta, 1975.

Roumani, Jacques. 'From Republic to Jamahiriya: Libya's Search for Political Community'. *The Middle East Journal*, 37, 2 (1983), 151-168.

St John, Ronald Bruce. 'The Determinants of Libyan Foreign Policy, 1969–1983'. *The Maghreb Review*, 8, 3-4 (1983), 96-103.

St John, Ronald Bruce. 'The Ideology of Mu'ammar al-Qadhdhafi: Theory and Practice'. *International Journal of Middle East Studies*, 15, 4 (1983), 471-490.

Schumacher, Edward. 'The United States and Libya', *Foreign Affairs*, 65, 2 (1986-87), 329-348.

Shembesh, Ali Muhammad. 'The Analysis of Libya's Foreign Policy, 1962–1973: A Study of the Impact of Environmental and Leadership Factors'. Emory University, 1975.

Waddams, Frank, C. *The Libyan Oil Industry.* London, 1980.

Wright, John. *Libya: A Modern History.* London and Baltimore, 1982.

Yost, David S. 'French Policy in Chad and the Libyan Challenge'. *Orbis*, 21, 1 (1983), 965-997.

Zartman, I. William and A.G. Kluge, 'Heroic Politics: The Foreign Policy of Libya', in *The Foreign Policies of Arab States*, Bahgat Korany and Ali E. Hillal Dessouki (eds.), Boulder, 1984.

Index

Abdelaziz, Muhammad 68
Abu Nidal 46
Afghanistan 76, 95, 149
Aflaq, Michel 30
African National Congress 47
African Petroleum Producers'
    Association 123
Afro-Asian movement 72
aid commitments/aid disbursement
    discrepancies 96, 100, 103, 122
air bases, British and American 14-
    15, 16, 27, 74, 86
Ajami, Fouad 26, 27
Algeria 19, 63-4, 67, 148
    accord with Tunisia, Mauritania
    104
    in Steadfastness Front 41
    Libyan relations with 57, 60,
    65-6, 68, 149
    Morocco and 59
    mutual defence pact with 60, 148
    oil policy of 108, 111, 113, 122
    Qaddafi support re West Sahara
    40, 98
    support for PLO 44
    war of independence in 16, 26
Amal movement 41
Amoseas oil company 109
Angola 95
anti-colonialism 16, 59
    see also colonialism
anti-imperialism 72
    see also imperialism
anti-royalist movements 14
Arab Federation 49
Arab League 14, 41-2, 50, 103, 135
Arab nationalism 16, 71, 95
    development of 23-4, 25
    Islam and 21, 24, 33-4
    Palestinian issue and 35
    Qaddafi and 21, 25, 26-8, 146
    sources of 21-3
    tenet of foreign policy 144, 146

Arab secularism 22-3, 30
Arab socialism 25, 26
Arab Socialist Union 129-30, 132
Arab summit meetings 16, 39, 43,
    51, 56, 83
Arab unity 95
    Qaddafi and 45, 49-51, 52, 54,
    58-60, 61-4, 69-70, 146, 147
    tenet of foreign policy 144, 146
    see also Pan-Arabism
Arab-African Union 67, 68, 149
Arab-Israeli War (1967) 94
    effects of 21, 26, 38-9
    reaction to in Libya 16-17
Arab-Israeli War (1973) 56, 59, 75,
    87, 116, 118
    PLO strengthened by 37
    Qaddafi and 56, 75, 117
    Sadat 26
Arabian Gulf Exploration Company
    115
Arafat, Yasser 37, 43, 44, 45
    on terrorist attacks in Europe 46
Arslan, Shakib 22
Arsuzi, Zaki 29
Assad, President Hafez al- 26, 45, 52,
    61
Association for the Propagation of
    Islam 36, 95
Austria 90

Baath Party 18, 30, 61
Baathism 14, 26, 36
Baghdad Pact 25
Bahrain, Libyan relations with 41
banks, nationalization of 110
Basic People's Congresses 127, 128,
    132, 134, 140
Beirut, loss of to PLO 42-3
Benghazi Declaration 54-7
Benin 96, 103
Benjedid, President Chadli 68

Bokassa, Jean Bedel 99
Bourguiba, President Habib 57, 58,
  64
Brezhnev, Leonid 75, 77
Britain 16
  air bases 14-15, 16, 27-8, 74, 86
  and trusteeship 12
  monarchy and 14-15
  Qaddafi reaction to 86-7
  reaction to US pressure on Libya
  89-90
British Petroleum company 115
Bureau to Export Revolution 95
Burkina Fasso *see* Upper Volta
Burundi 96, 97

Cameroons 100, 101, 102
Camp David Accords 41, 60, 76, 77
Carter, President James E. 81
Central African Republic 94, 96, 99,
  105, 148
Central America 38
Chad 29, 67
  break of relations with Israel 97
  French policy in 47, 87, 89, 94,
  103-4
  joint venture companies in 96
  Libyan involvement in 41, 44, 61,
  62, 66, 77, 83, 87, 94, 97, 100,
  103, 104, 119, 122, 133
  mineral resources of 99
  Muslim missionaries in 93
  proposed union with 61, 100-101,
  148
  support for Frolinat in 94
  withdrawal from 102, 122, 149
colonialism, neo-colonialism 26-7,
  119, 148
Congo 97
Council of Ministers 126, 127, 132
Cyrenaica 12, 13, 16, 17

Democratic Front for the Liberation
  of Palestine 42
demographic setting 12-13

Economic problems 121-2, 124, 139

economic-cum-cultural agreements
  96
Egypt 13, 16, 18, 19, 23, 31, 84, 145
  and Arab socialism 25-6
  and October War 117
  Arab unity and 50, 54, 60
  Free Officers' Movement 18, 25
  foreign policy of 60, 72, 143
  in Federation of Arab Republics
  52
  nationalism in 24, 25
  proposed union with 54-6, 62,
  131, 147
  relations with Libyan monarchy
  14, 15
  relations with Qaddafi regime 37,
  54, 56, 59, 60, 62, 66
  relations with Soviet Union 74-5
  Tripoli Charter and 51
Egypt-Israel Peace Treaty 41-2, 43,
  60, 77
Eisenhower Doctrine 15
ENI, Italian oil company 115
Esso company 109, 116
Ethiopia 70, 77, 94, 95, 101, 105, 148
European Economic Community 89
External Security Secretariat 140

Farouk, King 25
Fatah wing of PLO 37-8
  assumes leadership of PLO 39
  Libya ends support to 42, 132, 147
Federation of Arab Republics 52, 53,
  56, 57, 148
Fezzan 12, 16
First Nasserite Volunteers' Camp 38
foreign debt 121
Foreign Liaison Bureau 127, 135,
  140, 145
foreign policy 127, 128
  agreement with Sudan 104
  attacks colonialism, neo-
  colonialism 98
  border issues 99
  constant principles of 146-7
  continuity of 144-5
  control of natural resources 98-9,

122
decline of influence 99-102, 105
foreign policy process 140-41
ideological framework of 105, 144
in Africa vis-à-vis Israel 94-7, 103
interests and objectives 143-4, 145
lack of success of 149-50
Moroccan union 44-5, 66-7, 104
tactics of 147-9
France
and Libyan foreign policy 99, 100
and trusteeship 12
Libyan relations with 87
response to US actions against
Libya 88-9
war against Sanusi order 93
Free Unionist Officers' Movement
11, 125, 126
French rule in Maghreb 24
fuqaha (jurists) 32

Gabon 94, 96, 99, 100, 101, 102
Gafsa, attack on 64, 81
Gambia 96, 100, 103
Garang de Mabior, Colonel John 62
General People's Committee 127,
132
General People's Congress 126-7,
128, 132-5, 140-41
and Islam 29
breaks with Fatah 42
creation of suicide commandos 47
economic stress and 121, 122
issues reviewed by 132
powers of 133-4
geographical setting 12-13, 17
Ghana 100, 101, 102, 103, 105
Gorbachev, Mikhail 78, 79
governmental system 125-36, 140
see also Basic People's Congresses,
General People's Committee,
General People's Congress *and*
Revolutionary Command
Council
Greece 90
Green Book, The 31, 32, 34, 103, 133,
134, 137, 149

Green March, The 134
Group of Seventy-Seven 72
Guinea-Bissau 95, 99
Gulf Cooperation Council 90
Gulf states 23, 53, 61, 62, 85, 111,
112, 113, 119, 122

Hadith (the sayings) 31-2
Hassan, King 51, 57, 66, 68
'holy war' see *jihad*
Hunt, H.R. 112
Hunt, N.B. 115, 116
Husri, Sati al- 24
Hussein, King 39, 43, 44, 51

Idi Amin 97, 99
Idris al-Mahdi al-Sanusi,
Muhammad (King Idris) 14-17,
23, 26, 57, 73, 86, 144
ijma (general agreement) 30, 32
imperialism 36, 63, 69, 72
hostile forces of named 35
Qaddafi and 18, 50, 72, 95, 119,
149
independence
achievement of 14, 16, 24, 73
background to 12, 73
India, Islamic Legion recruitment in
47
International Centre for Combating
Imperialism, Zionism 47
international monetary relationships
116
Iran 90, 108, 114, 118, 120, 122
Libyan relations with 41, 147
major radical element in Middle
East 44
support for in Gulf War 61, 62,
70, 79
Iran-Contra affair 41, 91
Iran-Iraq war 41, 43, 61, 62, 70, 90,
91, 148
Iraq 19, 31, 60, 117, 119
and Arab nationalism 24
and Libyan oil policy 111
and PLO 44
and Syria 59, 61

and UAE 59
and United Arab Republic 25
Kuwait and 59
1958 coup in 24
relations with Libya 41, 61, 62
Irish Republican Army, Qaddafi
support for 38, 46, 86
Islam 13
component of Arab nationalism
21, 24, 33-4
element of foreign policy 95
Qaddafi on centrality of 21, 29,
30, 32-3, 35, 138, 145-6, 149
state religion 19
Islamic Call Society 145
Islamic Conference Organization 62
Islamic fundamentalism 145-6
Islamic jurisprudence 30, 32
Islamic Legion 36, 47, 95, 100, 101,
105
Islamic reform movement 21-3
Qaddafi and 22
Islamic Republic of the Sahel 101
Islamic tradition, Qaddafi and 18
Israel 35, 60, 116, 119, 143
and October War 117
influence in Africa 94, 95, 97, 102,
105, 146
Jordan river diversion 15
Libyan reaction to Israeli
independence 24
Italian colonial rule 17, 31, 86
resistance to 13, 16, 17, 23, 24
Italian-owned assets, confiscation
of 28, 86
Italo-Libyan struggle 28, 86
Italy
Libyan relations with 86, 89
response to US sanctions 89, 90
Ivory Coast 102

Jallud, Abdel-Salam 40, 45, 74, 79,
108, 115, 120
jihad (holy war)
Arab unity and 50
as solution to Palestine issue 35
Qaddafi approach to 35, 36

tenet of foreign policy 144
Jihad Fund 36, 95
joint venture companies 96, 103
Jordan 16, 50, 60, 62, 84
and Palestinians 59
Libyan relations with 41, 44, 132
move against PLO 39
not representing Palestinians 44
relations with Syria 61

Kanak Socialist National Liberation
Front (New Caledonia) 47, 48
Kawakibi, Abdel-Rahman al- 23, 26
Kemal, Mustafa (Atatürk) 23, 32
Kenya 102
Khomeini, Ayatollah 41
Kosygin, A.N. 75
Kuwait 114, 117
Libyan relations with 41
relations with Iraq 59

Lebanon
civil war in 40, 59, 90
Libyan relations with 41, 44
Libyan support for Shiites in 41
Lebanon-Israel accord 44
Lesotho 102
Liberia 96, 101, 102, 103
Libya–Egypt union 54-7, 62
Libya–Syria Union 61-2
Libyan Arab Socialist Union 29
Libyan embassies, become People's
Bureaux 135
Libyan guerrillas, in Syria or
Lebanon 38
Libyan Liberation Organization 139
Libyan National Democratic Group
139
Libyan National Oil Company 116
London, Libyan demonstration in
86-7

Maghrabi, Mahmud Suleiman al-
108
Malawi 94, 102
Mali 97, 105, 122
condemns Treaty of Oujda 67, 68

relations with Libya 97, 101, 103
Malta 86
    NATO facilities in 87-8
    off-shore oil dispute 88, 99
Maronite Christians 40
Mauritania 67, 68, 99, 122
    Libyan relations with 94, 98, 101,
    103
Mediterranean, oil in 122
Mengistu, Haile Mariam 101
migrant workers, expulsion of 13,
    62, 64, 68, 103, 122
military establishment 137-8
mineral resources 99, 122
Mobil oil company 112
monarchy, Libyan 11, 13, 17
    African policy of 93, 146
    and Arab unity 50
    and nationalism 16, 17
    and Palestinians 35
    dependence on West 14-15
    foreign policy of 14-16, 144-5
    legacy of 144
    methods of government 128
    oil policy 107, 108, 144
    political parties banned by 136
    RCC and corruption of 17, 18,
    28, 129, 145
Morocco 68
    Algeria and 59
    proposed union with 44-5, 66-7,
    104, 148, 149
    relations with Libya 50, 57, 66
Mozambique 95
Mubarak, President Husni 62
Mukhtar, Umar al- 17, 28
Muslim Brotherhood 61

Nahdah, al- (the awakening) 23
Nasser, President Gamal Abdel 14,
    56, 143, 145, 149
    and Pan-Arabism 25, 26, 59, 69
    and Six-Day War 16
    and Yemen 25
    concept of Islam 32-3, 146
    Czechoslovak arms deal 25
    death of 52, 58, 69

    foreign policy 72
    influence on Qaddafi 33, 72, 129,
    147
    positive neutrality and 72
    Qaddafi compared with 21, 126,
    146, 149
    role as Arab leader 21, 25, 126
    Suez crisis and 25
    three circle strategy 93
Nasserism 14, 26, 36
National Front for the Salvation of
    Libya 139
national identity 16-17, 18, 28
New Caledonia *see* Vanuatu
Nicaragua 44, 90
Niger 67
    break with Israel 97
    joint venture companies in 96
    mineral resources of 99
    relations with Libya 60, 94, 99,
    100, 101, 103
Nigeria 100, 101, 103, 105
non-aligned movement 62, 72, 84
non-alignment 71, 76, 87, 144
North Yemen 41
nuclear reactor 75-6, 77, 78
Numairi, President Jafar al- 53, 60
    overthrow of 62-3, 104
    Qaddafi and 53, 62

Oasis oil company 116
Occidental oil company 108-9, 113,
    116, 121
oil
    control 107, 108, 109, 112, 123
    discovery of 13, 107, 119
    European/Western reliance on 89
    Geneva agreements 114
    increased participation 114-16,
    118, 144
    Libyan Producers' Agreement
    111, 114, 115, 116
    nationalization 108, 109, 115,
    116, 123
    off-shore rights 60, 64, 66, 68, 88,
    99
    price collapse in 1985-6 89, 103

pricing of 107-8, 109-10, 112,
113, 114, 117-20 *passim*, 123, 144
production 107, 110, 111, 117-20
passim, 123, 144
revenues 107, 113, 123, 124
decline in 103, 120-23, 124
foreign policy and 67, 118-20,
123-4, 144
influence of 15, 17, 119
use of 73, 119
September agreements 109-10,
111
Tehran-Tripoli agreements
111-14
oil weapon 75, 81
effect in achieving Arab goals 39,
96
effect in support of Palestinians 37
following October war 117-18
power of oil-producing states
116-17
US dependence on ME oil 116
Oman revolt 59
Organization of African Unity 83,
146, 149
and Chad 100, 101
Israeli issue at 97
Libya and Polisario at 66
monarchy and 15, 93
planned Tripoli summit 102
policies against imperialism 98
Organization of Arab Petroleum
Exporting Countries 64
Organization of Petroleum
Exporting Countries 84, 108-12
passim, 114, 117, 118, 120, 121,
122-3
Ottoman Empire 59
Arab nationalism and 21, 26
Ottoman nationalism 21-2, 23
Oueddei, Goukouni 77
Oujda, Treaty of 66-9

Pakistan 76
Pakistan-India-Bangladesh issue 52
Palestine Liberation Organization
commitment to armed struggle 42

defeat in Lebanon (1982) 42-3
dialogue with Jordan 44
Fatah leadership of 37, 39
in Steadfastness Front 41
relations with Libya 45, 135
result of October war 37
role as 'sole legitimate
representative' 39, 42, 44, 135
terrorism incidents 39-40, 90
Palestinian issue 14, 18, 23, 35, 48
Palestinians 39, 42, 59
Arab unity and 39
Egypt-Israel Peace Treaty 42
improved status of 38-40
Pan-African unity 19
Pan-Arab Command 37
training camps in Libya denied 46
Pan-African Unity 19
Pan-Arab Command 37
Pan-Arabism 17, 18, 24-6
Baathist 14, 26
development and prospects 49
effects of Lebanon war 43, 146
in Egypt 25, 26
Nasserist 14, 15, 26
Qaddafi as new leader of 49-51
secular factor in 24
Six-Day war and 26
pan-Islamic unity 19
People's Committees 127, 128, 131,
132, 135
People's Congress 127, 128, 132, 136
Peres, Shimon 68
petit bourgeoisie 138-9
Philippines, minority Muslims in 38,
47
Polisario Front 66, 67, 68, 83, 98, 102
Pompidou, President Georges 87
Popular Front for the Liberation of
Palestine 37, 42
Popular Front for the Liberation of
Palestine — General Command 42
Popular Struggle Front 42
positive neutrality 95
closer Soviet relationship 75-7
early expressions of 71-3
early relations with US 79-81

European response 88-91
Libya and Europe 85-8
revision of US policy 81-5
Soviet early contacts 73-5
strains in Soviet relationship 77-9
tenet of foreign policy 144

Qaddafi, Colonel Muammar al-
and Arab nationalism 25, 26-8, 29, 30, 32, 33, 34, 37, 115, 119, 145, 149
and Arab unity 45, 49-51, 52, 54, 58-65, 69-70, 115, 146-9 *passim*
and Arafat and Fatah leadership 43, 45, 147
and Islam as component of nationalism 21, 29, 30, 32-3, 35, 138, 145-6, 149
and Numairi 53, 62
and October war 56, 75, 117
and Soviet Union 29, 73-9, 144
and US 29, 80, 84, 115
and West Sahara question 98
approach to *jihad* 36, 37, 38, 42, 43, 44, 47, 48, 50, 147
as Leader of the Revolution 133, 135, 136, 138
attacks Britain re Iran 115
attitude to oil companies 108, 110, 111, 115, 118, 124
call for *jihad* against West 44
Chairman of RCC 11, 126, 129
character, views of 125, 145
coup attempts on 137-8
debt to Nasser 26, 33, 50, 56
domestic intervention abroad 51, 70
East European visits 139-40
first major address 17-18
foreign policy 143, 145-9
    and diplomatic corps 135
    foreign policy process 140-41
    tactical flexibility 147-9
head of state 11, 126, 144
meets Palestinian radical groups 43, 44, 47
on Christian Arabs 30
on Palestinian issue 35, 37-8, 45, 48, 146, 147, 149
on political parties 136-7
on Revolutionary Committees' duties 134, 136
opposition to, from abroad 139-40
opposition to, internal 137-9
physical liquidation doctrine 139
positive neutrality 72-91; *see main entry*
proclaims popular revolution 130-31
proposed unions with
    Algeria 65
    Egypt 54-6, 62
    Morocco 44-5; *see main entry*
    Sudan 63
    Syria 61-2
    Tunisia 57-8, 65
Reagan and 81-4
reinstatement of *sharia* 30-31
rejects Arab secularism 30
relations with Sadat 41, 56-7, 76, 81, 117
relations with West Europe 85-8
religious views of 29-30, 31-2
secondary role in 1982 war 43
Secretary of General People's Committee 133
self-assessment of 34
support for national liberation groups 38, 40, 45-6, 62, 95, 98
support for Palestinians 37, 44
terrorism
    associated with 45-8, 78, 85, 149
    claims to oppose 38, 45, 46
    differentiates revolutionary violence and 38, 147
Third Universal Theory 28, 33, 34, 35, 38, 48, 72, 119, 140, 149
threats to join Warsaw Pact 71, 145
three-fold concept of freedom 27
visits Moscow 76, 77, 78
Qatar, relations with 41

qiyas (analogy) 30
Queen Elizabeth II, liner 55
Quran 29, 30, 31-2

Rawlings, Jerry 102
Reagan, President Ronald 44, 81, 83, 85, 88, 90-91, 120
Red Army Fraction, Red Brigades 45
Republic proclaimed 17
Revolutionary Command Council 11, 17-19, 27-8, 125-6, 132, 133
    abolition of 132
    aims and objectives of 128-9
    and Arab Socialist Union 129-30
    and foreign policy 140
    and monarchy 17, 18, 28, 129
    and Morocco 57
    and popular revolution 131
    in 1969 coup 125-6, 137
    Italian property confiscated 86
    nationalization of BP 115
    neutrality of 74
    oil policy 107-8, 110
    political parties banned 136
    support for Palestinians 36, 38
    use of oil revenues in foreign policy 96
Revolutionary Committees 134-6, 141
Rhodesia 98
Rogers plan 52
Rome and Vienna airport attacks 46, 83
Rwanda 99

Saadah, Antun 29
Sadat, President Anwar 68, 75
    and Arab unity 52, 53-6, 60
    Arab opposition to 41
    assassination of 62
    October war and 26, 117
    relations with Qaddafi 41, 56-7, 75, 76, 81, 117
    replaces Nasser 26, 52
    visits Jerusalem 41
Sadawi, Bashir al- 23
Sadr, Musa al- 41

Saharan Arab Democratic Republic 98
Sahel 93, 148
    Libyan influence in 57
    mercenaries from 36
    mineral resources in 122
    proposed Islamic Republic 101
Saiqa, Al- 42
Sanusi, Muhammad ibn Ali al- 13
Sanusi tradition, Sanusis 28, 33
Sanusiya order 13, 16, 17, 30, 93, 145
Saudi Arabia 23, 60, 117
    and oil concessions, pricing 114, 119, 122, 123
    and Gulf states 53, 62, 85
    condemns US air attack 85
    Libyan pilgrims expelled 45
    Libyan relations with 41, 61, 62, 66, 122
secularism, Qaddafi and 22, 32
Senegal 67, 93, 100
sharia, Islamic law 30-31, 55
Shevardnadze, Foreign Minister 79
Shultz, George 79
Sierra Leone 96
Sinai II accord 60
Sirte, Gulf of 12, 84
    shooting incident in 84
socialism, in Libya 29
Socialist People's Libyan Arab Jamahiriya, Libya renamed 132
Somalia 101, 103
South Africa, Republic of 94
South America 38
South Pacific, Libyan involvement in 47
South Yemen 41, 77
Soviet Union 90
    and trusteeship 12, 73
    arms supplied from 44, 74-6, 78, 81
    Egypt and 72
    interests in Middle East 14, 71, 75, 79, 90
    Qaddafi and 29, 72-9, 144
    qualified support of 144
    strains in Soviet relationship 77-8

support for Palestinians 75
Steadfastness and Confrontation
Front 42, 60, 76, 77, 81, 147
created 41
Libya and 41, 44
Sudan 67, 104, 105
1958 coup 24
1969 coup 53
alleged plot against 44
and Federation of Arab Republics
52, 53, 147
and Tripoli Charter 51
Libyan bombing of 78
Libyan relations with 53, 60,
62-3, 100, 101
military cooperation agreement
104
Sudanese People's Liberation
Movement 62, 63
Suez Canal 45, 107, 110
Suez crisis (1956) 25
suicide squads 47, 134
sunna (the way of the Prophet) 30
Swaziland 102
Syria 19, 31, 91
and Federation of Arab Republics
52, 147, 148
and Iraq 59, 61
and Jordan 61
and pan-Arabism 18, 24, 26
formation of UAR 25
in Steadfastness Front 41
Lebanese involvement 40
Libyan relations with 37, 41, 132,
147
major radical element in Middle
East 44
1949 coup in 24
Syrian Christians 22-3, 30
ties with PLO 39, 43

Tanzania 97, 102
terrorism 68, 90-91
European governments and 90
liberation movements and 147
Libyan-associated 38, 48, 78, 82,
84, 85, 149

People's Bureaux and 136
Qaddafi claims to oppose 38, 45,
46
Third Universal Theory 28-30, 31
alternative to capitalism and
communism 28, 29
devotion to Islam 13, 21, 33
nationalism in 21
Togo 96, 102
Tripoli, Libya
attacks on embassies 44, 136
Tripoli Charter 51-4
Tripolitania 12, 16, 17, 73
Tripolitania-Cyrenaica Defence
Committee 23
Tunisia 19, 23, 63, 68, 81
bilateral treaty with 14
nationalism in 24
offer of union with 58, 60, 63, 148
off-shore dispute with 60, 64, 66,
68, 88, 99
relations with 57, 64, 66, 68-9
Tunisian Armed Resistance 64
Turkey 23
Turkish cultural influence 21, 23

Uganda 94, 148
joint venture companies in 96
Libyan aid to 96, 99, 105
military aid to 92, 119
relations with 97, 100
ulama (religious scholars) 32, 33
unions and professional associations
127-8
United Arab Emirates 85
and Iraq 59
Libyan relations with 41
United Arab Republic 25, 49, 53
United Arab States 25, 49
United Nations 14, 24, 73, 117
vote equating Zionism with
racism 98
United States 16, 60
air bases 14-15, 16, 27-8, 74, 86
air raid on Libya 63, 68, 79, 84-5,
87, 90, 136, 138
and trusteeship 12

and proposed Libya–Morocco union 67–8
Arab reaction to 71
charges Libya with sponsoring dissidence 47
effect of devaluation 114
Libyan planes shot down 77, 82, 83
Libyan relations with 79–84, 120
Middle East policy of 80–81, 85, 91
monarchy and 11, 14–15
oil interests 80
opposition to Libyan tactics 88–9, 100, 102, 122
Qaddafi and 29, 44, 51, 69, 84, 119
Qaddafi support for militants in 38, 46
reaction to Libyan foreign policy 143
universal conscription 13, 133, 137
universities 128
Upper Volta 96, 99, 100, 103, 105

Vanuatu, New Caledonia 47, 48

Wage increases 133
Wahhabi movement 30
West Germany, relations with 15, 89
Western Europe
    Libyan relations with 85–6
    Muslim reaction to 71
    response to Libyan foreign policy 143
    response to terrorist links 90
    US asks for anti-Libyan cooperation 88
Western Sahara issue 59, 66, 67, 102, 148
    Libyan approach to 98

Yamani, Ahmed Zaki 123
Yemen 25

Zaire 87, 102, 103
    Libyan aid to 96, 98–9
    mineral resources 99
zakat (alms tax) 31, 36
Zionism 35–6, 63, 69
    Qaddafi and 18, 37, 50, 95